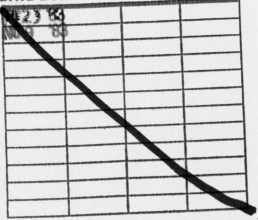

THE
TWENTY-FIFTH
AMENDMENT

The Twenty-Fifth Amendment

Its Complete History
and Earliest Applications

JOHN D. FEERICK

Foreword by
Birch Bayh

New York
Fordham University Press
1976

Printed in the United States of America

To my children,
MAUREEN, MARGARET, JEAN,
ROSEMARY, and JOHN

Contents

Foreword

As THIS NATION celebrates the two-hundredth anniversary of its birth, we should take special note of one unique feature of our great constitutional experiment. Unlike almost any other Western democracy, the United States has never been faced with a serious crisis in the line of succession to office of its chief executive and head of state. Our ability to avoid such a crisis throughout much of our earlier history was, perhaps, largely a matter of luck. Fortunately, we never had to confront the prospect of a double vacancy in the offices of both President and Vice President. Thus, one of two individuals specifically designated by the voters as President and next-in-line served in the office at all times.

The problem of the line of succession following the Vice President, however, long bothered many thoughtful Americans. But it was not until the mid-1960s, after the assassination of President Kennedy, that the Constitution was changed to provide a structural solution to the problem. As fate would have it, less than a decade after the ratification of the Twenty-Fifth Amendment, the unprecedented happened, and both offices were vacated during one presidential term. Twice Vice Presidents were then nominated by the President and approved by both Houses of the Congress under the new Amendment. When the first of these, Gerald R. Ford, became the thirty-eighth President of the United States, there was no serious question about the legitimacy of his claim to the office. One has only to imagine the divisiveness which would have been created had the White House been turned over to the opposing party in the person of the Speaker of the House to realize how significant an achievement this was.

The nation owes a great debt of gratitude to the author of this volume, John Feerick, not only for this comprehensive, scholarly, and highly readable history of the Twenty-Fifth Amendment, but for his expert guiding hand throughout the process of crafting the Amendment, obtaining its approval by Congress and ratification by the states, and implementing it for the first time. Mr. Feerick, who is a distinguished attorney in private practice in New York, gave freely of his time and talents in assisting those of us in public office in providing a solution to this crucial aspect of our constitutional system. In my view, his distinguished service should serve as an example to his colleagues at the bar of a man who has fulfilled his public responsibilities in an outstanding way.

BIRCH BAYH
United States Senator

Preface

This book is a sequel to my earlier book, *From Failing Hands: The Story of Presidential Succession* (1965). There, the development from 1607 to 1964 of our political and legal experiences with executive succession machinery was traced. *From Failing Hands*, among other things, constitutes a detailed account of presidential succession as reflected in the deaths and illnesses of Presidents and Vice Presidents, the crises reflected in those events, and the continuing growth in importance of the vice presidency.

This book focuses on the Twenty-Fifth Amendment—its meaning, legislative history, and applications in 1973 and 1974 following the resignations from office of Spiro T. Agnew and Richard M. Nixon. Necessarily, certain historical background material appearing in *From Failing Hands* is repeated in abbreviated form.

Here I have desired to complete to date the story of presidential succession initially undertaken in *From Failing Hands*. My present purpose has been fortified by the considerable interest shown in the Twenty-Fifth Amendment since its adoption on February 10, 1967. It has been the subject of fiction and non-fiction.* It has been criticized for being vague and undemocratic. It has been praised for making possible swift and orderly successions to the presidency and vice presidency upon the occurrence of some of the most extraordinary events in American history. Its vice presidential selection feature has been recommended as the best method for selecting all Vice Presidents. The repeal of that feature and the abolition of the vice presidency have also been suggested. Moreover, throughout the Watergate crisis the Amendment was alluded to as affording a means by which a President voluntarily and temporarily could transfer presidential power during an impeachment proceeding, and it was suggested as authorizing a Vice President and Cabinet to suspend, so to speak, a President during the period of an impeachment trial before the Senate.

Judging by all the attention the Amendment has received and by the number of presidential and vice presidential vacancies and illnesses which have occurred in our history, one can expect that the Twenty-Fifth Amendment will receive frequent application in the future history of our country. I hope that this book will serve as a useful reference work and afford greater understanding of an amendment which is unique in so many ways. It is the only part of the Constitution which confers an explicit power on the President's Cabinet, places specific time limits on congressional action, empowers persons other than the President to convene a special session of Congress, and assigns the House of Representatives a role in the appointive process. It also adds to the Vice President's constitutional duties, establishes a proce-

* See F. Knebel, *Night of Camp David* (1965); B. Bayh, *One Heartbeat Away* (1968).

dure in addition to impeachment by which a President can be prevented from discharging his powers and duties, and prescribes for the first time a method of filling a vice presidential vacancy. Finally, it is one of the longest amendments to the Constitution and its every detail is filled with considerable meaning.†

In the writing of this book I owe my greatest debt of gratitude to my wife, Emalie, and to our children.

I wish to express my special thanks to Linda Wood for editorial and substantive suggestions which greatly improved the manuscript, for invaluable assistance with the research and drafting of Part III, and for her cheerful help with numerous details. Although this book was started shortly before Agnew's resignation, I could not have finished it without Mrs. Wood's assistance since October 1974.

My debt to Gloria Frank and Linda Schurmann for typing and re-typing the manuscript and for helping me in so many ways is inexpressible.

I am particularly grateful to my colleagues Joseph T. C. Hart and Kurt Koegler, to my father-in-law, William B. Platt, Jr., and to my brother-in-law, Harold K. Platt, for taking the time to read the manuscript and making suggestions which improved it. Kurt Koegler was especially helpful with Chapters 13 and 14.

To the secretarial supervisors of my firm, Anthony Arbisi and Lorraine Meyer, I owe a debt of thanks for their understanding of my requests. I am grateful to my law partners for their encouragement in this undertaking; to Kathryn V. McCulloch and Finbarr O'Neill of the *Fordham Law Review* for their work in checking the accuracy of citations and quotations; and to the staff of Fordham University Press, especially Dr. Mary Beatrice Schulte, for many helpful suggestions and painstaking attention to detail.

I wish to acknowledge my deep gratitude to the American Bar Association, especially to Donald E. Channell and Lowell R. Beck of its Washington office at the time the Amendment was developed, for making possible my participation in that development. The contributions of Channell and Beck to the Amendment's success were immeasurable.

Finally, I am honored to have Senator Birch Bayh, the chief architect of the Twenty-Fifth Amendment, write the Foreword to this book.

JOHN D. FEERICK

† I have placed in a volume on file with the Fordham University School of Law Library copies of correspondence and memoranda which may shed additional light on the Amendment. For the fascinating inside story of the development of the Amendment, see Bayh, *One Heartbeat Away* (1968).

THE TWENTY-FIFTH AMENDMENT

I

The Problems

1

Presidential Inability

What is the extent of the term "disability" & who is to be the judge of it?

JOHN DICKINSON
August 27, 1787 [1]

WHEN THE FRAMERS OF THE CONSTITUTION met in Philadelphia in 1787, they brought with them almost two hundred years of experience with executive succession machinery.[2] Yet they did not spend much time discussing the subject at the Constitutional Convention of 1787. They seem to have thought they handled the matter adequately by providing for the office of Vice President and by inserting in the Constitution the following clause on presidential succession:

> In Case of the Removal of the President from Office, or of his Death, Resignation, or Inability to discharge the Powers and Duties of the said Office, the Same shall devolve on the Vice President, and the Congress may by Law provide for the Case of Removal, Death, Resignation or Inability, both of the President and Vice President, declaring what Officer shall then act as President, and such Officer shall act accordingly, until the Disability be removed, or a President shall be elected.[3]

The debates were silent on the meaning of "inability" and on who should determine its existence and termination.[4] Also untouched was the question of what happened when the President became disabled. Did the Vice President become President for the remainder of the term, or did he merely act as President for the duration of the inability? In the answer to this question, the antecedent of the words "the Same" became determinative. If the "Office" devolved, the Vice President presumably became President for the rest of the term; if "the Powers and Duties" devolved, he presumably would be Acting President. Moreover, since the clause did not differentiate among the covered contingencies, whatever devolved did so whether it was a case of removal, death, resignation, or inability.

This question and these fine distinctions did not surface until many years after the adoption of the Constitution. For the first 52 years of the existence of the presidency, our nation was remarkably fortunate. No President died in office, although three vacancies did occur in the vice presidency. In 1812 George Clinton, James Madison's first Vice President, died in office, and in the following term Madison's second Vice President, Elbridge Gerry, also died.* These deaths left the vice presidency unoccupied for a period of more than three years. Another vice presidential vacancy occurred when John C. Calhoun resigned in 1832, less than three months before the expiration of his term, in order to accept an appointment as United States Senator from South Carolina.

MADISON ILLNESS

A little more than a year prior to Gerry's death, President Madison suffered an illness which left him unable to conduct the affairs of state for three weeks, and set off widespread discussion of presidential succession. By a note of June 18, 1813, Madison postponed a meeting with a congressional delegation to discuss the nomination of Albert Gallatin, then Secretary of the Treasury, to be Envoy Extraordinary. The note read:

> James Madison is sorry that a continuance of his indisposition will not permit him to see the committee of the Senate today, nor can he at present fix a day when it will be in his power.[5]

Word traveled throughout the capital that Madison was critically ill of bilious fever, and attention focused on the possible succession of Vice President Elbridge Gerry, then almost 69 years old. French Minister Louis Serurier wrote on June 21:

> The thought of [Madison's] possible loss strikes everybody with consternation. It is certainly true that his death in the circumstances in which the Republic is placed, would be a veritable national calamity. The President who would succeed him for three and a half years is a respectable old man, but weak and worn out. All good Americans pray for the recovery of Mr. Madison.[6]

Daniel Webster delivered some congressional resolutions to Madison but found him too ill to read them.

There was speculation in the press that Madison might not survive. The *Alexandria Gazette* observed that the President's age (sixty-two), "added to the heavy weight with which the public burdens must bear upon his mind, in this calamitous crisis is enough to create serious doubts of his recovery." [7]

Both Houses of Congress became engrossed with the possibility of the President's death and the Vice President's succession. The presidential succession statute at that time ran first to the President pro tempore of

---

* Shortly before the vacancy caused by Gerry's death, President Madison risked death or capture by his personal involvement in the War of 1812. I. Brant, *James Madison, Commander in Chief, 1812–1836* 299–300 (1961).

the Senate and then to the Speaker of the House. There was a vacancy in
the Senate post because Madison had appointed the former President pro
tempore, William H. Crawford, as Minister to France. James Monroe
wrote that there was plotting in the Senate to fill the post of President
pro tempore because the deaths of both the President and the Vice President
were presumed to be near.[8] The *Federal Republican* newspaper
focused on the future of House Speaker Henry Clay. In an analogy to
the Duke of Gloucester who had murdered repeatedly to gain the throne
of England, the paper obliquely suggested that Clay would murder
Gerry to become President.[9]

Fortunately, Madison began a slow recovery from his illness. On
July 2 Dolly Madison wrote that his fever had subsided and that he was
improving. On July 7 it was announced that the President had resumed
the most urgent public business,[10] and a week later he met with a Senate
committee. In early August he journeyed four days from Washington to
his home in Montpelier where his health continued to improve. The
Federal Republican, however, sought to prolong the controversy and
reported on August 13 that the sickness had left Madison with only a
few months or perhaps a few days to live. "*We know* that his mind has
shared the fate of his body . . . not a few, who have recently visited
him, have left his chamber under a full conviction of the derangement
of his mind." [11] This account set off another series of rumors which were
quelled only by further accounts of his good health. When Madison
returned to Washington on October 24, 1813, it was obvious that his
recovery was complete.[12]

Vice President Gerry died the next year; Madison survived until 1836,
when he died at the age of 85.

TYLER PRECEDENT

The luck of the first fifty years ended on April 4, 1841, when President
William Henry Harrison, the oldest President at inauguration, died of
pneumonia. It was not until early the next day that a messenger, traveling by boat and horse, reached Vice President John Tyler in Williams-
burg, Virginia, to give him the news. Tyler immediately proceeded to
Washington and, shortly after his arrival on April 6, took the presidential
oath of office. Although he apparently held the view that he was President
without the oath, Tyler took it to remove any future questions of his
authority.[13] To make his view clear, Tyler had William Cranch, Chief
Judge of the United States Circuit Court for the District of Columbia,
prepare an appropriate certification:

> I, William Cranch, chief judge of the circuit court of the District of
> Columbia, certify that the above-named John Tyler personally appeared

before me this day, and although he deems himself qualified to perform the duties and exercise the powers and office of President on the death of William Henry Harrison, late President of the United States, without any other oath than that which he has taken as Vice-President, yet as doubts may *arise*, and for greater caution, took and subscribed the foregoing oath before me.[14]

After taking the oath, Tyler held his first Cabinet meeting. When asked by Secretary of State Daniel Webster whether he would continue Harrison's practice of assigning the President's vote no more weight than that of any member of the Cabinet, Tyler said: ". . . I can never consent to being dictated to. . . . I, as president, will be responsible for my administration." [15] Several days later he delivered an inaugural address, and on April 14 moved into the White House. Declared the *New York American* on April 16: "It is impossible for an American not to feel . . . great pride at the quiet, orderly, and, as it were, matter of course transition, by which so important a movement has been operated."

Tyler's ascendancy to the "office" of President was not without dispute. Protests were echoed by some newspapers, and leaders of the Whig Party referred to him as simply the "Acting President." When the Cabinet notified Tyler of Harrison's death, he was addressed as "Vice President," although the Cabinet quickly acquiesced in his assumption of the office of President. John Quincy Adams, a former President of the United States and then a member of the House of Representatives, noted in his diary for April 16, 1841:

> But it [Tyler's assumption of the title and office of the presidency] is a construction in direct violation both of the grammar and context of the Constitution, which confers upon the Vice-President, on the decease of the President, not the office, but the powers and duties of the said office.[16] *

Webster, on the other hand, reportedly held the view that the powers and duties of the President were inseparable from the office itself and that any succession by a Vice President to the presidential office was a succession for the remainder of the term.[17]

Upon the convening of the special session of the Twenty-Seventh Congress on May 31, 1841, Tyler's assumption of the presidential office came under attack.[18] When Representative Henry A. Wise of Virginia introduced a resolution calling for the formation of a committee "to wait on the President of the United States," Representative John McKeon of New York moved to strike "President" and substitute "Vice-President, now exercising the office of President." He stated that "a grave constitu-

---

* In his diary for April 4, 1841, Adams reported that the Constitution "makes the Vice-President of the United States, John Tyler, of Virginia, Acting President of the Union for four years less one month." 10 *The Memoirs of John Quincy Adams* 456 (Adams ed., 1876).

tional question" had been presented, which should be set "at rest for all future time." The House of Representatives rejected McKeon's suggestion and passed the Wise resolution, sending it to the Senate.

In the Senate the next day, Senator William Allen of Ohio urged that Tyler be addressed as "the Vice President, on whom by the death of the late President, the powers and duties of the office of President have devolved." Allen said that if a President were afflicted with a disease producing a temporary mental disability from which he subsequently recovered, he then could be reinstated to his powers and duties. He further stated that he had no objection to Tyler's calling himself President, provided it was understood that a person could become President only through election.

Senator Robert J. Walker of Mississippi disagreed. In his opinion, the Constitution provided for two separate contingencies. He stated that the Vice President succeeded to the "Office" of President in all cases because Article II, section 1, clause 6 was explicit: an officer appointed by Congress acts as President when both the President and the Vice President have died, resigned, been removed, or become disabled, but not so when a Vice President takes over upon the happening of any of these eventualities to the President. "This is the language and the meaning of the Constitution," he said. "Can there be any doubt on the subject?" Senator Allen thought that there was. He hypothesized a case of temporary disability, more easily contemplated by the Founding Fathers than death, he said, when a disabled President recovered to find the Vice President in his office.

> The question would then arise, which of the two officers should continue in the chair. . . . Was it [the office] to vibrate [assuming a struggle for power] between the two claimants? In what manner could a President of the United States—unimpeached, sane, and alive—cease to be President? There was none known to the Constitution. None.[19]

Senator Calhoun of South Carolina considered the entire discussion irrelevant, since there was a permanent vacancy in the presidential office. The House resolution passed the Senate, without change, by a vote of 38 to 8, and the Tyler precedent became firmly established in our history.*

GARFIELD INABILITY

Within the next 25 years the Tyler precedent was followed twice—by Vice President Millard Fillmore upon the death in office on July 9, 1850,

---

* Not everyone, of course, came to accept Tyler's succession to the office. Thus, when an impeachment resolution was introduced by a Whig congressman in January 1843,

of President Zachary Taylor, and by Vice President Andrew Johnson upon the death of Abraham Lincoln on April 15, 1865. Each succession to the office of President took place swiftly and without question.

On July 2, 1881, however, when the nation was confronted with its first case of prolonged presidential inability, the Tyler precedent became a formidable obstacle to the Vice President's acting as President.[20] That day President James A. Garfield was shot by an assassin and for the next eighty days wavered between life and death. Although at times it appeared that he would recover, he suffered frequent relapses and experienced periods of hallucinations. "Hope alternated with despair and days of physical strength and mental alertness inevitably gave way to days of extreme weakness and moments of mental aberration." [21] For most of the last eighty days of his life, Garfield was confined to bed. Only toward the end was he permitted to sit in a reclining chair. When he was moved to the New Jersey shore from the White House on September 6, "those watching were shocked by the change that had come over the great, strong man who had been the President of the United States." [22]

During the period of his inability, the number of Garfield's visitors was restricted. From July 2 through July 20, only his family and physicians were permitted to see him, and although occasional visits from members of the Cabinet were permitted thereafter, at no point did Vice President Chester A. Arthur confer with him. This may have been in part because they were not good friends and were from different factions of the Republican Party. The further fact that Garfield's assassin, Charles J. Guiteau, was motivated by a desire to have Arthur succeed to the presidency also initially turned public opinion against Arthur.

Arthur was in New York when informed of the shooting of Garfield. He was unwilling to go to Washington until officially notified of the President's death. But the Cabinet requested that he take the midnight train to the capital, and he arrived at approximately 8 A.M. on July 3. Arthur stayed at the home of Senator John P. Jones of Nevada, and the Cabinet paid daily visits to him. On July 13 Garfield's physicians expressed optimism about his full recovery, and with great relief Arthur returned to his home in New York where he remained secluded.[23] Arthur's conduct during the entire period of Garfield's inability was such that *The New York Times* observed in late August:

> Such impending fear as there might have been early in July of the dangers to the common weal from the President's sudden taking off has passed away. If his legal successor has not disarmed criticism, he has at least done nothing to sharpen it. . . . A change of Executive eight

---

Tyler was referred to as "Vice President, acting as President." 12 Cong. Globe, 27th Cong., 3d Sess. 144 (1843).

More than 100 years later an unsuccessful challenge would be made to Lyndon B. Johnson's succession on the ground that he had assumed the "office" of President in violation of the Constitution. *From Failing Hands* 10 & n.

weeks ago would have been felt as one of the most violent of the jars to which the institutions of the United States have been subjected. A change to-day would be effected merely amid a certain silent and watchful expectancy. . . .[24]

Garfield's only official act during the eighty days was the signing of an extradition paper on August 10. He was prevented from discharging his powers and duties by his doctors, who felt his only chance of survival lay in isolation from the burdens of public affairs. On one occasion when Garfield wanted to discuss the business of the executive department, a doctor forbade it, stating: "I told him that he must dismiss that subject from his mind until he was fully recovered. He said that it was on his mind and he had to let it off; but he obeyed me as implicitly as a schoolboy would obey his teacher, and he has said hardly anything since." [25]

The members of the Cabinet tried to keep the wheels of government turning. Whenever the President's condition became critical, the Cabinet would spend long hours of vigil at the White House. But there was much the Cabinet could not do. Important matters such as the handling of foreign affairs and the prosecution of post office swindlers were neglected. Accordingly, it was not surprising that in late August Secretary of State James Blaine prepared a paper on presidential inability and argued that since the Constitution contained no directions for replacing a disabled President, Arthur should be called to Washington to take over the presidency. Only a few Cabinet members agreed.[26] It is reported that a majority of the Cabinet, including Attorney General Wayne MacVeagh, were of the view that any succession by Arthur would be, by virtue of the Tyler precedent, to the President's office for the rest of the term.[27] Arthur, however, fearful of being labeled a usurper and of possibly killing Garfield, made it clear that he would not assume presidential responsibility.

Following Garfield's death on September 19, 1881, the debate over the meaning of the succession provision continued in the press, in the legal journals of the day, and in Congress.[28] When Arthur became President, there was no Vice President, President pro tempore of the Senate, or Speaker of the House—in short, no constitutional successor to the presidency. Arthur recognized the problem and, before leaving New York to accompany Garfield's body to Washington, he wrote a proclamation summoning the Senate into immediate special session so that it could elect a President pro tempore. He mailed it to the White House so that if he were struck down on his way to Washington a constitutional crisis would be averted. If he arrived in the capital safely, he planned to call the Senate into session himself and destroy the letter.[29] On October 10 the Senate convened in special session called by Arthur, and the independent David B. Davis of Illinois was ultimately selected to be President pro tempore.

In several messages to Congress, Arthur himself expressed concern over the ambiguities in the succession provision, stating in his message of December 6, 1881:

> Is the inability limited in its nature to long-continued intellectual incapacity, or has it a broader import? What must be its extent and duration? How must its existence be established? Has the President whose inability is the subject of inquiry any voice in determining whether or not it exists, or is the decision of that momentous and delicate question confided to the Vice-President, or is it contemplated by the Constitution that Congress should provide by law precisely what should constitute inability and how and by what tribunal or authority it should be ascertained? If the inability proves to be temporary in its nature, and during its continuance the Vice-President lawfully exercises the functions of the Executive, by what tenure does he hold his office? Does he continue as President for the remainder of the four years' term? Or would the elected President, if his inability should cease in the interval, be empowered to resume his office? And if, having such lawful authority, he should exercise it, would the Vice-President be thereupon empowered to resume his powers and duties as such? [30]

ARTHUR ILLNESS

Arthur's interest in the problem of presidential inability was not merely intellectual. In the summer of 1882 the Surgeon General examined him and found that he was suffering from Bright's disease, an almost inevitably fatal kidney affliction. Early in October an Associated Press release describing his illness appeared in newspapers across the country, but it was denied on the President's authority and labeled "pure fiction" by a "friendly" newspaper. The disease produced spasmodic nausea, mental depression, and indolence, and, according to one biographer, perhaps was responsible for Arthur's early distaste for the presidency and his somewhat casual approach to the duties of his office.[31]

In April 1883, on a vacation trip to Florida, Arthur suffered a severe attack of the disease, and the newspapers described his sudden and violent illness. The President's physician told reporters that he was suffering only from overexposure to the sun and indigestion caused by seasickness. In light of the President's travels, the explanation seemed reasonable. Arthur was intent upon concealing his condition from the public lest he become the object of sympathy, and reports of his ill health were dismissed as grossly exaggerated.[32] By June, Arthur had reduced his schedule so that he would not begin work until noon or one o'clock. Administration critics complained of "the shadow of repose that has come over the Government business." [33]

By early 1884, as the presidential election approached, Arthur enjoyed little Republican support. Each of the warring Republican factions found him objectionable. Yet Arthur refused to exclude himself from contention for the nomination. He feared that suspicions about his health would be raised which would cast doubt on his ability to handle the presidency, and that a withdrawal would indicate an insecurity about his record in office and his ability to be re-elected.[34] But Arthur did not make a serious effort to secure the nomination and asked all his Cabinet members to stay away from the Republican convention. Arthur also privately asked several supporters to abandon their efforts on his behalf because he did not wish to be re-elected.[35] His only stronghold in the convention balloting was the South, and on the fourth ballot James G. Blaine was selected as the Republican nominee. Arthur, by then helplessly ill, was relieved rather than disappointed by Blaine's nomination, but he played no role in the ensuing presidential campaign.

After the inauguration of Grover Cleveland as the twenty-second President, Arthur retired to private life and served briefly as counsel to his old New York law firm. He spent the last year of his life as an invalid, and died on November 18, 1886, at the age of 56.

With the passing of Arthur's administration, interest in solving the problem of presidential inability faded.

CLEVELAND INABILITY

Twelve years after Garfield's assassination another President of the United States suffered an inability.[36] On June 30, 1893, President Grover Cleveland issued a call for a special session of Congress to repeal the silver purchase provisions of the Sherman Act, and that night boarded a friend's yacht in New York City. For the next five days the President cruised in Long Island Sound. He then visited his summer home at Gray Gables on Buzzards Bay, Massachusetts, returned to the yacht for a few more days of cruising, and then revisited his summer home. There he remained until August 5 when he returned to Washington to address the special session of Congress on August 7.

Unknown to the public, all but one member of the Cabinet, and virtually every member of the government, including Vice President Adlai Stevenson,* was the fact that during the initial cruise Cleveland had undergone an operation for the removal of a cancerous growth on the roof of his mouth. The operation took place while Cleveland was unconscious and strapped to a chair propped up against the yacht's mast. A major part of his upper jaw was removed. No external incision was

* Stevenson would have been one of the last to be informed anyway because he did not enjoy a close relationship with Cleveland, and his views on the economy differed substantially from those of the President. M. Harwood, *In the Shadow of Presidents: The American Vice-Presidency and Succession System* 135–36 (1966).

made. At his summer home he was fitted with an artificial jaw, without which his speech would have been wholly unintelligible. During the second cruise in July, Cleveland underwent a second operation for the removal of suspicious tissue which was observed after the first operation.

On August 29, 1893, when Cleveland had recovered and was at his oratorical best, a letter appeared in the *Philadelphia Press* describing the operations in detail. The story was denounced as a hoax; a number of newspapers claimed there had been no operations. Some said Cleveland merely had a toothache, which required the extraction of a few teeth. Cleveland's doctors and members of the government either denied or refused to confirm the story. In view of his apparent good health, the public accepted the charge that the *Press* story had been a fake. One of the doctors who participated in the operations subsequently stated that he did more lying during this period than in all the rest of his life put together.[37]

Not until the publication of an article in *The Saturday Evening Post* in 1917 by one of Cleveland's doctors did the public learn the true facts. The doctor stated that the operations had been performed under complete secrecy because of the unstable financial situation in the country at that time. It was feared that the country might suffer an economic disaster if the public were informed that Cleveland had cancer. "What the consequences would have been had it become known at once we can only surmise, and shudder!"[38]

McKinley assassination

Cleveland's concealed inability was followed eight years later by a case of publicized presidential inability. On September 6, 1901, while attending a reception in Buffalo, New York, President William McKinley was struck by an assassin's bullet.[39] McKinley was taken to a nearby emergency hospital where he was given ether and underwent surgery. By the next day most of the members of his Cabinet and Vice President Theodore Roosevelt had assembled in Buffalo. During the next few days McKinley, although conscious, was confined to bed and unable to perform his presidential duties. His condition appeared to improve until September 12, when he suffered a relapse. He died in the early morning hours of September 14.

Wilson inability

On September 25, 1919, President Woodrow Wilson fell ill while on a speaking tour of the United States to gain support for the League of

Nations. The tour was canceled promptly, and the presidential train was ordered to return to Washington. The public was informed that the President had suffered a nervous breakdown. His illness was attributed variously to overwork, an apparent attack of influenza the previous April, and his trips to Europe in December 1918 and in March 1919.

On October 2, 1919, after his return to Washington, Wilson suffered a stroke which paralyzed the left side of his body. Dr. Cary T. Grayson, the President's close friend and physician, released a bulletin stating: "The President is a very sick man." From that time until the inauguration of Warren G. Harding on March 4, 1921, the country was without the services of an able President.[40] For more than six months after Wilson suffered the stroke, only a few people were permitted to see him. The ambiguous nature of the medical bulletins prompted wild rumors about his condition. Some stated that he had an abscess of the brain; others, that he had suffered a cerebral hemorrhage; and still others, that he had gone mad and was being kept a prisoner in the White House. "His mind was uninjured," said one historian later, "but his emotional balance was permanently upset. . . . What remained was not Woodrow Wilson but a shell and travesty of him." [41] Demands that the people be informed of his true health were ignored.

The facts were concealed not only from the public but also from the Congress and members of the Cabinet. Vice President Thomas R. Marshall, whom Wilson reportedly had described earlier as a "small-calibre man," [42] was kept almost completely ignorant and was forced to depend upon the newspapers and secondhand accounts for his information. He resented this and said that it would be tragic for the country if he ever had to act as President under such circumstances. A few members of the Cabinet, including Secretary of State Robert Lansing, were told about the President's true condition, but only in the strictest of confidence. The President's wife, Dr. Cary Grayson, and Joseph Tumulty, his secretary, controlled the flow of information.

While Wilson lay ill, unable to discharge the powers and duties of office, attempts were made to provide executive leadership. The day after the stroke Secretary of State Lansing suggested to Tumulty that the Vice President be called upon to act as President. Lansing read the succession provision to Tumulty, who responded: " 'I have read the Constitution and do not find myself in need of any tutoring at your hands of the provision you have just read.' " When Lansing said that either Dr. Grayson or Tumulty should certify the President disabled, Tumulty declared: " 'You may rest assured that while Woodrow Wilson is lying in the White House on the broad of his back I will not be a party to ousting him.' " [43] Grayson made it clear to Lansing that he also would oppose any attempt to have Wilson declared disabled.

A Cabinet meeting of October 6 was called at Lansing's initiative, and the subject of Marshall's acting as President was discussed.[44] Lansing noted that the Constitution was unclear on the meaning of "inability" and on who should determine its existence. He expressed the view that if Wilson were unable to attend to public matters, Marshall should act as President. Grayson and Tumulty arrived at the meeting and voiced Wilson's irritation over the fact that the meeting had been called without his authority. Predictably, the possibility of Marshall's acting as President was quickly dropped.

In the days and weeks which followed, there were repeated demands for Marshall to act as President. The confusion surrounding the succession provision, coupled with Marshall's strong reluctance to appear as a usurper and to incur the wrath of the President and Mrs. Wilson, all combined to prevent him from so acting. Marshall reportedly stated: "I am not going to get myself entangled with Mrs. Wilson. No politician ever exposes himself to the hatred of a woman, particularly if she's the wife of the President of the United States." [45]

As a result of the vacuum at the top, presidential leadership was assumed for all practical purposes by Mrs. Wilson, Grayson, and Tumulty. They decided who saw the President and what matters, documents, and notes were forwarded to him. Said Mrs. Wilson: "Woodrow Wilson was first my beloved husband whose life I was trying to save, fighting with my back to the wall—after that he was the President of the United States." [46] The possibility of Wilson's resigning seems to have been discussed and rejected, partly because it would remove his main incentive to recovery.[47] One doctor, Francis X. Dercum, strongly opposed resignation, believing it would be bad not only for Wilson but for the country, because of his view that Wilson's leadership was necessary for the establishment of the League of Nations.

Meanwhile, Robert Lansing took the initiative in convening the Cabinet more than twenty times between October 1919 and February 1920. At these meetings governmental problems were discussed and actions recommended. Prompted by his distress over Lansing's earlier suggestion that Marshall act as President and the convening of the Cabinet without his approval, Wilson dismissed Lansing as Secretary of State in February 1920. Wilson is reported to have said to Tumulty upon the dismissal: " 'Tumulty, it is never the wrong time to spike disloyalty. When Lansing sought to oust me, I was upon my back. I am on my feet now and I will not have disloyalty about me!' " [48]

As a result of the lack of presidential leadership by Wilson or by an Acting President, United States participation in the League of Nations was defeated in the Senate; numerous governmental vacancies went unfilled; twenty-eight bills became law by default of any action by the President; foreign diplomats were prevented from submitting their credentials to the President; letters and notes to the White House either went unanswered or were answered by Mrs. Wilson, or by the President in illegible handwriting; and, in many other ways, the business of government was brought to a standstill in 1919 and 1920.

Throughout the Wilson inability period, varying interpretations of the Constitution's succession provision were offered. Numerous proposals for dealing with the constitutional problem were introduced in Congress, and hearings were conducted by the House Judiciary Committee.[49] But the installation of a new administration once again pushed the matter aside.

HARDING DEATH

While on a speech-making tour in July 1923, President Warren Harding became ill. His ailment was initially diagnosed as acute indigestion. "There is every indication," said *The New York Times* on August 2, "that he ultimately will recover his health and strength. It may as well be understood by the country, however, that Mr. Harding will be an invalid for a considerable period, during which he will be unable to attend actively to important public business." Several hours later Harding was dead. His death was probably caused by a cerebral thrombosis, but since Mrs. Harding refused to permit an autopsy, the exact cause remains undetermined.[50]

ROOSEVELT "INABILITY"

The extent to which President Franklin D. Roosevelt was disabled, if at all, during the last year of his life is unclear. Also unclear is whether the outcome of the 1944 election would have been different had the American people had the relevant medical information. What is clear is that the President refused to acknowledge his medical condition lest his goals of ending World War II and of establishing an organization for world peace be thwarted.[51]

In early 1944 President Roosevelt underwent a physical examination which revealed hypertensive heart disease, accompanied by hardening of the arteries, hypertension, and acute bronchitis. Dr. Ross McIntire, the President's personal physician, and Dr. Howard Bruenn, the cardiologist who conducted the examination, agreed to keep the findings private and not to discuss them with either the President or his family. Bruenn also agreed to serve from that time on as the President's physician-in-attendance.

It appears that Roosevelt and McIntire previously had reached a tacit understanding under which Roosevelt would not question, and McIntire would not describe, the condition of his health. Thus, from April 1944 until his death a year later, Roosevelt did not ask Bruenn about his condition or treatment, or even about the need for a cardiologist.[52]

In May 1944, Roosevelt decided to seek a fourth term as President. Although he expressed his support for a number of vice presidential candidates, including Vice President Henry A. Wallace, Harry S Truman, William O. Douglas, and James F. Byrnes, he allowed the Democratic Party leaders to select the nominee. Following the Democratic Convention of 1944, which he did not attend, Roosevelt met with Truman only once prior to election day. At that meeting he asked Truman about his campaign plans. When Truman replied that he would travel by airplane, Roosevelt said: " 'No. Make it by train all the way. This time we may need you.' " [53]

In September and October 1944, rumors circulated about the President's health, and to offset their impact, Roosevelt took to the campaign trail in the two weeks before the election, delivering major speeches in New York, Philadelphia, Chicago, and Boston. After the excitement of his fourth election victory, Roosevelt relapsed into physical and mental fatigue. Duties which had never been troublesome now required his utmost concentration. He was beset with indecision about simple problems. His attention span was short, and his signature became an illegible scrawl. He lost weight, his appetite disappeared, and his blood pressure rose. McIntire, however, continued to conceal the true situation, maintaining that Roosevelt was in good health.

Former Secretary of State Dean Acheson wrote of Roosevelt's appearance at a meeting held a few days before his fourth inauguration: "We were all shocked by the President's appearance. Thin, gaunt, with sunken and darkly circled eyes, only the jaunty cigarette holder and his light-hearted brushing aside of difficulties recalled the FDR of former days." [54] Of Roosevelt on the day of his inauguration, John Gunther said: "I was terrified when I saw his face. I felt certain that he was going to die. All the light had gone out underneath the skin. It was like a parchment shade on a bulb that had been dimmed. . . . I could not get over the ravaged expression on his face. It was gray, gaunt, and sagging, and the muscles controlling the lips seemed to have lost part of their function." [55]

At his inauguration in January 1945 Roosevelt suffered severe chest pains, but neither of his physicians was called to render assistance or was even informed of the incident. The following month on the journey to Yalta Roosevelt's fatigue was noted by his entire staff. Lord Moran, Churchill's personal physician, observed that the President had symptoms of hardening of the arteries of the brain, which can cause insufficient blood supply to the brain and result in impaired powers of reasoning and concentration.[56] Secretary of State Edward R. Stettinius, Jr., observed that the attainment of world peace and the formation of the

United Nations were Roosevelt's primary goal at Yalta, while his other positions were negotiable.[57] Immediately upon his return from Yalta, where the emotional and intellectual demands had been exhausting, Roosevelt insisted on a personal report to Congress. His speech, delivered in a hoarse, weak voice, with trembling hands and frequent departures from the text, convinced many members of Congress that he was gravely ill.

Despite long rests at Hyde Park and Warm Springs, Roosevelt's health continued to decline. Occasionally, he had active days when he appeared to regain his strength. At other times advisers found him unable to discuss serious matters. He vacillated between intellectual acumen and a vacuous attitude which seemed impossible to penetrate. By March, he no longer could bathe or shave himself. His mind wandered and he awoke exhausted. His staff was forced to limit his appointments and shield him from routine problems.

As his dreams of peace dissolved with the continued controversy over a new Polish government, Roosevelt became depressed and saw fewer people. In increasing numbers, he signed messages written by others. Somehow he found the energy to involve himself in planning the United Nations organizational meeting in San Francisco, laboring over the smallest detail. Yet even here he vacillated, at one time planning to open the conference; later stating that he would not attend; and on the morning of his death suggesting that he might resign the presidency to head up the United Nations.

On April 12, less than three months into the term, Franklin Roosevelt died of a massive cerebral hemorrhage, and Harry S Truman was sworn in as President. Truman had had only two conversations with Roosevelt since inauguration day, both dealing with legislative matters. The development of the atom bomb was one of many matters not disclosed to Truman.[58] Fortunately, Truman was able to provide the country with effective leadership during the remainder of the term. As Winston Churchill told Truman in 1952: "I must confess, sir, I held you in very low regard then. I loathed your taking the place of Franklin Roosevelt. I misjudged you badly. Since that time, you, more than any other man, have saved Western civilization."

EISENHOWER INABILITIES

On September 24, 1955, while vacationing in Colorado, President Dwight D. Eisenhower suffered a heart attack, thus confronting the nation once again with a case of presidential inability.[59] The initial medical announcement said that the President had suffered "a digestive upset." After the President had been removed to a hospital and placed under oxygen, the public was advised that he had suffered a coronary thrombosis which would require complete rest for about a month. Fortunately, the heart attack occurred at a time when no emergencies existed in either the foreign or the domestic area. Congress, too, was out of session.

On the evening of September 24, Vice President Richard Nixon, Acting Attorney General William Rogers, and White House assistant Wilton Persons met to discuss arrangements for the operation of the executive branch during Eisenhower's inability. Among those consulted were Secretary of State John Foster Dulles and Treasury Secretary George M. Humphrey. It was decided that the Cabinet and White House staff should continue the administration of the government. The next day Nixon announced that "the President's well-defined policies and Government business would be carried out without delay." [60] After conferring with Rogers, Persons, presidential assistant Sherman Adams, and others, Nixon announced on the following day that the Cabinet would meet on Friday, September 30. An initial White House request for the Attorney General's opinion on the legality of a temporary delegation of presidential power was not acted upon, according to Attorney General Herbert Brownell, because there were "sufficient legal arrangements to carry on 'the day-to-day operations of the Government.'" [61] Consequently, no opinion was ever delivered.

On September 28, Nixon signed some ceremonial papers on the President's behalf. The National Security Council met the next day, with Nixon presiding for the first time; the Cabinet, the day after. The Cabinet accepted a recommendation of the National Security Council that Sherman Adams go to Denver to serve as liaison and administrative assistant to the President. Nixon initially thought that Adams should remain in Washington but was persuaded by Dulles that one person closely identified with the President should act as his official spokesman.[62] Dulles was influenced by the Wilson inability and by the apprehensions which had been created by the Cabinet meetings for which his uncle, Robert Lansing, had been dismissed. The Cabinet agreed on the following procedure:

(1) On actions which Cabinet members would normally take without consulting either the Cabinet or the President, there would be no change in procedure from the normal.

(2) Questions which would normally be brought before the Cabinet for discussion before decision should continue to be discussed there.

(3) *Decisions* which would require consultation with [the President] should go first to the Cabinet or the National Security Council for thorough discussion and possible recommendation and then go to Denver for . . . [the President's] consideration.

(4) The proper channel for submission to . . . [the President] of

matters requiring presidential decisions should be to General Persons in the White House and then through Governor Adams to . . . [the President] in Denver.⁶³

After the meeting, the following statement was released to the press:

After full discussion of pending matters, it was concluded that there are no obstacles to the orderly and uninterrupted conduct of the foreign and domestic affairs of the nation during the period of rest ordered by the President's physicians.

Governor Sherman Adams, the Assistant to the President, will leave for Denver today and will be available there, in consultation with the President's physicians, whenever it may later become appropriate to present any matters to the President.

The policies and programs of the administration as determined and approved by the President are well established along definite lines and are well known. Co-ordination of the activities of the several departments of the government within the framework of these policies will be continued by full co-operation among the responsible officers of these departments so that the functions of the government will be carried forward in an effective manner during the absence of the President.⁶⁴

On the day of the Cabinet meeting, Eisenhower, who had been kept practically incommunicado during the prior week and in an oxygen tent for most of it, performed his first official act by signing lists of foreign service officer appointments. Adams journeyed to Denver and reported the developments at the Cabinet meeting to the President. Several days later Eisenhower directed that all regularly scheduled meetings of the Cabinet and of the National Security Council be held under the chairmanship of the Vice President.⁶⁵ He wrote Nixon as follows: "I hope you will continue to have meetings of the National Security Council and of the Cabinet over which you will preside in accordance with procedures which you have followed at my request in the past during my absence from Washington." ⁶⁶ In the next few weeks a number of such meetings took place, with Adams usually traveling in from Denver and then returning to report to the President. Said Secretary of Agriculture Ezra Taft Benson:

[I]t had seemed to me that Nixon deferred too much to Sherman Adams; sometimes you wondered whether Sherm or Dick was running the meeting. On the one hand most major policy matters were held over until later. But there also was a spreading tendency for Cabinet officials to go ahead on their own—on things that before the heart attack would have been checked out with the President.⁶⁷

Eisenhower began to receive visitors during the second and third weeks of his illness and saw Nixon on October 8. He was allowed to walk on October 25, and was discharged from the hospital on Novem-

ber 11. He met with his Cabinet for the first time on November 22 at his Camp David retreat in the Catoctin Mountains. After convalescing in Georgia and Florida, the fully recovered President returned to Washington during the week of January 16, 1956, thereby ending this period of uncertainty.

Although the "committee system" worked well during Eisenhower's illness, Adams noted that it left everyone "uncomfortably aware of the Constitution's failure to provide for the direction of the government by an acting President when the President is temporarily disabled and unable to perform his functions." [68] Said Eisenhower of this period:

> I was not required to make any immediate operational decisions involving the use of the armed forces of the United States. Certainly, had there been an emergency such as the detection of incoming enemy bombers, on which I would have had to make a rapid decision regarding the use of United States retaliatory might, there could have been no question, *after* the first forty-eight hours of my heart attack, of my capacity to act according to my own judgment. *However*, had a situation arisen such as occurred in 1958 in which I eventually sent troops ashore in Lebanon, the concentration, the weighing of the pros and cons, and the final determination would have represented a burden, during the *first week* of my illness, which the doctors would likely have found unacceptable for a new cardiac patient to bear. As it was, with a period of rest, I was able to keep my mind clear, to talk to members of the government on matters of long-range interest, and to experience a satisfactory recovery [emphasis added].[69]

Nixon noted that:

> [The committee system] worked during the period of President Eisenhower's heart attack mainly because . . . there was no serious international crisis at that time. But had there been a serious international crisis requiring Presidential decisions, then . . . the committee system might not have worked.[70]

Nixon described his personal dilemma in these words:

> [A]side from the President, I was the only person in government elected by all the people; they had a right to expect leadership, if it were needed, rather than a vacuum. But any move on my part which could be interpreted, even incorrectly, as an attempt to usurp the powers of the presidency would disrupt the Eisenhower team, cause dissension in the nation, and disturb the President and his family.[71]

To avoid misunderstandings Nixon abstained from using the President's office in the White House and declined to sit in the President's chair at Cabinet meetings.

On two other occasions during the Eisenhower administration, the question of presidential inability was forcibly revived. On the morning of June 8, 1956, the public was advised that the President had "an upset stomach and headache" which required a postponement of his schedule for the day. Several hours later the President was removed from the White House on a stretcher and taken to Walter Reed Hospital. The public was told that he had had an attack of ileitis and was being taken to Walter Reed Hospital as a precautionary measure.

There, at 2:59 A.M. on June 9, the President underwent an operation for the removal of a non-malignant obstruction of the small intestine. The operation lasted for two hours, during which the President was unconscious. At a press conference later in the day Dr. Leonard Dudley Heaton, the commanding officer at Walter Reed Hospital, stated:

> We look for a rapid and complete recovery. . . . During the coming week he should be able to sign official papers and carry on those functions of the Government which are necessary. We should like to establish here that his cardiac condition had no relationship to this present illness. We do not expect his heart in any way to affect his convalescence. . . . I want you to know that there was nothing suggesting a malignant disease found at operation.[72]

By June 10 the President was up walking, and the following day he began performing official acts. By August 1 he was said to be in "fine shape" and on August 27 "completely recovered."

During his stay at Walter Reed, President Eisenhower said that he would resign if another illness should occur. He was profoundly disturbed about the operation and its significance for the nation. Said Nixon:

> On several occasions afterwards, he pointed out to me that for the two hours he was under anesthesia the country was without a Chief Executive, the armed forces without a Commander-in-Chief. In the event of a national emergency during those two hours, who would have had the undisputed authority to act for a completely disabled President? [73]

On November 25, 1957, another inability crisis struck when the President sustained a stroke which affected his ability to speak. The stroke occurred at "the worst time possible, short of outright war," according to Nixon, since Russia had just launched its first Sputnik and the country's military and scientific programs were under critical review.

The stroke, which was described initially to the public as a clot or spasm, prevented Eisenhower from attending a state dinner that night in honor of King Mohammed V of Morocco. He became very distressed and reportedly stated to a group of confidants, including Adams: " 'If I cannot attend to my duties, I am simply going to give up this job. Now that is all there is to it.' " Adams notified Nixon: " 'You may be President in the next twenty-four hours.' " [74]

On the next day Adams met with Brownell, Nixon, and Persons to discuss Eisenhower's condition. At the same time the medical bulletins indicated that the President's condition was improved. By December 2 he was back at work in the White House.

Eisenhower's inabilities focused attention on the Constitution's succession provision and its lack of clarity. In 1956 Eisenhower asked the Department of Justice to study the problem and recommend a solution. On February 8, 1957, the entire matter was reviewed at a Cabinet meeting. Attorney General Brownell informed the Cabinet that his staff could not reach a conclusion on what procedure should be followed if the President were unable to declare his own inability. Brownell himself and Adams favored the Vice President's making the determination, checked by the Cabinet, while Eisenhower expressed a preference for a commission consisting of the Chief Justice and some medical experts. A President, asserted Eisenhower, should be allowed to declare his own inability and its termination. He also believed that the 1947 succession law should be revised in favor of a Cabinet line of succession. Brownell and Nixon pointed out that an attempt to change the line of succession would cause a political controversy which might obfuscate the important problem of presidential inability. Thus, it was decided to propose a constitutional amendment of the type favored by Brownell.[75]

A meeting was held with legislative leaders on March 29, 1957, at which opposition to such an amendment was voiced. Speaker Sam Rayburn of Texas said that the public would be suspicious of any attempt by Eisenhower to turn over the government to another. Senator William Knowland of California, the Republican leader in the Senate, felt that a President's competency should be decided by a committee having congressional representation. "There being no unanimity and little enthusiasm among the Republican leaders, and strong opposition from Rayburn, it was apparent that the proposal would not get far and it didn't." [76]

Following Eisenhower's stroke, another attempt was made to get Congress to act on the problem. It, too, met with failure. According to Nixon, "the reason was purely political and obvious. The Democratic congressional leaders would not approve any plan which might put Richard Nixon in the White House before the 1960 election." [77] As a result of these failures, Eisenhower developed an ad hoc solution for any further cases of inability during his administration.*

KENNEDY ASSASSINATION

On November 22, 1963, the nation experienced one of its greatest tragedies when President John F. Kennedy, the youngest elected chief executive, was assassinated. Although the efforts made to save the President did not succeed, they underscored the absence of procedures

* See pp. 55–56, *infra.*

to deal with the case in which a President might linger on unconscious for days, weeks, or months. As James Reston noted in the November 23, 1963 issue of *The New York Times*:

> For an all too brief hour today, it was not clear again what would have happened if the young President, instead of being mortally wounded, had lingered for a long time between life and death, strong enough to survive but too weak to govern.[78]

Succession beyond the vice presidency also was highlighted because, shortly after Kennedy had been shot, rumors circulated that Vice President Lyndon B. Johnson had suffered a heart attack. Fortunately, these rumors were false, and the nation did not have to test the adequacy of the 1947 succession law.

NOTES

1. 2 *The Records of the Federal Convention of 1787* 427 (Farrand ed., 1911 & 1937).

2. For a summary of the colonial experience, see J. Feerick, *From Failing Hands* 23–38 (1965).

3. U. S. Const. art. II, § 1, cl. 6.

4. For the constitutional convention and post-convention history of the succession clause, see *From Failing Hands* 39–56.

5. I. Brant, *James Madison, Commander in Chief, 1812–1836* 184 (1961).

6. *Id.*

7. *Id.* 187.

8. *Id.*

9. *Id.*

10. *Id.* 188.

11. *Id.* 210.

12. *Id.* 219–20.

13. See *From Failing Hands* 91–92.

14. 4 J. Richardson, *A Compilation of the Messages and Papers of the Presidents, 1789–1902* 31–34 (1907).

15. H. Fraser, *Democracy in the Making* 160 (1938); R. Morgan, *A Whig Embattled: The Presidency under John Tyler* 59 & n. 8 (1954).

16. 10 *The Memoirs of John Quincy Adams* 463–64 (Adams ed., 1876).

17. R. Silva, *Presidential Succession* 15–16 & n. 8 (1951).

18. 10 Cong. Globe, 27th Cong., 1st Sess. 3–5 (1841).

19. *Id.* 5.

20. See generally *From Failing Hands* 117–39.

21. *Id.* 124.

22. R. Caldwell, *James A. Garfield: Party Chieftain* 355 (1931).

23. T. Reeves, *Gentleman Boss: The Life of Chester Alan Arthur* 238–43 (1975).

24. *N. Y. Times*, Aug. 27, 1881 at 4.

25. *Id.*, July 8, 1881 at 1.

26. Reeves 244–45; G. Howe, *Chester A. Arthur: A Quarter-Century of Machine Politics* 153 (1934).

27. Brownell, Presidential Disability: The Need for a Constitutional Amendment, 68 Yale L. J. 189, 193–94 (1958).

28. See *From Failing Hands* 133–39.

29. Reeves 247, 253.

30. 8 Richardson 65.

31. Reeves 317–18.

32. *Id.* 358–59.

33. *Id.* 360.

34. *Id.* 370.

35. *Id.* 373–74.

36. See *From Failing Hands* 147–51.

37. A. Nevins, *Grover Cleveland: A Study in Courage* 533 (1962).

38. W. Keen, The Surgical Operations on President Cleveland in 1893, 190 The Saturday Evening Post, Sept. 22, 1917 at 55.

39. See *From Failing Hands* 156–57.

40. See *id.* 162–80; and generally G. Smith, *When the Cheering Stopped: The Last Years of Woodrow Wilson* (1964).

41. Hearings on Presidential Inability and Vacancies in the Office of Vice President Before the Subcomm. on Constitutional Amendments of the Senate Comm. on the Judiciary, 88th Cong., 2d Sess. 112 (1964) (quoting historian John M. Blum).

42. H. Eaton, *Presidential Timber: A History of Nominating Conventions, 1868–1960* 244–45 (1964).

43. J. Tumulty, *Woodrow Wilson as I Know Him* 443–44 (1921).

44. *The Cabinet Diaries of Josephus Daniels: 1913–1921* 445 (Cronon ed., 1963).

45. CBS Reports, The Crisis of Presidential Succession (January 8, 1964) (remarks of Arthur Krock).

46. E. Wilson, *My Memoir* 290 (1939).

47. *From Failing Hands* 173.

48. Tumulty 445.

49. *From Failing Hands* 179.

50. *Id.* 184.

51. See J. Bishop, *FDR's Last Year* ix–x (1974); W. Manchester, *The Glory and the Dream* 321–27 (1973).

52. Bishop 10.

53. *Id.* 130.

54. D. Acheson, *Present at the Creation* 103 (1969).

55. J. Gunther, *Roosevelt in Retrospect: A Profile in History* 28–29 (1950).

56. Bishop 295–96.

57. E. Stettinius, *Roosevelt and the Russians: The Yalta Conference* 25 (1949); Bishop 295–96.

58. *From Failing Hands* 199–201.

59. *Id.* 211–29.

60. *N. Y. Times*, Sept. 26, 1955 at 1.

61. *Id.*, Sept. 28, 1955 at 1.

62. S. Adams, *Firsthand Report: The Story of the Eisenhower Administration* 186–87 (1961).

63. D. Eisenhower, *The White House Years: Mandate for Change* 540 (1963).

64. R. Donovan, *Eisenhower: The Inside Story* 373 (1956).

65. Eisenhower 538.

66. *Id.* 541.

67. E. Benson, *Cross Fire: The Eight Years with Eisenhower* 282 (1962).

68. Adams 192.
69. Eisenhower 545.
70. CBS Reports, The Crisis of Presidential Succession (January 8, 1964).
71. R. Nixon, *Six Crises* 143 (1962).
72. *N. Y. Times*, June 10, 1956 at 60.
73. Nixon 168.
74. *From Failing Hands* 225–26.
75. Adams 200.
76. *Id.* 200–01.
77. Nixon 177.
78. *N. Y. Times*, Nov. 23, 1963 at 7.

2

Vice Presidential Vacancy

[M]y country has in its wisdom contrived for me the most insignificant office that ever the invention of man contrived or his imagination conceived. . . . I can do neither good nor evil. . . .

JOHN ADAMS
December 19, 1793 [1]

CREATION OF OFFICE

FROM MAY 29 through September 4, 1787, the framers of the Constitution spent a considerable amount of time on the executive article.[2] A consensus on a single executive developed early in the Convention, but the method of selecting that executive was not so easily settled. Numerous proposals were advanced, including election by Congress, by the people, and by electors chosen either by the state legislatures or by the people from districts in each state. An election by Congress, for which both the Virginia and the New Jersey Plans of government had provided, was approved by the Convention on a number of occasions between June 1 and August 24, unanimously on July 17. Direct popular election, on the other hand, was rejected by substantial margins on July 17 * and August 24, and a proposal that the President be selected by electors chosen by the people was also defeated on August 24. Since the method of election had not been finally approved at the end of August, the Convention appointed a Committee of Eleven to resolve this and a number of other items.

In a partial report delivered on September 4, the committee proposed that the President be selected by an electoral college system under which the state legislatures would appoint, in such manner as they should decide, presidential electors to make the choice. On the following day a congressional election of the President was rejected, 8 to 2, and on September 6 and 7 the Convention approved the committee's proposal. Although an electoral college method of election was adopted, many

* Said delegate George Mason of Virginia: "[I]t would be as unnatural to refer the choice of a proper character for chief Magistrate to the people, as it would, to refer a trial of colours to a blind man. The extent of the Country renders it impossible that the people can have the requisite capacity to judge of the respective pretentions of the Candidates." 2 *The Records of the Federal Convention of 1787* 31 (Farrand ed., 1911 & 1937).

delegates believed that Congress nevertheless would often make the final decision, since it would be difficult for any candidate to receive a majority of the electoral votes. Thus, delegate George Mason predicted that it would not be "once out of fifty" elections when the President would receive a majority of the electoral votes.[3]

In view of the controversy over the executive article throughout the debates, it is not surprising that the vice presidency was created in the closing days of the Constitutional Convention of 1787. The need for a successor to the President, however, had been recognized from the beginning of the Convention. Both Hamilton's plan of government of June 18, 1787, and the August 6 report of the Committee on Detail provided that the President of the Senate, who was to be elected from among its members, should discharge the powers and duties of the President in the event of the President's death, resignation, removal, or disability.[4] On August 27, when election of the President by Congress was still the favored method at the Convention, Gouverneur Morris of Pennsylvania objected to the President of the Senate's being the "provisional successor" and suggested the Chief Justice.[5] James Madison of Virginia also objected to the President of the Senate, fearing that the Senate might delay the appointment of a President if its presiding officer was the immediate successor. He suggested that during a presidential vacancy the executive powers be administered by a council to the President.† Hugh Williamson of North Carolina suggested that Congress be empowered to provide for occasional successors, and then successfully moved that the entire subject be postponed.

On September 4, the Convention's Committee of Eleven recommended an office of Vice President and an electoral college selection of both the President and the Vice President.[6] These proposals were favorably acted upon on September 6 and 7.

The discussion of September 7 on the office of Vice President focused almost entirely on the Vice President's position as President of the Senate. Elbridge Gerry of Massachusetts, the only framer to become a Vice President, thought that the proposed office, which combined the functions of presidential successor and presiding officer of the Senate, violated the principle of separation of powers since it allowed for executive interference in the legislature.[7] Gouverneur Morris dismissed this notion, arguing that the Vice President could be expected to be independent of the President ("the vice president then will be the first heir apparent that ever loved his father"), and that it mattered little whether the successor was a Vice President who was also President of the Senate or a senator who was elected President of the Senate.[8] Roger Sherman of Connecticut voiced concern that, unless there were a Vice President, some senator

† Current at the time was a suggestion of a council to the President consisting of the Speaker, the President of the Senate, the Chief Justice, and the heads of certain executive departments.

would frequently be deprived of his vote by being made President of the Senate, with the right to vote only when the Senate was deadlocked. He also feared that the Vice President "would be without employment" if he were not also President of the Senate.[9] Hugh Williamson stated that "such an officer as vice-President was not wanted." [10] At the conclusion of this discussion the delegates, by a vote of 8 to 2, decided that the Vice President should be *ex officio* President of the Senate.

The Convention paid little attention to the Vice President's role as a presidential successor. Similarly, scant attention was paid to the office in the state ratifying conventions.[11] The limited discussion of the post-Convention period centered principally on the office's blending of legislative and executive functions. Some objected to the Vice President as unnecessary and useless. George Clinton of New York, later to be Vice President, referred to the office as dangerous and unnecessary, because it blended executive and legislative powers.[12] Only oblique references were made in the state ratifying convention debates to the succession provision. The weight of the available evidence indicates that the framers contemplated that the Vice President would not become President but would act as President in the event of the President's death, resignation, removal, or inability.[13] ‡ In that way, a President would not be ousted from office in a case where he recovered from an inability.

The Vice President was given only two duties by the Constitution: (1) to preside over the Senate, in which capacity he could vote when the Senate was "equally divided," and also open the certificates containing the votes of the presidential electors, and (2) to discharge the powers and duties of the President in case of his death, resignation, removal, or inability. What his actual role would be was clouded in such mystery that Alexander Hamilton was impelled to declare in Number 68 of *The Federalist*:

> The appointment of an extraordinary person as Vice President has been objected to as superfluous, if not mischievous. It has been alleged that it would have been preferable to have authorized the Senate to elect out of their own body an officer answering that description. But two considerations seem to justify the ideas of the convention in this respect. One is that, to secure at all times the possibility of a definite resolution of the body, it is necessary that the President should have only a casting vote. And to take the senator of any State from his seat as senator, to place him in that of President of the Senate, would be to exchange, in regard to the State from which he came, a constant for a contingent vote. The other consideration is that, as the Vice President may occasionally become a substitute for the President in the supreme executive magistracy, all the reasons which recommend the mode of election prescribed for the one apply with great if not with equal force to the manner of appointing the other.[14]

‡ The author explains this conclusion in detail in *From Failing Hands* 40–51.

The Vice President, like the President, was to serve for four years. He was to be elected at the same time and generally in the same manner, and was to be subject to impeachment. While the Constitution provided that the Chief Justice would preside at an impeachment trial of the President, no presiding officer was specified for a trial of the Vice President. Presumably, the President pro tempore of the Senate would preside, since it would be incongruous for an impeached Vice President to preside over his own trial, and since the Constitution provides for the President pro tempore to serve as President of the Senate in the absence of the Vice President.

In contrast to its prescribed oath of office for the President, the Constitution prescribed no oath for the Vice President; one had to be created by an act of Congress of June 1, 1789.[15] Similarly, the Constitution failed to mention any qualifications for the vice presidency, but not through oversight or lack of deliberation. The Vice President would necessarily have the same qualifications as the President (i.e., be a natural-born citizen, of at least thirty-five years of age, and for fourteen years a resident within the United States) because, under the original method of election, presidential electors would vote for two persons for President and the person obtaining the second highest number of votes for President would be Vice President. The method was designed to place in the office of Vice President a person equal in stature to the President.[16]

Its purpose was frustrated early, however, because the electors began to distinguish the two votes in their own minds, casting the first for the candidate they considered suitable for the presidency and the second for their vice presidential choice. This practice surfaced in 1800 when most of the Republican electors voted for Aaron Burr and Thomas Jefferson, intending Burr for Vice President and Jefferson for President. Burr received as many votes as did Jefferson, so the election of President fell to the House of Representatives.[17]

The election of 1800, coupled with the 1796 election of a President and Vice President of different parties, led to the adoption of the Twelfth Amendment in 1804, providing that henceforth electors would cast distinct votes for President and Vice President. The candidate who received a majority of the electoral votes for each office would be elected. If no candidate obtained a majority, the House of Representatives would choose a President "from the persons having the highest numbers not exceeding three on the list of those voted for as President . . ."; and the Senate would choose a Vice President from "the two highest numbers on the list" of those voted for as Vice President. If it happened that the election of a President fell to the House of Representatives and the House failed to elect a President by the date set for his term to begin, the Twelfth Amendment provided that the Vice President–elect would "act" as President. Ironically, there is evidence indicating that the framers of the amendment believed that under this language the Vice President would, if he so acted, become President for the full term.[18] * In order to ensure that the Vice President would have the same qualifications as the President, the Twelfth Amendment provided that "no person constitutionally ineligible to the office of President shall be eligible to that of Vice-President. . . ."

DECLINE AND RISE OF OFFICE

Shortly after the passage of the Constitution, a number of matters concerning the vice presidency came under discussion in the Congress which revealed the low opinion most congressmen held for the office. In a discussion regarding titles, one senator reportedly suggested that the Vice President be referred to as "his Superfluous Excellency." [19] In the debates over an annual salary for the Vice President, some members of the House of Representatives felt that his work would be so sporadic that he should be paid only on a per diem basis.[20] Others, including James Madison, believed that to withhold an annual salary would be offensive to the dignity of the second officer of the government. Said Madison:

> If he is to be considered as the apparent successor of the President, to qualify himself the better for that office, he must withdraw from his other avocations, and direct his attention to the obtaining a perfect knowledge of his intended business. . . . [I]f we mean to carry the constitution into full effect, we ought to make provision for his support, adequate to the merits and nature of the office.[21]

The Congress finally agreed upon an annual salary of $5,000 which was to remain the Vice President's salary for the next sixty-five years.

The paradox which became evident in these debates was the tremendous gap between what the Vice President was and what he could be. As Vice President John Adams declared:

> I am possessed of two separate powers, the one in *esse* and the other in *posse*. I am Vice-President. In this I am nothing, but I may be everything. But I am president also of the Senate.[22]

Although two of the first three Vice Presidents became Presidents in their own right (Adams and Jefferson), the notion that the vice presidency was a sure springboard to the presidency ceased with the adoption of the Twelfth Amendment and the rise of political parties. It was not until 1836 that a third Vice President was elected President, and then not again until the twentieth century. As a result of the Twelfth Amendment, political considerations rather than ability became paramount in

---

* The Twentieth Amendment, which modified the Twelfth, makes clear that the Vice President serves only until a President shall qualify. See Appendix B.

the selection of a Vice President. Senator Alexander White of Virginia was remarkably perceptive when he said during the debates on the amendment that

> character, talents, virtue, and merit, will not be sought after, in the candidate. The question will not be asked, is he capable? is he honest? But can he by his name, by his connexions, by his wealth, by his local situation, by his influence, or his intrigues, best promote the election of a President? [23]

Other members of Congress went so far as to advocate the abolition of the office itself. Indeed, on November 23, 1803, a vote on such a motion was defeated in the Senate by the margin of 19 to 12, and in the House of Representatives on December 7, 1803, by 85 to 27.[24]

As predicted, in ensuing years the vice presidency became a very limited and often disparaged office:

> The adoption of the Twelfth Amendment in 1804 marks a great turning point in the history of the Vice Presidency, and the turn was definitely for the worse. . . . Even without the Twelfth Amendment political party practice was pointing the Vice Presidency toward a decline. But by specifying that each elector would cast one ballot for President and a separate ballot for Vice President the amendment made the descent of the Vice Presidency clearer and more understandable.[25]

Thus, Vice Presidents in the nineteenth century rarely were given any executive responsibilities. They did not take part in meetings of the President's Cabinet, and their role as President of the Senate became little more than a diversion. No longer followed were such pre–Twelfth Amendment precedents as the Vice President's deciding disputed questions regarding the certificates of the presidential electors and participating in Senate debates. Few nineteenth-century Vice Presidents left any legacy for future occupants of their office. In 1840, because of a two-thirds vote requirement, the Democratic National Convention was unable to select any vice presidential candidate to run with its presidential candidate, Martin Van Buren. The incumbent Vice President, Richard Johnson, failed to secure his party's renomination. Four years later an almost unanimous nomination to the vice presidency by the Democratic Party was rejected by Senator Silas Wright of New York.

In general, it may be said that the names of the nineteenth-century Vice Presidents—e.g., Richard M. Johnson, George M. Dallas, William R. King, Hannibal Hamlin, Schuyler Colfax, Henry Wilson, William A. Wheeler, Thomas A. Hendricks, and Levi P. Morton—are wholly unfamiliar to most Americans. Although Vice Presidents John Tyler, Millard Fillmore, Andrew Johnson, and Chester Arthur succeeded to the presidency upon the deaths of Presidents, none subsequently was nominated by his party to run for President in his own right.

The vice presidency did not experience a "renaissance" until the twentieth century. In this century, the role of the Vice President has steadily grown. He has become a regular member of the President's Cabinet,[26] a member of the National Security Council, the head of some executive agencies, a presidential representative on good will and diplomatic tours around the world, and a participant in some of the ceremonial and political functions of the President.[27] And, in this century, the four Vice Presidents who succeeded to the presidency upon the death of a President subsequently were re-elected President, and two other Vice Presidents secured the presidential nominations of their party.*

While the Vice President's duties have been minimal during much of our history and his effectiveness has depended almost completely on his relationship with the President, the office proved to be of vital importance on numerous occasions in the period between 1841 and 1964. Eight times during that period Vice Presidents succeeded to the presidency upon the death of the President; eight times the country was led successfully through the trauma caused by the loss of the President.

Yet the vice presidency had been vacant often in the period prior to 1965.† In addition to the eight vacancies created by a Vice President's succession to the presidency, the office also was vacant when Vice Presidents George Clinton, Elbridge Gerry, William R. King, Henry Wilson, Thomas A. Hendricks, Garret A. Hobart, and James S. Sherman died in office, and when John C. Calhoun resigned to become a United States senator. Between July 9, 1850, and March 4, 1857, the office was occupied for less than two months; and between September 19, 1881, and March 4, 1889, for less than nine months. In each of James Madison's two terms as President, the Vice President died. Gaps for more than three years each occurred following the succession of Tyler, Andrew Johnson, Arthur, Theodore Roosevelt, and Truman to the presidency.

Despite vacancies totaling more than thirty-seven years, no serious effort was made to devise a means for filling a vice presidential vacancy until after the assassination of President Kennedy. It was then that politicians and scholars alike finally concluded that the nation required a Vice President at all times.

* The four who succeeded were Theodore Roosevelt, upon President McKinley's assassination; Calvin Coolidge, upon President Harding's death in office; Harry S Truman, upon President F. D. Roosevelt's death; and Lyndon B. Johnson, upon President Kennedy's assassination. Former Vice Presidents Hubert Humphrey and Richard Nixon were chosen as the presidential candidates of their respective parties in 1968.
† See Appendix D.

NOTES

1. 1 *The Works of John Adams* 460 (Adams ed., 1856).
2. See Feerick, The Electoral College: Why It Was Created, 54 A.B.A.J. 249, 250–52 (1968).
3. 3 J. Elliot, *The Debates in the Several State Conventions on the Adoption of the Federal Constitution* 493 (2d ed. 1836).
4. 3 *The Records of the Federal Convention of 1787* 625 (Farrand ed., 1911 & 1937); 2 Farrand 186.
5. 2 Farrand 427.
6. *Id*. 493–95.
7. *Id*. 536–37.
8. *Id*. 537.
9. *Id*.
10. *Id*.
11. See Field, The Vice-Presidency of the United States, 56 American L. Rev. 365, 369–72 (1922).
12. 2 *The Federalist and Other Constitutional Papers* 628 (Scott ed., 1894).
13. *From Failing Hands* 55–56.
14. *The Federalist* No. 68 at 456 (Ford ed., 1898).
15. 1 Stat. 23. See Learned, The Vice-President's Oath of Office, 104 Nation 248 (1917); and Feerick, The Vice-Presidency and the Problems of Presidential Succession and Inability, 32 Fordham L. Rev. 457, 462 & n. 31 (1964).
16. See N. Peirce, *The People's President* 60–61, 71 (1968); and Feerick, The Electoral College—Why It Ought To Be Abolished, 37 Fordham L. Rev. 1, 17 (1968).
17. Peirce 65–71.
18. *From Failing Hands* 74–75.
19. *Id*. 66.
20. Annals of Cong., 1st Cong., 1st Sess. 672 (1789).
21. *Id*. 674.
22. W. Maclay, *The Journal of William Maclay* 2 (1927).
23. Annals of Cong., 8th Cong., 1st Sess. 144 (1803); see *From Failing Hands* 72–75. For an analysis of the effect of the amendment, see Wilmerding, The Vice Presidency, 68 Pol. Sci. Q. 17, 29–31 (1953).
24. Annals of Cong., 8th Cong., 1st Sess. 84, 682 (1803). On April 12, 1808, Senator James Hillhouse of Connecticut proposed an amendment to abolish the office altogether. *Id*., 10th Cong., 1st Sess. 357 (1808).
25. E. Waugh, *Second Consul* 50 (1956).
26. See L. Hatch, *A History of the Vice-Presidency of the United States* 419 (Shoup ed., 1934); Learned, *The President's Cabinet* (1912); Paullin, The Vice-President and the Cabinet, 29 Am. Hist. Rev. 496, 498 & nn. 13 & 14 (1924).
27. See generally M. Dorman, *The Second Man* (1968); M. Harwood, *In the Shadow of Presidents: The American Vice-Presidency and Succession System* (1966).

3

Succession Beyond the Vice Presidency

> Mr. Burke said, that he had consulted a gentleman skilled in
> the doctrine of chances, who, after considering the subject, had
> informed him, that there was an equal chance that such a
> contingency would not happen more than once in eight hun-
> dred and forty years.
>
> Annals of Cong., 1st Cong., 3d Sess. 1914 (1791)

AS THE FRAMERS DEBATED the executive article, they realized that a
vacancy could occur in the presidency during the course of a term. Indeed, they remembered situations in America's past involving the death,
resignation, absence, and removal of colonial governors. Fortunately,
there had been procedures to handle such contingencies.[1] In the royal
colonies there was an office of lieutenant governor, and provision was
made for either the governor's council or the senior councillor to assume
the reins of government in the event that there were no governor or
lieutenant governor. In the early history of the proprietary colonies, the
governor was given the power to deputize a successor, and at times
exercised the power from his deathbed; later, the senior councillor was
designated to act as governor in the event of a vacancy. It is of interest
that the charters of Connecticut and Rhode Island provided for a governor and deputy governor elected by the people, and authorized the
legislature to fill a vacancy occurring in either of these offices—a power
which was used on numerous occasions.

The first state constitutions adopted after the Declaration of Independence all contained provisions for dealing with executive succession. A
lieutenant governor was the immediate successor in several of the
colonies, the president of the governor's council in a few, and the presiding officer of the upper house of the legislature in others. Several colonies
continued the line of succession beyond the immediate successor. For
example, New York ran the line of succession from the lieutenant
governor to the legislative officers, and Delaware and North Carolina
from the presiding officer of the upper house to the speaker of the lower
house.

This pre-Convention experience undoubtedly shaped the provisions of
Article II, section 1, clause 6 of the Constitution with respect to a line of
succession beyond the vice presidency. It was late in the Constitutional

Convention of 1787 when Hugh Williamson declared that Congress "ought to have power to provide for occasional successors . . ." to the President. Accepting his suggestion, Edmund Randolph of Virginia on September 7 moved to expand the provision providing for a Vice President's succession in the event of a President's death, resignation, removal, absence, or inability.* At the time of Randolph's proposal the provision simply stated:

[I]n case of his [the President's] removal as aforesaid, death, absence, resignation or inability to discharge the powers or duties of his office, the vice-president shall exercise those powers and duties until another President be chosen, or until the inability of the President be removed.

Randolph's suggested addition was:

The Legislature may declare by law what officer of the U.S.—shall act as President in case of the death, resignation, or disability of the President and Vice-President; and such officer shall act accordingly *until the time of electing a President shall arrive* [emphasis added].[2]

Madison objected that the italicized words would prevent the filling of a vacancy by means of a special election of the President. He suggested as an alternative the expression "until such disability be removed, or a President shall be elected." A few delegates opposed Madison's proposed change, believing that it would be difficult to schedule a special election. Other delegates objected to the limitation that Congress could appoint only officers of the United States. These objections notwithstanding, Randolph's suggestion with Madison's amendment was accepted by a vote of 6 to 4. The debates at the Virginia ratifying convention clearly show that the intent was to allow for a special election, at least in the event of a double vacancy. There, George Mason objected to the succession provision on the ground that it did not provide for an immediate election in case of a presidential vacancy. In reply, Madison stated that if both the President and the Vice President should die, another election would take place immediately, but that in default of such election the successor appointed by Congress could serve only for the remainder of the term.[3]

Unfortunately, the various congressional enactments prescribing a line of succession beyond the vice presidency have never been very

---

* The "absence" contingency was deleted subsequently from the succession provision by the Committee on Style. No doubt, it had been included initially because of the colonial practice under which a governor's absence from the colony resulted in the assumption of his powers and duties by the person next in line. *From Failing Hands* 23–38. The intent in using it seems to have been to cover situations when a President might be absent from the seat of government. It was dropped by the Committee on Style probably because of the belief that the term "inability" was broad enough to cover such situations. The term "disability," which seems to have been used interchangeably with "inability," was dropped only from the first part of the provision. *Id.* 48–50.

satisfactory. Each reflected considerations of the personalities occupying the particular offices at the time, and each assigned the responsibility of succession to an official who had been chosen for his office for reasons other than his qualifications as a potential President.

THE 1792 LAW

The first succession law was formulated at the time when Thomas Jefferson was serving as Secretary of State.[4] His political foe, Alexander Hamilton, was serving both as Secretary of the Treasury and as leader of the Federalist Party, which then controlled the United States Senate. The view was very much current that should the Secretary of State be placed first in the statutory line of succession, Hamilton's pretense as head of the Cabinet would be exposed and Jefferson's potential as a future President enhanced.

A bill was presented in the First Congress providing that some officer, whose designation was left blank, should act as President whenever there were vacancies in the offices of President and Vice President.[5] Suggestions subsequently were made to name the officer variously as the Secretary of State, the Secretary of the Treasury, the Chief Justice, the President pro tempore, and the Speaker. One of those objecting to the Chief Justice was James Madison, who felt that this would be an excessive merging of the executive and the judiciary. Madison was also opposed to the selection of the President pro tempore since he would be holding two offices simultaneously—those of senator and of Acting President—and that as a senator he would be subject to instruction by his state. In Madison's view, the Secretary of State was the preferable successor, but others felt that the designation of the Secretary of State would give too much power to the President in the selection of a potential successor. It is not surprising, then, that no consensus developed in the First Congress, and that the entire subject was dropped—but not until after some delegates had expressed their views concerning the need for immediate action. One member of Congress observed that dual vacancies would not happen once in 100 years; another, that there was an equal chance that the situation would not happen more than once in 840 years. In contrast, Representative William B. Giles of Virginia urged that the matter be dealt with promptly before any such calamity occurred. "Suppose," he said, "the Vice President should die, then the fate of this Government would remain in the hands of the President who, by resigning, would destroy its organization, without leaving a constitutional mode of filling the vacancy." [6]

In the Second Congress, on November 30, 1791, the Senate passed a bill dealing with the selection of presidential electors. Section 9 of the bill named the President pro tempore and the Speaker successively as the persons to administer the government in the event of vacancies in the offices of both President and Vice President. When the bill came under scrutiny in the House by the Committee of the Whole, a motion to eliminate Section 9 entirely was made and defeated. Also made and defeated was a motion to remove the President pro tempore and the Speaker from the line of succession.

At the committee stage, a number of representatives expressed the view that neither the President pro tempore nor the Speaker was an officer in the sense contemplated by the Constitution.* Thus, Representative Giles declared that "if they had been considered as such, it is probable they would have been designated in the Constitution; the Constitution refers to some permanent officer to be created pursuant to the provisions therein contained." [7] Said Representative Hugh Williamson: "[T]his extensive construction of the meaning of the word officer, would render it proper to point out any person in the United States, whether connected with the Government or not, as a proper person to fill the vacancy contemplated." [8] Other representatives, however, felt that they were officers. "If [the Speaker] is not an officer," said Representative Elbridge Gerry of Massachusetts, "what is he?" [9] Gerry, however, objected to Section 9 on the ground that it blended the executive and legislative branches. Representative James Hillhouse of Connecticut preferred a legislative succession and registered a general objection to any provision by which the President could appoint his own successor, since it would take "away the choice from the people . . . violating the first principle of a free elective Government." [10]

When on January 2, 1792, the Committee of the Whole reported the bill to the House, a motion to strike out the President pro tempore was defeated narrowly while one to eliminate the Speaker was carried. Voting in favor of these motions were a number of framers, including Madison, Williamson, Abraham Baldwin of Georgia, and Thomas Fitzsimmons of Pennsylvania. Elbridge Gerry joined in the motion to eliminate the Speaker, but not the President pro tempore. Thereupon, the bill was returned to the committee, which removed the President pro tempore from the line of succession and substituted the Secretary of State. The House then passed the bill and forwarded it to the Senate. [11]

In the Senate—the result in no small measure of Hamilton's influence and the opposition to Jefferson—the House amendment was rejected, and

---

* In the First Congress, Representative Alexander White of Virginia had advanced this argument, with which Representative Roger Sherman of Connecticut had disagreed. Annals of Cong., 1st Cong., 3d Sess. 1902–03 (1791). Representative William L. Smith of South Carolina also questioned whether Congress could provide for an officer to serve only until a special presidential election were held to elect a new President and Vice President. In his view the Constitution provided only for a regular quadrennial election. *Id.* 1902.

the President pro tempore and the Speaker were again inserted. On February 21, 1792, the bill was returned to the House, which withdrew its amendment, 31 to 24. The bill became law on March 1, 1792, when it was signed by President George Washington.[12]

Section 10 of the act provided that whenever the offices of President and Vice President became vacant, the Secretary of State was to notify the governor of every state that electors were to be appointed within thirty-four days prior to the first Wednesday of the ensuing December. If less than two months remained before that date and if the term of the last President and Vice President were not to end in the following March, the election would take place in December in the year next ensuing, with the newly elected President and Vice President taking office in the following March.† If the term were to end in March, no election at all would take place. The bill seems to have contemplated a four-year term for a specially elected President and Vice President.

Shortly after the law of 1792 was passed, James Madison expressed his opposition to it, in a letter to Edmund Pendleton, the governor of Virginia. He questioned the constitutionality of placing the legislative officers in the line of succession, stating:

> It may be questioned whether these [the President pro tempore and the Speaker] are officers in the Constitutional sense. . . . If officers, whether both could be introduced. . . . As they are created by the Constitution, they would probably have been there designated if contemplated for such service, instead of being left to the legislative selection.[13]

He also stated that the Speaker and the President pro tempore

> will retain their Legislative stations, and then incompatible functions will be blended; or the incompatibility will supersede those stations, & then those being the substratum of the adventitious functions, these must fail also. The Constitution says Congress may declare what officers, &c., which seems to make it not an appointment or a translation, but an annexation of one office or trust to another office.[14] *

For the next ninety-four years, the President pro tempore and the Speaker were the only successors after the Vice President. Although four Presidents and five Vice Presidents died in office during this period, a double vacancy did not occur. Accordingly, the 1792 law was never implemented. Close calls did occur. In 1844 President Tyler's life was endangered by an explosion, and in 1853 President Franklin Pierce

† Hence, depending on when the dual vacancies occurred, the 1792 law left open the possibility of the statutory successors' serving for a period of up to seventeen months.
* In her pioneer work on presidential succession, Ruth Silva argues persuasively that the framers intended the Vice President and the officer designated by Congress to serve only as an Acting President, while continuing to occupy the position they held at the commencement of such service. R. Silva, *Presidential Succession* (1951).

suffered from a serious case of malaria. Had anything happened to these Presidents, there would have been no Vice Presidents to serve in their places.†

THE 1886 LAW

Dissatisfaction with the act of 1792 reached a peak in the 1880s.‡ Of major importance was the fact that when Arthur succeeded to the presidency upon Garfield's death, there was neither a President pro tempore nor a Speaker to act as President in the event that something happened to Arthur. Both positions remained unfilled for a period of several weeks. Similarly, when Vice President Thomas Hendricks died in November 1885, there was no President pro tempore or Speaker to succeed if the President were to die.

These events generated considerable discussion in Congress on the problems of presidential succession and presidential inability.[15] Numerous objections to the act of 1792 were voiced. It was argued time and again during this period—particularly by Senators George F. Hoar of Massachusetts, Samuel B. Maxey of Texas, James B. Beck of Kentucky, and Augustus H. Garland of Massachusetts—that the President pro tempore and the Speaker were not officers of the United States within the meaning of the succession provision. James Madison was cited as authority for this proposition, as was the *Blount* impeachment, which had been interpreted as deciding that a member of Congress is not an officer of the United States.[16] § Parts of the Constitution itself were cited in support of this position.* An officer under the succession provision, they said, was

† These events are described in *From Failing Hands* 97, 105.

‡ Prior to the 1880s, various suggestions for reform had been voiced. For example, in 1856 the Senate Judiciary Committee recommended that the line of succession be extended to the Chief Justice of the Supreme Court and then the associate justices according to seniority. S. Rep. No. 260, 34th Cong., 1st Sess. 5 (1856). The committee also expressed the view that the special election feature of the 1792 law was constitutional, and that any specially elected President would serve a full four-year term. Eleven years later, a unanimous House Judiciary Committee said that Congress had no power to provide for a special presidential election. Cong. Globe, 39th Cong., 2d Sess. 691 (1867). In 1868, shortly after his impeachment trial, President Johnson recommended changing the line of succession to the members of the Cabinet, stating that the legislative officers had a stake in removing the President by resort to the impeachment process.

§ Senator William Blount of Tennessee was impeached by the House in 1797. When he was tried in the Senate, his lawyers pleaded lack of jurisdiction on the ground, among others, that a senator was not a civil officer and thus not subject to impeachment. The Senate dismissed the case, giving no reason for its decision. Since Blount had been expelled before the dismissal, another interpretation is that a member of Congress loses his status as a civil officer, and therefore may not be impeached, after he is expelled from Congress. See U. S. Const. art. II, § 4.

* See U. S. Const. art. II, § 1, cl. 2, where a distinction is made between senators and representatives, on the one hand, and "officers," on the other: "[N]o Senator or Representative, or Person holding an Office of Trust or Profit under the United States . . .";

a permanent officer, who receives his commission from the President and remains in that office while acting as President.[17] As Senator Hoar stated:

> [T]he Presidency is annexed by law to an office. It is not a person holding an office at the time succeeding to the Presidency, but it is an officer continuing in that office who is to perform as an annex or incident merely to another office the great duties of the Presidency itself. The moment he lays down or becomes incapable to perform the duties of the principal office to which the Presidency is annexed, that moment he must lay down or be incapable of performing the duties of the Presidency itself. . . .[18]

It was urged that the Speaker and the President pro tempore as members of Congress could not be "officers of the United States" in the constitutional sense because Article I, section 6 provided that "no Person holding any Office under the United States, shall be a Member of either House during his Continuance in Office." It also was pointed out that if either became Acting President while continuing to serve as a presiding officer and member of Congress, his tenure as Acting President would be subject to the will of his respective House and it could be ended abruptly if he was replaced as a presiding officer or lost his legislative seat at the polls. This objection to the 1792 law was more than academic since the law was predicated on the premise that the President pro tempore and the Speaker were not eligible to act as President unless they retained their offices while so acting. This prompted the additional objection that the law violated the principle of separation of powers, since the President pro tempore or the Speaker, as presiding officer of his House, was entitled to vote and participate in congressional debates. A further objection was voiced to the President pro tempore on the ground that in the case of an impeachment trial of the President when there was no Vice President, as in 1868, he would be placed in a difficult position, raising questions of propriety and legitimacy. Thus, Senator William M. Evarts of New York argued that the Constitution did not contemplate that the House could impeach and the Senate convict and then replace the President with one of their own members.[19] Another criticism of the 1792 law was that it rendered possible a political transfer of the administration when the opposition party controlled Congress.

Most of the critics of the 1792 law favored a Cabinet line of succession, believing that there was no doubt about a Cabinet member's status as an "officer" and that such a line would produce continuity of administration and policy. It also was asserted that the Secretary of State usually

---

and U. S. Const. amend. XIV, § 3: "No Person shall be a Senator or Representative in Congress . . . or hold any office, civil or military, under the United States. . . ." It also was argued that a President pro tempore is not even an officer of the Senate, since U. S. Const. art. I, § 3, cl. 5, provides: "The Senate shall chuse their other Officers, and also a President pro tempore. . . ." See 14 Cong. Rec. 913 (1883).

would be better qualified for the discharge of executive duties than either the President pro tempore or the Speaker. Opposition to a Cabinet line of succession centered on the arguments that the original law was written by the Founding Fathers, and that the President would be able to appoint his own successor, which would be contrary, it was reasoned, to the elective principle of democracy.

The arguments for a Cabinet line of succession prevailed with the adoption of the act of January 19, 1886.[20] † That act removed the President pro tempore and the Speaker from the line of succession, and substituted the heads of the executive departments in the following order: Secretary of State, Secretary of the Treasury, Secretary of War, Attorney General, Postmaster General, Secretary of the Navy, and Secretary of the Interior.

Although some of the advocates of the 1886 law thought that the special election provision of the 1792 act was unwise or even unconstitutional, the following provision nonetheless was inserted in the 1886 act:

> [T]he Secretary of State . . . shall act as President until the disability of the President or Vice President is removed or *a President shall be elected*; Provided, That whenever the powers and duties of . . . President . . . shall devolve upon any of the persons named herein, if Congress be not in session, or if it would not meet in accordance with law within twenty days thereafter, it shall be the duty of the person upon whom said powers and duties shall devolve to issue a proclamation convening Congress in extraordinary session, giving twenty days' notice of the meeting [emphasis added].‡

Although the matter is far from clear, it appears that this provision was designed to permit Congress to decide whether or not to call a special election.[21] §

Between 1886 and 1945 three Presidents and two Vice Presidents died in office. But since a double vacancy did not occur, it was unnecessary to resort to the act of 1886.

THE 1947 LAW

After the death of President Roosevelt on April 12, 1945, and the succession of Vice President Harry S Truman to the presidency, criticism of

† See Appendix C.

‡ This provision is the same as that placed in U. S. Const. art. II, § 1, cl. 6 to allow for a special presidential election. See p. 36, *supra*.

§ The clause which provided that the Acting President serve "until . . . a President shall be elected" was severely criticized in Hamlin, The Presidential Succession Act of 1886, 18 Harvard L. Rev. 182, 191–93 (1905), where it was said to be both confusing and unwise in that the tenure of the successor was not fixed (i.e., whether or not it was for the rest of the presidential term or until a special election took place), and thereby it allowed Congress to harass an acting executive should it choose to do so. Cf. Silva, The Presidential Succession Act of 1947, 47 Michigan L. Rev. 451, 472–75 (1949).

the 1886 act manifested itself.[22] Forty-four-year-old Edward R. Stettinius, Jr., a former steel executive who lacked a clear-cut political affiliation and substantial government experience, was then Secretary of State. Truman later wrote that he felt strongly that the successor to the President should have held elective office and that until he could persuade Congress to make a statutory change in the line of succession he preferred to replace Stettinius with a person with an elective background. Truman regarded James F. Byrnes, then sixty-eight years old and in poor health, as the best qualified candidate in light of his years of congressional and executive service; nor was Truman unaware of the political advantage of appointing Byrnes, who had expected to be Roosevelt's vice presidential choice in 1944.[23] He offered Byrnes the position of Secretary of State when returning from the Roosevelt funeral at Hyde Park, but delayed announcing his choice until the conclusion of the San Francisco United Nations organizational meeting at which Stettinius represented the United States. The conference ended June 26, Stettinius resigned June 27, and the appointment of Byrnes was announced June 30.[24]

Shortly before the Stettinius resignation, Truman sent a special message to Congress, in which he declared:

[B]y reason of the tragic death of the late President, it now lies within my power to nominate the person who would be my immediate successor in the event of my own death or inability to act.

I do not believe that in a democracy this power should rest with the Chief Executive.

Insofar as possible, the office of the President should be filled by an elective officer. There is no officer in our system of government, besides the President and Vice President, who has been elected by all the voters of the country.

The Speaker of the House of Representatives, who is elected in his own district, is also elected to be the presiding officer of the House by a vote of all the Representatives of all the people of the country. As a result, I believe that the Speaker is the official in the Federal Government, whose selection next to that of the President and Vice President, can be most accurately said to stem from the people themselves.[25]

In placing the Speaker ahead of the President pro tempore, Truman stated that members of the House are closer to the people than those of the Senate, since they are elected every two years. Hence the Speaker would be closer than the President pro tempore. Truman also recommended that whoever succeeded after the Vice President should serve as President only until a new President and Vice President are chosen, either at the time of the next congressional election or by means of a special election. The newly elected team would fill out the existing term.

On June 25, 1945, Representative Hatton W. Sumners of Texas introduced a bill embodying the President's recommendations and placing the Speaker and the President pro tempore ahead of the Cabinet in the line of succession.[26] It was debated briefly in the House on June 29, with supporting statements made by Representatives Estes Kefauver of Tennessee, John M. Robsion of Kentucky, Sumners, Chauncey W. Reed of Illinois, Earl C. Michener of Michigan, and A. S. Mike Monroney of Oklahoma.[27] The enactment of the first succession law and its long acceptance, the Supreme Court decision in *Lamar* v. *United States*,[28] * and parts of the Constitution itself were referred to in support of the contention that a law placing the Speaker and the President pro tempore in the line of succession would be constitutional. Representative Kefauver argued that Article I, section 2, clause 5 of the Constitution, which provides that the "House of Representatives shall chuse their Speaker and other Officers . . . ," shows that the Speaker is an officer. Representatives John W. Gwynne of Iowa, Charles E. Hancock of New York, and Raymond S. Springer of Indiana reiterated the arguments of others from past Congresses that the Speaker and President pro tempore were not officers within the meaning of the succession clause. The special election feature of the Sumners bill was attacked by Representative Robsion, who stated that it would require conforming changes in state election laws and constitutions.† He was joined by others. Kefauver observed: "[I]t probably would upset things too much within a period of four years to have four people fill the office of President—the President, the Vice President, the Speaker of the House—and then have an election to get the fourth person." [29] Said Representative Monroney: "I feel that the Speaker should continue to fill that unexpired term of the Presidency in order to avoid creating disunity and division which always occurs in a national election at a time when we would need the greatest unity in our country." [30] These representatives succeeded in eliminating the election provision altogether. As amended, the Sumners bill passed the House and was forwarded to the Senate, where it became pigeonholed in committee.

The 1946 congressional elections placed the opposition party in the majority in Congress. Yet President Truman still asked for action on his succession recommendations, in spite of the fact that their enactment would place a Republican Speaker, Joseph W. Martin of Massachusetts, first in the line of succession. In June 1947 the Senate gave serious con-

* In that case, the Court held that a member of the House of Representatives was an officer within the meaning of a penal statute making it a crime for one to impersonate an officer of the government. The Court was careful to note that the issue presented was not a constitutional one. In the course of its opinion, the Court stated: "[W]hen the relations of members of the House of Representatives to the Government of the United States are borne in mind and the nature and character of their duties and responsibilities are considered, we are clearly of the opinion that such members are embraced by the comprehensive terms of the statute." 241 U. S. 103, 112 (1916).

† As reported from committee, the bill provided for a special election to fill vacancies in the offices of President and Vice President if such should occur ninety days or more before the midterm congressional elections.

sideration to a bill (similar to the Sumners bill) which had been introduced several months before by Senator Kenneth S. Wherry of Nebraska. Unlike the Sumners bill, it contained no special election provision and it expressly required the Speaker and the President pro tempore to resign from Congress before they could act as President.[31] The Senate debate on the Wherry bill was similar to the debate on the Sumners bill. Thus, during the debates of June 1947, objections were voiced that the Speaker and the President pro tempore are not officers; that if an officer resigns his office he cannot act as President; that it would violate the principle of separation of powers for a member of Congress to act as President; that it was unlikely the Speaker and the President pro tempore would act in a case of a presidential inability, and that they are not elected on the basis of their qualifications for the presidency.[32] An amendment to place the President pro tempore ahead of the Speaker was proposed by Senator Richard B. Russell of Georgia. It was narrowly defeated, largely because Senator Arthur Vandenberg of Michigan, the then President pro tempore, argued that the Speaker was "the officer reflecting the largest measure of popular and representative expression at the instant moment of his succession." [33] An amendment proposed by Senator Brien McMahon of Connecticut for a special election provision was defeated. McMahon's proposal provided for the last electoral college to select a new President and Vice President whenever vacancies in both offices occurred 120 or more days before the end of the term. Senator Wherry objected to this amendment on the grounds that Congress lacked the power to legislate a special election, that the Constitution provided only for four-year terms, and that it would interfere with the power of the states to say how their electors are to be chosen.[34] Also defeated was a proposal by Senator Alexander Wiley of Wisconsin to add the highest-ranking military or naval officers to the line of succession after the Cabinet heads. The bill finally was put to a vote and was passed, 50 to 35. On July 10 it passed the House, 365 to 11, and on July 18 it became law with President Truman's signature.[35] *

The 1947 law provides that

If, by reason of death, resignation, removal from office, inability, or failure to qualify, there is neither a President nor Vice-President to discharge the powers and duties of the office of President, then the Speaker . . . shall, upon his resignation as Speaker and as Representative in Congress, act as President.

If there is no Speaker at the time, then the President pro tempore acts as President, upon his resignation as President pro tempore and as senator. If either the Speaker or the President pro tempore acts, he does so until the end of the presidential term except in cases of failure to qualify or of

* See Appendix C.

inability, in which cases he acts until a President or Vice President qualifies or recovers from an inability. If the President pro tempore acts, he cannot be replaced by a new Speaker. If a President pro tempore acting as President should die while in office, he would be replaced by the new Speaker, or in the absence of a Speaker, by the new President pro tempore. The act is not clear on whether a new Speaker, elected after a Speaker had resigned to act as President, is next in line. The legislative history of the act suggests that he would be.[36] Furthermore, the act does not state that the Speaker or the President pro tempore must take the presidential oath, although the legislative history indicates that such was intended.[37] His resigning from Congress and taking the oath would probably be simultaneous so that, it may be argued, at the time at which he acts as President, he would still be an "officer."

If there should be no Speaker or President pro tempore at the time of an emergency, then the line of succession runs to the highest on the following list who is not under a disability which precludes his discharging the powers and duties of the President: Secretary of State, Secretary of the Treasury, Secretary of Defense, Attorney General, Postmaster General, Secretary of the Interior, Secretary of Agriculture, Secretary of Commerce, Secretary of Labor.† The act provides that a Cabinet officer automatically resign his departmental position upon taking the presidential oath of office. He acts as President for the rest of the term or until a President, Vice President, Speaker, or President pro tempore is available. The 1947 law makes it clear that no one may act as President who does not have the constitutional requirements for the presidency.‡

Although the 1947 act has never been applied, the act's imperfections were highlighted on several occasions when the Speaker became the heir apparent. From President Kennedy's assassination until January 20, 1965, Speaker John W. McCormack, more than seventy years of age, stood at the top of the line and lamented that circumstance:

> I have lived for 14 months in the position of the man who, in the event of an unfortunate event happening to the occupant of the White House, under the law then would have assumed the Office of Chief Executive of our country.[38]

Shortly after the assassination, when a reporter asked McCormack whether he might resign as Speaker to permit a younger person to become next in line, he declared: "I was elected Speaker and I'm staying Speaker. I'm amazed, just amazed, that you can ask that. Are there no

† The Secretaries of Health, Education and Welfare, of Housing and Urban Development, and of Transportation have been added to the line of succession since 1947. The Postmaster General was removed from the line at the creation of the Postal Service in 1970.

‡ The 1792 law was unclear on this point, thereby giving rise to a view that an Acting President did not have to possess the presidential qualifications specified in U. S. Const. art. II, § 1, cl. 6, which refers to eligibility to the "office" of President.

limits to decency?" [39] Similarly, following the resignations from office of Spiro T. Agnew and Richard M. Nixon, there were long periods of time during which Speaker Carl Albert stood first in line under extraordinary circumstances. After Agnew's resignation, the problem of Albert's position as successor was compounded since the House of Representatives had almost concurrently begun an impeachment inquiry into the President's conduct in office. Albert's succession during either of these periods would have shifted control of the White House to a different political party. Of the possibility of such succession, Albert reportedly said to a friend: "Lord help me. I pray every night it doesn't happen." [40]

NOTES

1. *From Failing Hands* 23–38.
2. 2 *The Records of the Federal Convention of 1787* 499, 535 (Farrand ed., 1911 & 1937).
3. 3 J. Elliot, *The Debates in the Several State Conventions on the Adoption of the Federal Constitution* 487–88 (2d ed. 1836).
4. *From Failing Hands* 57–62.
5. Annals of Cong., 1st Cong., 3d Sess. 1813 (1790).
6. *Id.* 1865.
7. 2 Annals of Cong., 2d Cong., 1st Sess. 281 (1791).
8. *Id.* 282.
9. *Id.* 281.
10. *Id.* 282.
11. *From Failing Hands* 59–60.
12. 1 Stat. 240.
13. 6 *Writings of James Madison* 95 & n. 1 (Hunt ed., 1906).
14. *Id.* 95–96.
15. *From Failing Hands* 140–46.
16. 2 Annals of Congress, 5th Cong., 3d Sess. 2245–416 (1798–99).
17. *From Failing Hands* 144–45.
18. 14 Cong. Rec. 689 (1882).
19. 17 Cong. Rec. 250 (1885).
20. 24 Stat. 1.
21. Hamlin, The Presidential Succession Act of 1886, 18 Harvard L. Rev. 182, 191 (1905).
22. *From Failing Hands* 204–10.
23. H. Truman, *Memoirs*, Vol. I, *Year of Decisions* 23 (1955).
24. *Id.* 326.
25. H. Truman, Special Message to the Congress on the Succession to the Presidency, June 19, 1945, *Public Papers of the Presidents of the United States* 129 (1961); 91 Cong. Rec. 6272 (1945).
26. H. R. 3587, 79th Cong., 1st Sess. (1945).
27. 91 Cong. Rec. 7010–22 (1945).
28. 241 U. S. 103 (1916).
29. 91 Cong. Rec. 7017 (1945).
30. *Id.* 7013.
31. S. 564, 80th Cong., 1st Sess. (1947).
32. *From Failing Hands* 207–08; 93 Cong. Rec. 7767–70 (1947).

33. 93 Cong. Rec. 7781 (1947).
34. *Id.* 7783–84.
35. 3 U.S.C. § 19 (1964), as amended, 3 U.S.C. § 19 (1970).
36. 93 Cong. Rec. 8622, 8626, 7696 (1947); 91 Cong. Rec. 7009 (1945).
37. 93 Cong. Rec. 7772 (1947); 91 Cong. Rec. 7026 (1945); see also Feerick, The Vice-Presidency and the Problems of Presidential Succession and Inability, 32 Fordham L. Rev. 482–83 & n. 159 (1964).
38. 111 Cong. Rec. 7967 (1965).
39. *N. Y. Herald–Tribune*, Dec. 12, 1963 at 1.
40. J. F. terHorst, *Gerald Ford and the Future of the Presidency* 145 (1974).

II

The Solution

4

Early Steps to Solve the Inability Problem

> We are very fortunate that this country now has a young,
> vigorous and obviously healthy President. This will allow us
> to explore these problems in detail without any implication that
> the present holder of that high office is not in good health.
>
> ESTES KEFAUVER
> June 11, 1963 [1]

1881–1961

DURING AND IMMEDIATELY AFTER the inabilities of Presidents James Garfield and Woodrow Wilson, proposals were introduced in Congress to combat the inability problem.

In the Garfield period, debate raged over the meaning of "inability," the status of a Vice President who succeeded in the event of a presidential inability, and the question of who had the power to determine whether an inability existed.[2] Professor Theodore W. Dwight of Columbia Law School argued that inability was limited to mental incapacity; others said that it applied to any kind of inability, of the body or mind, temporary or permanent, which prevented the discharge of the powers and duties of President; and others said that it must be of an obvious nature and that there must be an urgent need for executive action. Senators Charles W. Jones of Florida and George F. Hoar of Massachusetts argued that a Vice President who succeeded in a case of inability would serve for the rest of the term regardless of whether the President recovered. The framers of the Constitution, said Jones, had deliberately substituted the word "devolve" for "exercise" and had intended the so-called special election clause ("until . . . a President shall be elected") as a limitation on the tenure of an officer appointed by Congress but not on a Vice President, who was elected for a period of four years.[3] The predominant view, however, was to the contrary: namely, that in a case of inability, the Vice President acted temporarily until the President recovered. On the question of who had the power to declare a President disabled, a number of persons contended that the "necessary and proper" clause of Article I, section 8 gave Congress the power to adopt legislation on the subject. One point of view held that Congress itself was the only tribunal for deciding when an inability existed; another, that Congress could only provide by law the definition of an inability but could not declare of it-self that an inability actually existed. Others contended that the Consti-tution gave the Vice President the power to determine when a President was disabled. Yet another position was that the Constitution left the question to the President and Vice President. A further view was that the Vice President could act only at the request of the Cabinet or Presi-dent.

In the Wilson period one group of proposals introduced in Congress gave the Supreme Court the power to declare a President disabled when-ever it was authorized so to act by resolution of Congress; another pro-posal authorized the Secretary of State to convene the Cabinet to inquire into a President's ability to discharge his powers and duties whenever the President had been unable to do so for a period of six consecutive weeks, with a majority of the Cabinet empowered to declare him dis-abled.[4] These proposals were considered at hearings of the House Judi-ciary Committee; but considerable disagreement arose concerning the status of a Vice President who succeeded in a case of inability—that is, whether he replaced the President for the rest of the term.

These efforts at reform failed, in large part because of the varying views on the subject and the lack of any consensus on a single proposal. From 1921 to 1955 practically no attention was given to the problem, apart from an isolated speech or article about the importance of finding a solution.[5] In September 1955, shortly before President Eisenhower's heart attack, the chairman of the House Judiciary Committee, Emanuel Celler of New York, ordered the committee staff to undertake a study of presidential inability. The staff subsequently distributed to a number of jurists, political scientists, and public officials a questionnaire seeking their views on such questions as, what was intended by the term "in-ability"? Should a definition be enacted into law? Who should initiate and make the determination of inability? Of cessation of inability? Is a consti-tutional amendment necessary? [6]

The replies were extremely varied. Although a substantial majority of those who responded suggested that no definition of inability be enacted into law, and that in the event of a temporary inability the Vice President would succeed only to the powers and duties of President, there was little agreement on the remaining areas.[7] Thus, a wide variety of proposals were advanced on who should initiate the question of inability. Many felt that the agency for initiation should be different from that of determina-tion. Among the agencies proposed for the functions of initiation and determination were Congress, the Cabinet, the Vice President, the Supreme Court, a permanent commission of private citizens appointed by the Supreme Court, a panel of medical specialists appointed by the Chief Justice, a council consisting of Cabinet members and congressional leaders, a commission consisting of Supreme Court justices and other federal judges, a special body created by Congress, and combinations of these agencies. There was a similar variance of views with respect to the method of ascertaining the end of an inability.

From the replies, the Judiciary Committee staff formulated five proposals—one in the form of a bill, one a joint resolution, and the others as constitutional amendments.[8] All permitted the President to declare his own inability, and four provided that he could declare the end of his inability whether he had made the initial determination or not. In the case of a President who could not declare his own inability, two proposals empowered the Vice President to make the determination of inability; two, the Cabinet; and one, a medical panel appointed by the Chief Justice.

Against the backdrop of Eisenhower's first heart attack, a subcommittee of the House Judiciary Committee held hearings on the subject in 1956. Following the hearings, its members met in executive session to attempt to reach agreement on a single proposal, but without success. In the following year, Attorney General Herbert Brownell presented to the subcommittee on behalf of the administration a proposed constitutional amendment containing the following provisions: The President could declare his own inability, and the Vice President would discharge the powers and duties of President. If the President failed to declare his inability or was unable to do so, the Vice President, "if satisfied of the President's inability, and upon approval in writing of a majority of the heads of executive departments who are members of the President's Cabinet . . . ," would act as President. In either case, the President would resume his powers and duties upon his written declaration of recovery.[9]

The feature of the administration's proposal which came under particularly heavy criticism was the provision permitting the President to declare the end to his inability. Representative Kenneth B. Keating of New York leveled the sharpest attack, stating: "I can see . . . the danger of a chaotic condition by having the Vice President say the President was unable, and the next day the President saying, 'I am able,' and then the Vice President the next day saying he is unable, so that you would have a day-by-day President." [10] In response, Brownell argued that public opinion would ultimately decide the matter since the Vice President would not act without the suppport of the nation and could not act without the Cabinet's approval. Brownell stated that, since the President was elected by the people, there should be no obstruction to his resuming his powers and duties. If either the President or Vice President should act arbitrarily or irresponsibly, said Brownell, then the remedy of impeachment would be available.[11] But the impeachment alternative was generally regarded as unsatisfactory because there was doubt that a President could be impeached for an inability, and the process itself would be lengthy and effect a permanent removal from office.

Various other proposals were presented to the subcommittee, involving either separately or in combination the Vice President, Cabinet, Congress, Supreme Court, or an inability commission. One member of the subcommittee, Representative Keating, favored a ten-member inability commission, consisting of the Vice President, as a non-voting member, the Chief Justice, the senior Associate Justice, the Speaker and minority leader of the House, the majority and minority leaders of the Senate, the Attorney General, and the Secretaries of State and of the Treasury. The concurrence of six would be necessary for determination of inability. But Chairman Celler preferred leaving the entire process in the hands of the President and Vice President, with the President empowered to declare the end of any inability.

While the House Judiciary Committee was reviewing the matter, former President Truman set forth a proposal of his own in a copyrighted article for *The New York Times*. He suggested a commission of seven, consisting of the Vice President, the Chief Justice of the Supreme Court, the Speaker of the House, and the majority and minority leaders of the House and Senate. Truman's commission would be empowered to select a group of medical authorities from the top medical schools in the country and to call a special session of Congress if it were in recess. If the medical group found the President "truly incapacitated," the commission would so inform Congress. If Congress agreed by a two-thirds vote of its membership, the Vice President would become President for the remainder of the term.[12]

In the light of these differing views, it is not surprising that the House Judiciary Committee failed to reach any agreement, and that, as a result, the efforts at reform came to a halt in the House.

In early 1958, after Eisenhower's third illness, the Subcommittee on Constitutional Amendments of the Senate Judiciary Committee, under the chairmanship of Estes Kefauver, took up the cudgels.[13] Hearings were held,* and the administration proposal was reintroduced, with a new provision to cover the case of a President's disagreeing with a determination of inability made by the Vice President and Cabinet. This change provided that when the President declared his inability ended, he would not resume his powers and duties for seven days, unless he and the Vice President agreed to an earlier resumption. If the Vice President, with the approval of a majority of the Cabinet, disagreed with the President's declaration of recovery, he could bring the issue before Congress

---

* During the course of these hearings Senator Keating released a letter from Chief Justice Earl Warren concerning the undesirability of having the Supreme Court participate in the determination of a President's inability: "It has been the belief of all of us that because of the separation of powers in our Government, the nature of the judicial process, the possibility of a controversy of this character coming to the Court, and the danger of disqualification which might result in lack of a quorum, it would be inadvisable for any member of the Court to serve on such a Commission." Hearings on Presidential Inability Before the Subcomm. on Constitutional Amendments of the Senate Comm. on the Judiciary, 85th Cong., 2d Sess. 14 (1958).

for decision. If a majority of the House found that the President was disabled and the Senate concurred by a two-thirds vote, the Vice President then would discharge the powers and duties of President until the Vice President proclaimed the end of the inability, or a majority of both Houses decided that the inability had ended, or until the end of the term.

On March 12, 1958, the subcommittee approved a resolution essentially the same as the administration's revised proposal, but Congress subsequently adjourned without acting on the proposal. In the following year the proposal again was favorably reported by the subcommittee, but again neither its parent committee nor the Senate took any action.[14]

Although during the hearings there had been general agreement on the need for a constitutional amendment to confirm the Tyler precedent with respect to cases of death, resignation, and removal, and to provide for an Acting President in a case of inability, considerable disagreement arose over the mechanics of determining the beginning and ending of an inability. Each of the numerous proposals advanced had its adherents and critics. None had sufficient support for passage.

As Congress pondered the problem, with no foreseeable solution, President Eisenhower became increasingly concerned about the recurrence of another case of inability during his administration. He therefore conceived and drafted an informal agreement which offered an imaginative and practical approach to the problem. He showed it to Vice President Nixon and Attorney General Rogers and, after incorporating their suggestions, set forth this approach in a letter, copies of which were sent to Nixon, Rogers, and Secretary of State Dulles. Said Eisenhower about this agreement:

> We decided and this was the thing that frightened me: suppose something happens to you in the turn of a stroke that might incapacitate you mentally and you wouldn't know it, and the people around you, wanting to protect you, would probably keep this away from the public. So I decided that what we must do is make the Vice President decide when the President can no longer carry on, and then he should take over the duties, and when the President became convinced that he could take back his duties, he would be the one to decide.[15]

The letter was released to the public on March 3, 1958, and provided as follows:

> (1) In the event of inability the President would—if possible—so inform the Vice President, and the Vice President would serve as Acting President, exercising the powers and duties of the office until the inability had ended.
>
> (2) In the event of an inability which would prevent the President from so communicating with the Vice President, the Vice President, after such consultation as seems to him appropriate under the circumstances, would

decide upon the devolution of the powers and duties of the Office and
would serve as Acting President until the inability had ended.

(3) The President, in either event, would determine when the inability
had ended and at that time would resume the full exercise of the powers
and duties of the Office.[16]

This informal understanding was later adopted by President Kennedy
and Vice President Johnson,* President Johnson and House Speaker Mc-
Cormack, and President Johnson and Vice President Humphrey.[17]
Though it did not have the force of law and depended entirely on the
good will of the incumbent President and Vice President, the agreement
nevertheless constituted the first significant step toward solving the inability problem.

1961–1963

The end of the Eisenhower administration and the election of a young,
vigorous President reduced the problem of presidential inability to a low
priority. Only a few members of Congress continued to press for action.
Two of these, Senators Kefauver and Keating, put aside their previous
proposals and joined in sponsoring a proposed constitutional amendment,
known as S. J. Res. 35, which authorized Congress to adopt by statute
specific procedures for determining the beginning and ending of an
inability.† The proposal had actually been formulated in 1958 by the
Committee on the Federal Constitution of the New York State Bar
Association and was subsequently endorsed by the New York State Bar
Association, the American Bar Association, and The Association of the
Bar of the City of New York.[18] Said Keating about his sponsorship of
S. J. Res. 35:

. . . Senator Kefauver and I . . . agreed that if anything was going to
be done, all of the detailed procedures which had been productive of
delay and controversy had best be scrapped for the time being in favor of
merely authorizing Congress in a constitutional amendment to deal with

* Released at the time of such adoption was an opinion of Attorney General
Robert F. Kennedy's which declared the agreement to be "clearly constitutional and as
close to spelling out a practical solution to the problem as is possible." According to the
opinion, the Constitution empowered the Vice President to determine the existence of an
inability and authorized the President to declare its end. 42 Op. Att'y Gen. No. 5 (1961).

† S. J. Res. 35 provided that: "In case of the removal of the President from office or
of his death or resignation, the said office shall devolve on the Vice President. In case of
the inability of the President to discharge the powers and duties of the said office, the
said powers and duties shall devolve on the Vice President, until the inability be removed. The Congress may by law provide for the case of removal, death, resignation or
inability, both of the President and Vice President, declaring what officer shall then be
President, or in case of inability, act as President, and such officer shall be or act as
President accordingly, until a President shall be elected or, in case of inability, until the
inability shall be earlier removed. The commencement and termination of any inability
shall be determined by such method as Congress shall by law provide."

particular methods by ordinary legislation. This, we agreed, would later allow Congress to pick and choose the best form among all the proposals without suffering the handicap of having to rally a two-thirds majority in each House to do it.[19]

Thereupon, in June 1963 Senator Kefauver convened hearings of his Subcommittee on Constitutional Amendments. At the outset Kefauver remarked that " 'the essence of statesmanship is to act in advance to eliminate situations of potential danger. . . . [We should] take advantage of our present good fortune to prepare now for the possible crises of the future!' " [20] At these hearings Deputy Attorney General Nicholas deB. Katzenbach, Lewis F. Powell, Jr., who was soon to become President of the American Bar Association and later a justice of the Supreme Court, and representatives from the New York bar associations expressed their support for S. J. Res. 35. One witness, attorney Richard Hansen of Nebraska, advocated a limitation on S. J. Res. 35's blanket power to Congress to the effect that any method legislated by Congress must be compatible with the principle of separation of powers.

On June 25, 1963, the subcommittee favorably reported S. J. Res. 35 to the full committee. The sudden death of Senator Kefauver in August 1963 brought progress to a halt, but three months later the tragic death of President Kennedy forcefully catapulted the problem into full national concern. As Senator Keating stated:

> As distasteful as it is to entertain the thought, a matter of inches spelled the difference between the painless death of John F. Kennedy and the possibility of his permanent incapacity to exercise the duties of the highest office of the land.[21]

Keating added:

> The death of Estes Kefauver and John F. Kennedy provides a dual lesson for us. First, it is a grim reminder of the universality of tragedy, that no man, no matter his station, is immune from the accidents of fate that befall ordinary mortals.
>
> Secondly, however, it cautions those who survive of the difficulty of clearly foreseeing the absolutely incredible. Human legislation partakes always of human fallibility. No act of lawmaking, no matter how carefully conceived and executed, can possibly safeguard against all the freak contingencies of our existence. The best we can hope to achieve is the best practical solution which will meet the needs of crises we can readily envision.[22]

NOTES

1. Hearings on Presidential Inability Before the Subcomm. on Constitutional Amendments of the Senate Comm. on the Judiciary, 88th Cong., 1st Sess. 10 (1963).

2. *From Failing Hands* 133–35.

3. 13 Cong. Rec. 124, 142–43, 191–93 (1881).

4. *From Failing Hands* 179.

5. *Id.* 238.

6. Staff of the House Comm. on the Judiciary, 84th Cong., 2d Sess., Presidential Inability 3 (Comm. Print 1956).

7. House Comm. on the Judiciary, 85th Cong., 1st Sess., Presidential Inability: An Analysis of Replies to a Questionnaire and Testimony at a Hearing on Presidential Inability 4, 49 (Comm. Print 1957).

8. Hearings Before the Special Comm. on Study of Presidential Inability of the House Comm. on the Judiciary, 84th Cong., 2d Sess. 3–6 (1956).

9. Hearings Before the Special Subcomm. on Study of Presidential Inability of the House Comm. on the Judiciary, 85th Cong., 1st Sess. 7–8 (1957).

10. *Id.* 29.

11. *Id.* 29–30.

12. *N. Y. Times*, June 24, 1957 at 1, 14.

13. Hearings on Presidential Inability Before the Subcomm. on Constitutional Amendments of the Senate Comm. on the Judiciary, 85th Cong., 2d Sess. 1 (1958).

14. *From Failing Hands* 241–42.

15. CBS Reports, The Crisis of Presidential Succession, January 8, 1964.

16. White House Press Release, March 3, 1958. See Nixon, *Six Crises* 178–80.

17. *From Failing Hands* 229 & n.

18. For a good statement of the history, see 1963 Senate Hearings 67–70.

19. Senate Comm. on the Judiciary, Report on Presidential Inability and Vacancies in the Office of Vice President, S. Rep. No. 1382, 88th Cong., 2d Sess. 18 (1964).

20. 1963 Senate Hearings 10.

21. Hearings on Presidential Inability and Vacancies in the Office of Vice President Before the Subcomm. on Constitutional Amendments of the Senate Comm. on the Judiciary, 88th Cong., 2d Sess. 22 (1964).

22. *Id.*

5

Senate Passage of S. J. Res. 139

> [T]he problems of Presidential succession and Presidential Inability . . . have a ringing urgency today with the tragedy of our martyred President so fresh in our memory.
>
> BIRCH BAYH
> January 22, 1964 [1]

FOLLOWING PRESIDENT KENNEDY'S DEATH, there descended on Congress a flurry of proposals dealing with the problem of presidential inability, most of which also sought to deal with the related problem of presidential succession. The presence of a seventy-two-year-old Speaker and an eighty-six-year-old President pro tempore at the top of the line of succession underscored the imperfections of the 1947 succession law. Neither had been chosen for his position with an eye toward possible succession to the presidency, and neither was viewed by the public as a person of presidential stature.

Senator Birch Bayh of Indiana, Kefauver's successor as chairman of the Subcommittee on Constitutional Amendments, announced in December 1963 that the subcommittee would hold hearings on both problems early in 1964. Almost simultaneously with this announcement, Bayh and several other senators proposed a constitutional amendment (S. J. Res. 139) containing provisions on inability, filling a vice presidential vacancy, and succession beyond the vice presidency.[2] * The inability provisions were essentially the same as those in the revised Eisenhower administration approach. The vice presidential vacancy feature specified that the President must nominate within thirty days a new Vice President, who would take office upon confirmation by a majority of both Houses of Congress. The Bayh proposal also provided for a Cabinet line of succession (starting with the Secretary of State) in the event of double vacancies in the offices of President and Vice President.

At the same time and in coordination with Bayh's initiatives, the

---

* At a meeting of the Senate Judiciary Committee on December 4, 1963, before introducing the proposal, Senator Bayh and Senator Sam J. Ervin of North Carolina pointed out critically that under S. J. Res. 35 a President could be declared disabled by a simple majority of both Houses, since that is the required vote for passage of a law, and S. J. Res. 35 left it to Congress to establish by law the procedures for determining a case of presidential inability. Bayh, *One Heartbeat Away* 30 (1968). Of course, any bill passed by Congress is subject to a presidential veto, which requires a two-thirds vote of each House of Congress to be overridden.

American Bar Association (ABA) called a special conference of twelve lawyers to examine the problems and offer recommendations. The attending lawyers were former Attorney General Brownell; President Walter E. Craig of the ABA; Professor Paul A. Freund of Harvard Law School, one of the nation's foremost authorities on the Constitution; Jonathan C. Gibson of Chicago, chairman of the Committee on Jurisprudence and Law Reform of the ABA; Richard Hansen, author of *The Year We Had No President*; James C. Kirby, Jr., a former chief counsel to the Subcommittee on Constitutional Amendments; former Deputy Attorney General Ross L. Malone; Dean Charles B. Nutting of the George Washington Law Center; Lewis F. Powell, Jr.; Martin Taylor of New York, chairman of the Committee on the Federal Constitution of the New York State Bar Association; Edward L. Wright of Arkansas, chairman of the House of Delegates of the ABA; and the author.

From this two-day conference on January 20 and 21, 1964, the following consensus developed:

1. Agreements between the President and Vice President or person next in line of succession provide a partial solution, but not an acceptable permanent solution of the problem.

2. An amendment to the Constitution of the United States should be adopted to resolve the problems which would arise in the event of the inability of the President to discharge the powers and duties of his office.

3. The amendment should provide that in the event of the inability of the President the powers and duties, but not the office, shall devolve upon the Vice President or person next in line of succession for the duration of the inability of the President or until expiration of his term of office.

4. The amendment should provide that the inability of the President may be established by declaration in writing of the President. In the event that the President does not make known his inability, it may be established by action of the Vice President or person next in line of succession with concurrence of a majority of the Cabinet or by action of such other body as the Congress may by law provide.

5. The amendment should provide that the ability of the President to resume the powers and duties of his office shall be established by his declaration in writing. In the event that the Vice President and a majority of the Cabinet or such other body as Congress may by law provide shall not concur in the declaration of the President, the continuing inability of the President may then be determined by the vote of two-thirds of the elected members of each House of the Congress.

The Conference also considered the related question of Presidential succession. It was the consensus that:

1. The Constitution should be amended to provide that in the event of the death, resignation or removal of the President, the Vice President or the person next in line of succession shall succeed to the office for the unexpired term.

2. It is highly desirable that the office of Vice President be filled at all times. An amendment to the Constitution should be adopted providing that when a vacancy occurs in the office of Vice President, the President shall nominate a person who, upon approval by a majority of the elected members of Congress meeting in joint session, shall then become Vice President for the unexpired term.[3]

The consensus was released immediately to the press, endorsed by the ABA on February 17, and formally presented to the Subcommittee on Constitutional Amendments on February 24, 1964 by ABA President Craig and Lewis F. Powell.

SENATE HEARINGS

At the hearings of the Subcommittee on Constitutional Amendments held during the months of January, February, and March 1964, a majority of the witnesses expressed their support for the inability provisions of the ABA consensus, which closely followed those of the Eisenhower administration.[4] These included Brownell, Professor Freund, Ruth Silva, a noted scholar on presidential succession, Richard Nixon, and Powell. Although some of the proponents felt that Congress had the power to legislate procedures, there was wide agreement that a constitutional amendment was necessary and desirable to remove all doubts.[5]

The witnesses who favored the involvement of the Vice President and Cabinet in determining cases of presidential inability gave various reasons for the combination. The Vice President, it was said, should have a voice in the process because it would be his duty to act as President once the determination had been made. Consequently, he should not be forced to take over under circumstances which he felt to be improper. On the other hand, it was urged that he not have the sole power of determination since he would be an interested party and therefore possibly reluctant to make a determination. Said Professor Freund:

[T]hat officer should be spared the task of shouldering the responsibility alone. Leaving aside actual self-interest, the very appearance of self-interest might impel him to refrain from a decision which by objective standards ought to be taken.[6]

For this very reason, Professor James MacGregor Burns of Williams College testified that "[t]he Vice President is the worst person to decide Presidential inability," adding: "Not because he would want to make a grab for power—though this is always possible—but the opposite: he would hesitate to take any action that would give an appearance of over-eagerness or that might be used against him in the next election." [7]

The Cabinet was said to be the best possible body to assist the Vice

President in making his determination because its members are close to the President and likely to be aware of any inability and to know whether the circumstances require that the Vice President act as President. Furthermore, the use of the Cabinet would be consistent with the principle of separation of powers and would inspire public confidence. Brownell considered that the Cabinet's basic loyalty would be to the President, and he observed: "I believe that this system would guard against any such rash action or any danger that the decision might be made by persons who are unfriendly to the President." [8] Drawing on his experience, Brownell remarked that the performance of the Vice President and Cabinet during the period following Eisenhower's heart attack had met with public approval. In contrast, Burns argued that the use of the Cabinet was not desirable since its members would want to support either the President or the Vice President and, therefore, would be incapable of making an objective decision.

As for the ABA's recommendation that any constitutional amendment authorize Congress to substitute another body for the Cabinet,* Lewis Powell testified that such a provision would lend flexibility should subsequent experience indicate that a different procedure would be more desirable. In such an event, that new body could be established by statute.[9]

With respect to the ABA recommendation that a disagreement about the President's recovery should be resolved by Congress, with a two-thirds vote of each House necessary to prevent the President's return, Powell stated:

> Obviously, vital principles of government are involved. The independence of the executive branch must be preserved, and a President who has regained his health should not be harassed by a possibly hostile Congress. Yet, there must be a means to protect the country from the situation (however remote) where a disabled President seeks to resume office. It is believed that the recommendation provides appropriate safeguards for and a proper balancing of the interests involved.[10]

By having the Vice President continue to act as President pending Congress' decision, Freund said, the ABA recommendation guards against the return of the powers and duties of the presidency to "one whose capacity was in serious doubt." [11]

In a letter to Senator Bayh dated March 2, 1964, former President Eisenhower indicated his basic agreement with the ABA recommendations, stating:

> Many systems have been proposed but each seems to be so cumbersome in character as to preclude prompt action in emergency. My personal

---

* This joining of a key feature of S. J. Res. 35 was suggested at the ABA Conference by Vincent Doyle, then of the American Law Division of the Library of Congress. The feature from S. J. Res. 35 provided that: "The commencement and termination of any inability shall be determined by such method as Congress shall by law provide."

conclusion is that the matter should be left strictly to the two individuals concerned, the President and the Vice President, subject possibly to a concurring majority opinion of the President's Cabinet.[12]

Eisenhower further suggested that if there were a disagreement between the President and the Vice President and Cabinet, the issue should be referred to a commission consisting of the three ranking Cabinet officials, the Speaker and minority leader of the House, the President pro tempore and minority leader of the Senate, and four medical persons who would be selected by the Cabinet and whose credentials were recognized by the American Medical Association. The findings of this commission would then be submitted to Congress for approval.† Eisenhower concluded:

> There is, of course, no completely foolproof method covering every contingency and every possibility that could arise in the circumstances now under discussion. We must trust that men of good will and common-sense, operating within constitutional guidelines governing these matters, will make such decisions that their actions will gain and hold the approval of the mainstream of American thinking.

Professor Silva, however, thought it unnecessary to make provision for a disagreement, considering such an eventuality to be remote. In her opinion there should be no check on the President's resuming his powers and duties; still, she felt that the "two-thirds vote" was a "sufficiently heavy majority to protect the integrity of the office" of President. Silva further urged on grounds of separation of powers and protection of the integrity of the presidency that Congress not be given the power to change the Cabinet as the body to act with the Vice President.[13] She, like Brownell, argued that an inability commission would be undesirable, because the question of inability is more than a medical problem. Brownell had also observed that a commission composed of persons outside the executive branch "runs a good chance of coming out with a split decision," with possible catastrophic effects on the country.[14]

Senator Roman L. Hruska of Nebraska submitted his own proposal, which required that the determination of a President's inability be kept within the executive branch. In his view the Cabinet was the best possible body to make the determination. Instead of giving Congress carte blanche authority to designate any other body as a replacement for the Cabinet, as did S. J. Res. 139, Hruska strongly urged that any constitutional amendment limit Congress to designating only another body within the executive branch as a replacement for the Cabinet. In that way, he said, the doctrine of separation of powers would be respected, and the President would be accorded "every fair intendment for continuation" as President and "for his restoration to full Presidential powers. . . ."[15] "[T]he people have a right," declared Hruska, that the President "serve

† On May 25, 1964, at a conference convened by the ABA, Eisenhower moved away from the idea of a commission and expressed his confidence in the ability of Congress, on its own, to resolve such an issue. See Bayh, *One Heartbeat Away* 119–24 (1968).

the full term to which he was elected, except if there is some very grave disability visited upon him, nervous, mental, or physical." [16] Hruska observed that his proposal guarded against such potential abuses as Congress' using the inability procedures as a pretext to oust a healthy President rather than resort to the impeachment process; Congress' impairing the independence of the presidency; and the judiciary's being injected into the process in such a way as to impair its independence and preclude an impartial decision should an inability issue later reach the courts.[17]

A number of other witnesses expressed contrary views about the desirability of a constitutional amendment empowering the Vice President and Cabinet to declare a President disabled. Professors Clinton Rossiter of Cornell University and Richard Neustadt of Columbia University suggested merely the passage of a joint resolution by Congress endorsing the informal letter agreement approach originally adopted by Eisenhower.[18] In response to Bayh's observation that the informal arrangement did not deal with a disagreement, Neustadt asserted: "I don't know that constitutions can protect you against madmen. The people on the scene at the time have to do that. . . . So, I would leave it alone and assume that there are going to be a lot of sensible and responsible people around to work something out pragmatically." [19] If any group had authority to remove the President, he said, it would hang "over the head of every incoming President." [20] In Rossiter's view, the disability problem was "insoluble" because "a period of clearly established Presidential disability in any case is going to be a messy situation, one in which caution, perhaps even timidity, must mark the posture of an Acting President. . . ." [21]

On the other hand, Professor Burns favored a constitutional amendment allowing Congress to establish an inability commission composed of the Chief Justice, who would represent the political neutrality of the Supreme Court, two ranking Cabinet members, representing the interests of the disabled President, and the Speaker and President pro tempore, representing both Houses of Congress.[22] Each member would have the power to appoint a doctor to gather the facts, and the commission would have the power to certify the Vice President as Acting President or, in the case of a continuing inability, as President. Burns predicted that such a group could act quickly and authoritatively. Other witnesses also preferred the inability commission approach. Francis Biddle, Attorney General under Franklin D. Roosevelt, recommended a commission of three Cabinet officials with the power to declare an inability temporary or permanent.[23] If the inability should be declared permanent, the commission's findings would have to be approved by Congress. In addition to supporting the use of the Cabinet, Professor Freund suggested the creation by statute of a disability commission appointed by the President at the beginning of his term, and including in its membership former Presidents, members of the Cabinet and of Congress, and a medical expert.[24] Such a commission, said Freund, "would have the advantage of being a disinterested group, designated by the President himself, and prepared to take action without any hint of extraneous motivations."

Senator Keating and New York lawyer Martin Taylor urged that a constitutional amendment along the lines of S. J. Res. 35 be adopted.[25] They argued that the Constitution should not contain the detail in S. J. Res. 139, stating that an amendment with so much detail would be hard to ratify. Although they conceded that S. J. Res. 35 itself did not solve the inability problem since procedures would have to be adopted by Congress after its ratification, they asserted that the approach gave Congress flexibility to adopt procedures which could be easily changed if unforeseen defects appeared.[26] Sidney Hyman, noted author of books on the presidency, offered another choice. He suggested that the Vice President be given the power to declare a President disabled, stating:

> Furthermore, I would prefer vesting that discretionary power in one man who would always be the object of jealous watchfulness, than to vest it in any committee of men whose chief actors could not be singled out and called to account for what they did.[27]

Although there were varied views on the inability problem, most of the witnesses who testified at the 1964 hearings emphasized the need for finding a solution. As Senator Bayh stated:

> Here we have a constitutional gap—a blind spot, if you will. We must fill this gap if we are to protect our Nation from the possibility of floundering in the sea of public confusion and uncertainty which ofttimes exists at times of national peril and tragedy.[28]

As a national consensus on the inability problem gradually began to take shape along the lines of the ABA approach, widespread agreement manifested itself at the hearings on the need for a Vice President at all times. Said Senator Bayh: "It is significant that every measure placed before this committee since President Kennedy's assassination agrees on one vital point—that we shall have a Vice President." [29] A Vice President, he said, "would provide for an orderly transfer of Executive authority in the event of the death of a President—a transfer that would win popular consent and inspire national confidence. . . ." [30] The need was underscored by President Johnson, then serving without a Vice President, in a press interview in March 1964,[31] and by a number of leading scholars in response to a questionnaire which Senator Hubert Humphrey of Minnesota had circulated.[32] Bayh had expressed the basic rationale for keeping the vice presidency filled when he introduced his proposal on December 12, 1963:

Mr. President, there have been a number of instances of succession to the Presidency on the part of the Vice President. Each case has demonstrated the weakness of a system whereby there is no replacement of the Vice President.

The accelerated pace of international affairs, plus the overwhelming problems of modern military security, make it almost imperative that we change our system to provide for not only a President but a Vice President at all times.

The modern concept of the Vice Presidency is that of a man "standing in the wings"—even if reluctantly—ready at all times to take the burden. He must know the job of the President. He must keep current on all national and international developments. He must, in fact, be something of an "assistant President," such as Vice President Johnson was in the fields of space and civil rights and in carrying the flag of the United States to foreign countries on good will missions and on matters of great diplomatic concern.[33]

The measures and recommendations presented to Bayh's subcommittee differed on the means of filling a vice presidential vacancy.

Presidential Nomination

In the hearings a number of witnesses expressed the view that the best way to handle a vice presidential vacancy was to give the President the power to nominate a replacement who would take office if approved by Congress. Bayh emphasized that such a procedure would ensure the selection of a person with whom the President could work, and a reasonable continuity of executive policy should the Vice President succeed to the presidency.[34] Said Powell on behalf of the ABA's recommendation in favor of this approach:

It is true that this procedure would give the President the power to choose his potential successor. But with the safeguard of congressional approval, it is believed that this is sound in theory and in substantial conformity with current nominating practice. It is desirable that the President and Vice President enjoy harmonious relations and mutual confidence. The importance of this compatibility is recognized in the modern practice of both major parties in according the presidential candidate the privilege of choosing his running mate subject to convention approval. In the proposed amendment, the President would choose his Vice President subject to congressional approval.[35]

Freund testified:

The Vice Presidency should have a popular base and at the same time be in harmony with the Presidency. These objectives can best be achieved by associating the Congress and the President in the selection, with the opportunity for informal consultation to be expected in such a process.[36]

Under this procedure, said political scientist Clinton Rossiter:

[T]he three great political branches of our Government—President, Senate, and House—[would be joined] in a solemn and responsible act which strikes me as much the most sensible and convenient way to handle this delicate and vital problem.[37]

Favoring such a proposal, Senator Frank E. Moss of Utah stated:

[I]t is foolhardy in these days of instant crisis to have a Presidential succession law which could place a member of the opposite political party in the White House, with perhaps only an hour or two in which to become acquainted with all of the details of an explosive situation and be required to act.[38]

Moss added that if inquiry revealed that a nominee had a weakness or disability, Congress, as the representative of the will and views of the people, could reject the choice.

One major criticism of the proposal was that Congress' confirmatory role would be illusory, because it would be reluctant to reject a presidential nomination which was made after an incumbent President's death in office and a Vice President's succession. Hence, it was reasoned, the President actually would be picking his successor. Said Senator Jacob Javits of New York:

[T]here is a great difference between an informal practice at conventions which can always be overturned, which is not law, but is practice, and the cementing of an idea into the Constitution. I do not think it is a good idea for the law to say that the President chooses his successor . . . whatever may be the practice in party conventions.[39]

Another objection voiced against the proposal was that the advantage of speed said to be inherent in it could be overcome by congressional opposition to the nominee and resulting congressional "foot dragging." [40] A presidential nomination approach, others argued, would present a controversial political issue at a time when unity in the nation was most needed. Senator Mike Monroney said that an election in Congress would not be "wise during a period where the country is in mourning over the loss of its Chief Executive." [41] Keating concisely summarized the major objections:

[C]ongressional confirmation is likely to be meaningless at best and divisive at worst.

Meaningless, if the country is in its usual mood of rallying behind the new President and giving him his way during more or less of a "honeymoon" period, in which case confirmation would be expected as a matter of rote. Or divisive, if the Presidential nomination of a potential successor is looked upon by his opposition as an opportunity to make real trouble from the start.[42]

Thus, it was suggested by some that the President be required to submit to Congress a list of names (between two and five) from which Congress would choose the Vice President. Senator Frank Church of Idaho proposed that the President submit a list of several names to the Senate and that those ratified by the Senate be presented to the House for final selection.[43] These proposals were criticized because the President might not get the person with whom he could best work, and because no one person might be able to obtain the necessary number of votes for selection.

Those inclined toward a presidential nomination approach differed on whether the name or names should be submitted to one or both Houses of Congress. A few preferred the Senate on the grounds that it could be assembled more quickly than the House, and, further, that it had the constitutional role of confirming presidential nominations such as ambassadors, Cabinet members, and Supreme Court justices.[44] It was noted further that, under the Constitution, the Senate was assigned the role of choosing the Vice President when no candidate for that office received a majority of the electoral votes. Other witnesses preferred using the House alone because it was the more representative body. A greater number, however, favored participation by both Houses because it would elevate the selection of a Vice President above other presidential nominations. Moreover, it was observed that the two Houses together approximate the number of members of the electoral college.[45]

In the group which favored both Houses, there was a difference of opinion on whether the Houses should meet separately or jointly. If they met separately, it was argued, there could be considerable delay in the confirmation process and either House could reject the nominee or prevent any action at all. If they met jointly, on the other hand, the delay would be minimized and a majority of those present could be in a position to approve the President's choice. It was noted, however, that if every member had an equal vote in the joint session, the voice of the House would be more than four times greater than that of the Senate. Action by a joint session also would require the adoption of a new set of congressional rules, since there existed no established rules of procedure for such a session.

Congressional Selection

Senators Ervin and Javits urged that Congress alone fill any vice presidential vacancy. Ervin listed three reasons why such a plan "best meets the country's needs":

> It satisfies our requirement, ably voiced by President Truman, that the potential President should be democratically selected. For under this system, he will be selected by the people's representatives.

Second, the need for continuity is met. There will always be a Vice President who can participate in the making of and be briefed on the policies of the existing administration.

Finally, the successor to the Presidency will be chosen at a time when attention can be focused on the qualities necessary to make a good President, not those necessary for some other office, and the Congress will be able to select from among all our great men, public and private, in making their choice.[46]

Ervin also proposed that, in the event that both the presidency and the vice presidency become vacant at the same time, Congress should select both a new President and a new Vice President within ten days. In the interim the presidency would temporarily be filled according to the statutory succession law.

When Bayh asked Ervin if he had any objection to a presidential nomination approach, in order to guarantee continuity of party and administration, Ervin indicated that he had no serious objection, although he felt that a uniform rule should apply to both single and dual vacancies.[47] James C. Kirby, Jr., former chief counsel to the subcommittee, noted with respect to S. J. Res. 139:

If both offices become vacant then the existing line of succession established by Congress would give us a President, and then he would nominate and Congress would elect a new Vice President to join him. . . . We would fill both offices.

The obvious disadvantage is that both could be nonelected officials, but we wrestle in an area here where there are no good solutions. The nature of the problem is such that any solution is going to be partially undesirable, and one must choose between conflicting considerations and accept the fact that any proposal is going to be subject to some disadvantage and criticism.[48]

To ensure that the views of the President would not be excluded, and to meet the objection that Congress might select a person of the other party,[49] Javits offered an amendment to his proposal which would give the President a veto over any congressional selection.[50] He said that a veto power was particularly important because Congress might be "organized by the party of which the President is not a member." He argued that giving Congress the primary role would maximize public participation, whereas a system of presidential initiative would make Congress' role in a period of crisis perfunctory and thereby allow the President to choose his successor. Javits also suggested that the new Vice President be chosen from the groups named in the 1947 succession law—that is, the members of Congress and the President's Cabinet—so that Congress could act quickly, adding that the selection of a person already holding a high position of trust would ensure public confidence in the result.[51]

Senator Moss observed that if Congress chose the nominee,

the President then is under the pressure . . . to take the choice of the Congress and he would be inclined to do that. But yet this might not accord with what he would think could be a smooth-working team. . . . If he turned it down . . . [m]any would be incensed with the President. He turned down something that the Congress had all agreed upon. Rather than get this smooth, effectual transfer we are talking about, I think you might precipitate a greater internal crisis here. . . .[52]

Two Elected Vice Presidents

Senator Keating became the principal sponsor of the proposal to provide for the election of a President and two Vice Presidents every four years. One would be an Executive Vice President and the other a Legislative Vice President.[53] The Executive Vice President would be available to undertake assignments for the President and be first in the line of succession. The other would be President of the Senate, second in line, and also available for executive assignments. Critics argued that the proposal would aggravate the ticket-balancing tendency in selecting Vice Presidents, and that few people would be interested in being a Vice President under such a plan. Keating replied that the parties would act responsibly in picking the two; that most senators, representatives, and governors would be interested in either office, if the opportunity were presented; and that there is an abundance of work which the President could delegate to the two.[54] Former Vice President Nixon, however, argued that

> by dividing the already limited functions of the office, we would be downgrading the vice presidency at a time when it is imperative that we add to its prestige and importance.[55]

Richard Neustadt commented that the vice presidency is a "very frustrating position," and that it is difficult for a President and Vice President to develop a graceful relationship. "[T]o complicate that with a third man," said Neustadt, would "multiply the difficulties inherent in the relationship." [56]

The Keating proposal gained little support.[57] *

The Electoral College

During these hearings Nixon urged that the last electoral college be reconvened and, with the President's recommendation, that it select a

---

* A somewhat related suggestion was advanced by Professor Ruth Miner of Wisconsin State College, who proposed that the political parties name a second Vice President at convention time and that Congress provide by statute that the person so designated by the incoming party shall serve as President in the event the elected President and Vice President were unable to complete their terms, or as Vice President if a vacancy developed in that office. 1964 Senate Hearings 265–68.

new Vice President.† In advancing this proposal, Nixon reasoned that the procedures of S. J. Res. 139 might not work when Congress was controlled by the opposition party. He said:

> The Congress 20 per cent of the time during the history of our country has been under the control of a party other than that of the President of the United States. It seems to me then that the electoral college has that advantage over the Congress as the elective body which will select or approve the selection of the new Vice President.[58]

In contrast, the last electoral college would always contain a majority from the President's own party. It would also ensure, said Nixon, that the Vice President would be chosen through the elective process: "[W]hoever is to hold the Executive power in this Nation should be one who represents and has come from and has been approved by the electoral process rather than the appointive process." Nixon added that the hearings should make clear that the President has a right to a Vice President "who is compatible with his views." ‡

But other witnesses criticized use of the electoral college. Kirby testified that to revitalize and dignify the college "would be a great mistake," recalling Senator Kefauver's observation: " 'The electoral college is a loaded pistol pointed at our system of government. Its continued existence is a game of Russian roulette.' " [59] Silva argued that the use of the electoral college "would be a step away from democratic control" since it would have no current mandate from the voters,[60] and would encourage discretion in a body which should have none. Brownell observed that the person chosen by the college might not be compatible with the President.[61] Bayh succinctly summarized the principal criticisms, stating that "[t]he electoral college is not chosen, as is Congress, to exercise any considered judgment or reasoning"; that it is not "equipped . . . to conduct hearings on the qualifications" of a nominee for Vice President; that it "would be a cumbersome body to try to assemble quickly"; and that the people would hesitate to have electors unknown to them decide on the confirmation of a Vice President.[62]

As a consequence of these and other criticisms, the electoral college proposal garnered little support.

New Election

No witness before the subcommittee advocated a special election to fill a vice presidential vacancy. Javits, noting that theoretically it would be the best idea, stated that he did "not think it is practically feasible in short

---

† A similar proposal was advanced in the First Congress. Annals of Cong., 1st Cong., 3d Sess. 1911–12 (1791).

‡ Another proponent of this proposal at the time of the hearings was former President Truman.

enough time to provide the rapid continuity of both the Nation's highest offices which is so vitally necessary." [63] Clinton Rossiter stated that there "would be simply too much turmoil and chaos and expense to have a special nationwide election to choose a new Vice President." [64] Bayh noted that "a time of traumatic shock . . . is hardly conducive to a well-reasoned selection by popular vote." [65] It would represent, said Lewis Powell, "a new and drastic departure from our historic system of quadrennial presidential elections and would introduce various complications into our political structure." [66] Similar views were expressed by other witnesses,[67] with the result that no support developed for the idea.

Other Proposals

While most proposals for filling a vacancy in the vice presidency contemplated a constitutional amendment, some did not. Governor Nelson A. Rockefeller of New York expressed a preference for a statutory office of First Secretary.* The First Secretary would be appointed by the President, by and with the advice and consent of the Senate, would be a member of the Cabinet and of the National Security Council, and would assist the President in the areas of national security and international affairs. Said the Governor:

> An individual with the knowledge and experience gained from this position would be well suited to succeed to the Presidency in the absence of a Vice President. He would provide the essential continuity of Government in our international relations and leadership of the machinery of Government.[68]

This proposal was criticized by Richard Nixon, who alleged that it would downgrade the office of Vice President and make it possible for an appointed official to succeed to the presidency.[69]

Senator Eugene J. McCarthy of Minnesota proposed the creation of a statutory office of Deputy President to be filled within thirty days after a vacancy had occurred in the vice presidency. The President would appoint, subject to Senate confirmation, a person from among the members of Congress, the Cabinet, the justices of the Supreme Court, and the governors of the states. The Deputy President would be placed first in the line of succession. According to Senator McCarthy,

> the choice of the Deputy President would be made under politically realistic conditions. A weakness of our previous succession laws has been that the designated successor often attained his position for reasons and considerations quite apart from the possibility of succession.[70]

* The interesting story of why Rockefeller was not called to testify is described in Bayh, *One Heartbeat Away* 73–74.

Added McCarthy:

> The succession law should respect the mandate of the people, who vote not only for a man but also, in a broad way, for his party and his program. The elevation of a leader of another party in midterm is undesirable in principle and could have most unfortunate practical effects.

Neustadt suggested that the 1947 law be amended to provide for an office of Acting Vice President to be filled by the President, by and with the advice and consent of the Senate, in case of a vice presidential vacancy. Said Neustadt:

> [T]his appeals to me because it is the nearest thing I can envisage to contemporary practice . . . to the common law of the Constitution as it has operated.[71]

He argued that a case of succession should produce

> no break, no sharp break, in the continuity of the administration and party installed in the Executive by the last national election.[72]

Throughout the hearings numerous witnesses expressed their opposition to the statutory line of succession and suggested instead a Cabinet line of succession after the Vice President.[73] Rossiter declared "that the act of 1947 is a poor one, in many ways one of the poorest ever to emerge from this stately and distinguished body." [74] One proposal advanced was that in the event of succession by a Cabinet member, he should serve as Acting President until a new election could be held at midterm or at the end of the four-year term.[75] Another provided that whenever the Vice President or statutory successor succeeded, a new President and Vice President would be chosen by special election to fill out the existing term.[76] There was general recognition, however, that the problem of succession beyond the vice presidency would be minimized if a procedure for filling a vice presidential vacancy were established.

COMMITTEE ACTION

Following the completion of the Senate hearings and after consideration of the various proposals pending before it, the subcommittee, on May 27, 1964,* reported favorably on S. J. Res. 139, with amendments, and recommended its submission to the state legislatures.[77] The amendments completely eliminated the provision for a Cabinet line of succession beyond the vice presidency. This was done partly because of the concern that the presence of such a provision would be viewed as a criticism of

---

* This was two days after a national forum on the problem convened by the ABA. At that forum Emanuel Celler, then Chairman of the House Judiciary Committee, Eisenhower, and others expressed their support for the ABA consensus.

Speaker McCormack and therefore would jeopardize passage of the proposal in the House of Representatives, and partly because of the belief that the provisions designed to keep the vice presidency filled at all times would minimize the importance of the statutory line of succession.

The amendments also conformed the provisions of S. J. Res. 139 to the consensus recommendations of the ABA.

The committee amendments to S. J. Res. 139 are shown below. Provisions of the initial resolution which were omitted are enclosed in brackets, new matter is italicized, and provisions which remained unchanged are shown in regular text.

SECTION 1. In case of the removal of the President from office[,] or of his death or resignation, the Vice President shall become President [for the unexpired portion of the then current term]. [Within a period of thirty days thereafter, the new President shall nominate a Vice President who shall take office upon confirmation by both Houses of Congress by a majority of those present and voting.]

SEC. 2. [In case of the removal of the Vice President from office, or of his death or resignation,] *Whenever there is a vacancy in the office of the Vice President,* the President [within a period of thirty days thereafter,] shall nominate a Vice President who shall take office upon confirmation by *a majority vote* of both Houses of Congress [by a majority vote of those present and voting].

SEC. 3. If the President [shall] declares in writing that he is unable to discharge the powers and duties of his office, such powers and duties shall be discharged by the Vice President as Acting President.

SEC. 4. If the President does not so declare, *and* the Vice President [, if satisfied that such inability exists, shall, upon the written approval] *with the written concurrence* of a majority of the heads of the executive departments [in office,] *or such other body as Congress may by law provide, transmits to the Congress his written declaration that the President is unable to discharge the powers and duties of his office, the Vice President shall immediately* assume the [discharge of the] powers and duties *of the office* as Acting President.

SEC. 5. [Whenever the President makes public announcement in writing that his inability has terminated, he shall resume the discharge of the powers and duties of his office on the seventh day after making such announcement, or at such earlier time after such announcement as he and the Vice President may determine. But if the Vice President, with the written approval of a majority of the heads of executive departments in office at the time of such announcement, transmits to the Congress his written declaration that in his opinion the President's inability has not terminated, the Congress shall thereupon consider the issue. If the Congress is not then in session, it shall assemble in special session on the call of the Vice President. If the Congress determines by concurrent resolution, adopted with the approval of two-thirds of the Members present in each House, that the inability of the President has not terminated, thereupon, notwithstanding any further announcement by the President, the Vice President shall discharge such powers and duties as Acting President until the occurrence of the earliest of the following events: (1) the Acting President proclaims that the President's inability has ended, (2) the Congress determines by concurrent resolution, adopted with the approval of a majority of the Members present in each House, that the President's inability has ended, or (3) the President's term ends.] *Whenever the President transmits to the Congress his written declaration that no inability exists, he shall resume the powers and duties of his office unless the Vice President, with the written concurrence of a majority of the heads of the executive departments or such other body as Congress may by law provide, transmits within two days to the Congress his written declaration that the President is unable to discharge the powers and duties of his office. Thereupon Congress shall immediately decide the issue. If the Congress determines by two-thirds vote of both Houses that the President is unable to discharge the powers and duties of the office, the Vice President shall continue to discharge the same as Acting President; otherwise the President shall resume the powers and duties of his office.*

[SEC. 6. (a) (1) If, by reason of death, resignation, removal from office, inability, or failure to qualify, there is neither a President nor Vice President to discharge the powers and duties of the office of President, then the officer of the United States who is highest on the following list, and who is not under disability to discharge the powers and duties of the office of President, shall act as President: Secretary of State, Secretary of Treasury, Secretary of Defense, Attorney General, Postmaster General, Secretary of Interior, Secretary of Agriculture, Secretary of Commerce, Secretary of Labor, Secretary of Health, Education, and Welfare, and such other heads of executive departments as may be established hereafter and in order of their establishment.

(2) The same rule shall apply in the case of the death, resignation, removal from office, or inability of an individual acting as President under this section.

(3) To qualify under this section, an individual must have been appointed, by and with the advice and consent of the Senate, prior to the time of the death, resignation, removal from office, or inability of the President and Vice President, and must not be under impeachment by the House of Representatives at the time the powers and duties of the office of President devolve upon him.

(b) In case of the death, resignation, or removal of both the President and Vice President, his successor shall be President until the expiration of the then current presidential term. In case of the inability of the President and Vice President to discharge the powers and duties of the office of President, his successor, as designated in this section, shall be subject to the provisions of sections 3, 4, and 5 of this article as if he were a Vice President acting in case of disability of the President.

(c) The taking of the oath of office by an individual specified in the list of paragraph (1) of subsection (a) shall be held to constitute his resignation from the office by virtue of the holding of which he qualifies to act as President.

(d) During the period that any individual acts as President under this section, his compensation shall be at the rate then provided by law in the case of the President.]

[SEC. 7. This article shall be inoperative unless it shall have been ratified as an amendment to the Constitution by the legislatures of three-fourths of the several States within seven years from the date of its submission.]

In summary:

1. The words in Section 1 "for the unexpired portion of the then current term" were dropped as redundant.

2. The second sentence of Section 1 was placed in Section 2 and the term "vacancy" was substituted for the specific contingencies of death, removal, and resignation. Also the terminology "a majority vote of those present and voting" was changed in favor of the expression "a majority vote of both Houses of Congress." These changes were not intended to alter the substance of S. J. Res. 139 but rather either to simplify the language or to bring it into harmony with other provisions of the Constitution. One substantive change was the deletion from S. J. Res. 139 of the provision calling for a presidential nomination of a new Vice President "within thirty days."

3. Only minor word changes were made in Section 3.

4. A number of changes were made in Section 4, including the incorporation of the "such other body" and "concurrence" terminology from the ABA consensus and the inclusion of a requirement that Congress be notified of an inability determination.

5. Section 5 was considerably shortened by the amendments to follow the recommendations of the ABA consensus. The reference to Congress' being out of session was dropped; the Vice President was required to notify Congress within two days, instead of seven, of a determination that the President had not recovered from the inability; and the language listing the events which would end a Vice President's service as Acting President was eliminated.

Although the amendments closely followed the ABA recommendations, there were exceptions. For example, the amended S. J. Res. 139 made no reference to the manner in which a President's inability was to be determined when there was no Vice President. The ABA had proposed that the person next in succession would act in place of the Vice President. Apparently, the committee considered that this contingency would be remote if the provisions on the vice presidential vacancy were adopted. The use of a statutory successor also opened the possibility of Congress' controlling a case of presidential inability, since S. J. Res. 139 gave it the power to substitute another body for the Cabinet.

S. J. Res. 139 also did not cover the case of a vice presidential inability occurring either alone or concurrently with a presidential inability. Nor did it deal with simultaneous vacancies in the offices of President and Vice President. But these omissions were the result of a policy judgment, not of oversight. Said Senator Ervin:

> There was a consensus . . . that amending the Constitution is a rather difficult task, and that proposals for changes should be held to a minimum rather than expanded. The underlying thought, which I believe to be absolutely sound, was that every proposal additional to filling vacancies in the Vice-Presidency and coping with Presidential inability would cause some loss of support in the subcommittee, the full committee, the Congress, or the country at large, and thus endanger the prospect of any accomplishment.[78]

The full Judiciary Committee approved the revised S. J. Res. 139 on August 4 and issued a supporting report on August 13, 1964,[79] * thereby setting the stage for action by the Senate.

SENATE ACTION

On Monday, September 28, 1964, Senator Bayh, as principal sponsor of the proposal, opened the floor debate on S. J. Res. 139. In urging the adoption of its provision to keep the vice presidency filled at all times, Bayh stated:

> We pray that we may never be faced with the supreme test—the loss of a President and a Vice President within the same 4-year term of office. But in the event that history does not treat us so kindly in the future as it has in the past, we must be prepared for such an eventuality. For, whatever tragedy may befall our national leaders, the Nation must continue in stability, functioning to preserve a society in which freedom may prosper.[80]

Bayh reviewed the history of the vice presidency, showing how it had developed from an object of satire to an integral part of the executive machinery. The procedure of Section 2 allowing the President to nominate, he said, was designed to give the President someone with whom he could work closely, and to provide for continuity of authority, direction, and program. The requirement of confirmation by Congress, he said, would assure that the representatives of the people would "act as the voice of the people" and "have the final determination as to who the Vice President should be." [81] Bayh also pointed out that, by taking the

---

* Accompanying the report were individual views by Senators Hruska and Keating. Hruska stated his preference for a constitutional amendment which did not set forth a specific inability procedure and limited the determination to the executive branch. Keating expressed his continuing support for S. J. Res. 35, but said that he would vote for S. J. Res. 139 if his proposal were not accepted.

votes of members of both Houses, "we would arrive at a number identical with that now composing the electoral college."

Reviewing the course which S. J. Res. 139 had run, Senator Ervin recalled that one group of senators feared that vesting the power of selection solely in Congress could result in friction between the person designated as Vice President and the President, as well as interrupt continuity if a Congress of the opposition party were to select a member of its party to be Vice President.[82] Bayh concurred:

> The people, by voting in an election, should be the ones to decide a change of policy and a change of direction in our Government, and not some illness, some assassin's bullet, or some other unfortunate situation which would remove a President from the scene.[83]

Bayh observed that one of the major problems under Section 2 was the possibility that the President and Congress would be of different parties. Under such circumstances, the majority party might tend "to delay or play politics with" a nomination, but, Bayh affirmed, "I believe . . . that at a time of national crisis the public would not tolerate the playing of politics in the choice of a Vice President." [84]

Little opposition to S. J. Res. 139 developed during the debate of September 28. Senator Monroney, however, questioned the philosophy of allowing the President to pick his successor. He said that he could think of nothing worse for a newly installed President than to have his nomination for Vice President

> tied up in a long confirmation fight, with the ultimate possibility of rejection; and with a rival party in the majority in both Houses, or even rivalry in the majority party, over the choice of the nominee, with perhaps leading Members in either House being anxious to come in the line of authority, and one or the other Houses refusing to confirm.[85]

In Monroney's opinion, the selection of two Vice Presidents by the people in the regular quadrennial election was the best solution.

> [T]his would be an expression of the entire electorate of the United States, and thus bless the office or ratify the offices of first Vice President and second Vice President with the vote and the acceptance of the entire electorate.
>
> I recognize the fact that the joint resolution must be a compromise; but I question one bit of the philosophy in the selection of the successor by the nomination of one man, placing in the supreme line of authority over 180 million Americans one man chosen absolutely by the President, by sending the nomination to Congress, and saying, "This is my man. I choose him for my successor." [86]

In response, Bayh pointed out that the two Vice Presidents proposal was not accepted in committee because of the feeling that it might reverse the trend of making the Vice President a full-fledged, working member of the executive branch; that it might cause friction between the President and his Vice Presidents as well as between the two Vice Presidents; and that it might accentuate the ticket-balancing rather than the "best man" criteria in the selection process.[87] Bayh also said that the committee did not adopt the proposal requiring the nomination of several names because of its belief that, if the President had to choose from many possibilities, he would be put on the spot in selecting the several to be presented to Congress. The selection of his first choice, it was reasoned, would lead to a more peaceful transition.[88] "What better opportunity is there," said Bayh, "for the people to express their wishes than through those who serve in Congress?" [89]

In contrast to the vice presidential vacancy procedure, no opposition surfaced with respect to the procedures on presidential inability. Bayh reviewed the inability problem in detail, pointing out the unsettled questions raised by Article II, section 1, clause 6 of the Constitution and the cases of inability which had occurred since the adoption of the Constitution. Regarding the private agreement approach first entered into between Eisenhower and Nixon, Bayh observed that it could be subject to serious constitutional challenge, open the door to usurpation, and would not enjoy the confidence of the public as would a constitutional amendment. He emphasized the national consensus which had developed in support of S. J. Res. 139, and was joined in his support of the proposal by Senators Alan Bible of Nevada, Ervin, Philip Hart of Michigan, James Pearson of Kansas, and Leverett Saltonstall of Massachusetts, as well as by some senators who had expressed different views on the means of filling a vice presidential vacancy, such as Senators Church and Javits. Senator Ervin praised Section 1 of the proposal "because it would lay to rest the constitutional ghost that has been stalking to and fro in America ever since that time [i.e., Tyler's succession]." [90] "Although we cannot foresee every eventuality that might befall our Government," said Saltonstall, "this makes adequate provision for the uninterrupted conduct of our Nation's affairs." [91] Said Bible: ". . . I know that no single proposal will ever satisfy everyone. But I believe we have at last confronted and met the problem." [92] Concluded Senate Majority Leader Mike Mansfield of Montana: "I believe this is a momentous and historic occasion. . . . [T]he proposed joint resolution . . . is a foundation which will set well in the building which is this Republic." [93]

At the conclusion of the remarks of the nine senators who participated in the discussion, S. J. Res. 139 was passed without dissent. On the following day, however, Senator John Stennis of Mississippi said that he intended to move to reconsider the vote on the ground that it would be setting a dangerous precedent to have a proposed constitutional amendment approved by a voice vote and without at least a quorum present.[94] After a brief discussion, a roll call vote was taken, and the sixty-five senators present on September 29 all voted in favor. This marked the first time in history that a House of Congress approved a proposal dealing with presidential inability.[95] Although the year ended without any affirmative action in the House of Representatives, the momentum for a solution had clearly been established.

NOTES

1. Hearings on Presidential Inability and Vacancies in the Office of Vice President Before the Subcomm. on Constitutional Amendments of the Senate Comm. on the Judiciary, 88th Cong., 2d Sess. 1 (1964).
2. S. J. Res. 139, 88th Cong., 1st Sess. (1963).
3. *From Failing Hands* 245. The work of the ABA conference is described in detail in *id.* 246–54. Bayh, *One Heartbeat Away* 45–50 (1968). Kirby, A Breakthrough on Presidential Inability: The ABA Conference Consensus, 17 Vanderbilt L. Rev. 463 (1964).
4. 1964 Senate Hearings.
5. See, e.g., *id.* 91, 128–29, 223.
6. *Id.* 129.
7. *Id.* 115.
8. *Id.* 139.
9. *Id.* 92.
10. *Id.* 93.
11. *Id.* 130.
12. *Id.* 232.
13. *Id.* 161.
14. *Id.* 136–37.
15. *Id.* 71.
16. *Id.*
17. *Id.* 70–74.
18. *Id.* 166, 214.
19. *Id.* 173.
20. *Id.* 169.
21. *Id.* 216.
22. *Id.* 115.
23. *Id.* 144.
24. *Id.* 130.
25. *Id.* 24–25, 107–08.
26. *Id.* 23–24, 100, 105–07.
27. *Id.* 184.
28. *Id.* 3.
29. *Id.* 1–2.
30. *Id.* 3.
31. *N. Y. Times*, March 16, 1964 at 1, 19.
32. *Id.*, Feb. 16, 1964 at 48.
33. 109 Cong. Rec. 24421 (1963).
34. 1964 Senate Hearings 4.
35. *Id.* 93–94.
36. *Id.* 130–31.
37. *Id.* 218.
38. *Id.* 59.

39. *Id.* 56.

40. *Id.* 29, 55–56.

41. *Id.* 31.

42. *Id.* 28–29.

43. *Id.* 78–82.

44. *Id.* 168, 182–83, 210.

45. *Id.* 42.

46. *Id.* 19.

47. *Id.* 21.

48. *Id.* 49.

49. *Id.* 28, 89 (Report and Recommendations of the Standing Comm. on Jurisprudence and Law Reform of the ABA).

50. *Id.* 53.

51. *Id.* 52–53.

52. *Id.* 62.

53. *Id.* 26–27.

54. *Id.* 28.

55. Nixon, We Need a Vice President *Now*, 237 The Saturday Evening Post, Jan. 18, 1964 at 6.

56. 1964 Senate Hearings 177.

57. For objections, see *id.* 5, 48, 125–26, 164–65, 217.

58. *Id.* 240.

59. *Id.* 42.

60. *Id.* 164.

61. *Id.* 138.

62. *Id.* 5.

63. *Id.* 52.

64. *Id.* 218.

65. *Id.* 4.

66. *Id.* 94.

67. *Id.* 79, 89 (Report and Recommendations of the Standing Comm. on Jurisprudence and Law Reform of the ABA).

68. *Id.* 188.

69. *Id.* 246.

70. *Id.* 207–08.

71. *Id.* 168.

72. *Id.* 167.

73. *Id.* 117, 138, 206, 232, 261–62.

74. *Id.* 217.

75. *Id.* 272.

76. *Id.* 9.

77. Bayh 127–28.

78. 110 Cong. Rec. 22992 (1964).

79. Senate Comm. on the Judiciary, Report on Presidential Inability and Vacancies in the Office of Vice President, S. Rep. No. 1382, 88th Cong., 2d Sess. (1964).

80. 110 Cong. Rec. 22986 (1964).

81. *Id.* 22988, 22996.

82. *Id.* 22988.

83. *Id.*

84. *Id.*

85. *Id.* 22996.

86. *Id.* 22990.

87. *Id.* 22995–96.

88. *Id.* 22999.
89. *Id.* 22996.
90. *Id.* 22988.
91. *Id.* 22993.
92. *Id.* 22995.
93. *Id.* 23001.
94. *Id.* 23019.
95. *Id.* 23061.

6

Congress Acts

> The provisions of these measures have been carefully considered and are the product of many of our finest constitutional and legal minds. . . . I urge the Congress to approve them forthwith for submission to ratification by the States.
>
> LYNDON B. JOHNSON
> January 28, 1965 [1]

THE FAILURE OF THE HOUSE OF REPRESENTATIVES to take any action in 1964 is not surprising, since it was anxious not to do anything which might be interpreted as a slap at its Speaker. With the election of Johnson and Humphrey and the arrival of the new year, this possibility, for all practical purposes, no longer existed. The momentum for a solution was quickly reinforced by President Johnson himself in his state of the union message of January 4, 1965, in which he promised to "propose laws to insure the necessary continuity of leadership should the President become disabled or die." [2] Two days later S. J. Res. 1, which was identical to S. J. Res. 139 as passed by the Senate in September 1964, was introduced by Senator Bayh and co-sponsored by more than seventy other senators. An identical measure was introduced in the House as H. R. J. Res. 1 by Representative Emanuel Celler, Chairman of the House Judiciary Committee. Representatives William M. McCulloch of Ohio and Richard H. Poff of Virginia, senior Republican members of the House Judiciary Committee, introduced similar proposals, but with the difference that if the President on the one hand and the Vice President and Cabinet on the other disagreed on whether a President had recovered from an inability, Congress would have ten days in which to decide the issue. If it failed to do so within such period, the President would automatically resume his powers and duties. In contrast, S. J. Res. 1 and H. R. J. Res. 1 merely required Congress to decide the issue "immediately."

On January 28, 1965, President Johnson sent a special message to Congress endorsing S. J. Res. 1 and H. R. J. Res. 1 and urging prompt action on these resolutions. Said the President:

> Favorable action by the Congress on the measures here recommended will, I believe, assure the orderly continuity in the Presidency that is imperative to the success and stability of our system. Action on these measures now will allay future anxiety among our own people, and among

the peoples of the world, in the event senseless tragedy or unforeseeable disability should strike again at either or both of the principal Offices of our constitutional system. If we act now, without undue delay, we shall have moved closer to achieving perfection of the great constitutional document on which the strength and success of our system have rested for nearly two centuries.[3]

ACTION IN THE SENATE

On January 29, 1965, the Senate Subcommittee on Constitutional Amendments held a one-day hearing at which Attorney General–designate Katzenbach, former Attorney General Brownell, President Powell of the ABA, and others testified in support of S. J. Res. 1. Katzenbach presented his interpretations of the proposed amendment in several vital areas, offered a number of suggestions, and concluded by stating that

Senate Joint Resolution 1 represents as formidable a consensus of considered opinion on any proposed amendment to the Constitution as one is likely to find. It may not satisfy in every respect the views of all scholars and statesmen who have studied the problem. . . . But, it . . . "would responsibly meet the pressing need. . . ." [4]

In view of the widespread sentiment that the procedures should be written into the Constitution, Katzenbach stated that he saw no reason why he should insist upon the preference he had expressed in 1963 in favor of a constitutional amendment empowering Congress to establish procedures for handling cases of inability by statute. He added: "The debate has already gone on much too long. Above all, we should be concerned with substance, not form. It is to the credit of Senate Joint Resolution 1 that it provides for immediate, self-implementing procedures that are not dependent on further congressional or Presidential action." [5]

Among the suggestions * made by Katzenbach in his testimony were the addition of language to Section 3 to ensure that the recovery procedures of Section 5 applied only to instances in which the President had been declared disabled without his consent. A President thereby would be encouraged, said Katzenbach, to declare his own inability, since he would be permitted to resume his powers and duties upon his own written declaration of recovery. Katzenbach also stated that the language used in Section 5 to the effect that "Congress will immediately decide" an issue of disagreement was so vague that more precise language should be found or appropriate provisions made in the congressional rules for the speedy handling of such an issue. He stated that he understood the "immediately decide" language to mean "that if a decision were not

* These ultimately were reflected in several language changes made in S. J. Res. 1 by the committee after the close of the hearings. See pp. 89–90, *infra*.

reached by the Congress immediately, the powers and duties of the Office would revert to the President." [6] Recognizing that there could be debate on whether Congress had acted soon enough, he added: "There is no word that you can use that completely resolves that problem. I do not know what 'immediately' means, except it means as soon as you can darn well do it." [7] On balance, however, Katzenbach thought it unwise to specify a time limit in the Constitution itself, since different circumstances might require different time-periods.

Katzenbach also established important legislative history concerning the voting requirement terminology used in Sections 2 and 5, stating that it meant to him a majority and two-thirds, respectively, of the members of each House present at the time of the vote, providing there existed a quorum. Focusing on Section 5 of S. J. Res. 1, he said that he assumed that, with the concurrence of the Vice President acting as President, the President could resume his powers and duties before the expiration of the two days specified. Katzenbach raised a further question concerning a situation in which there is disagreement about the President's recovery at a time when Congress is out of session. He suggested that additional language be considered to ensure that the Vice President could not delay the process by his failure to call Congress into session.

During the course of his testimony Katzenbach engaged in significant colloquies with Senators Bayh and Hruska on the rationale for Section 5's involving Congress in the inability process. He emphasized that Congress could not initiate but only affirm a decision which had been made in the executive branch. The inclusion of Congress, he noted, was a safeguard against usurpation by the Vice President and Cabinet. He further stated:

> I continue to believe that it would be important that that decision would be affirmed as overwhelmingly as this contemplates by elected representatives and that we would get an additional measure of security out of that. I do not say that from any lack of confidence in the integrity of the Cabinet, or in the decision that they would make. I say it as I said before, because I do believe that in that kind of a crisis, which, thank God, we have never had in this country and I hope never will, it would be so important to join ranks on both sides of the aisle and to create that kind of confidence among the public of the United States by their elected representatives joining in this very unpleasant and terribly important determination so that as we have in the past, this country could indicate that in such crisis, it can and will unite. [8]

As for the possibility of confusion and chaos if a majority but less than two-thirds of the Senate believed the President to be disabled, Katzenbach stated:

> On this, it would be my hope that if that situation ever evolved, you would have 100 Senators who would agree. Because it simply becomes

an impossible situation, and if it is a close question and a difficult one, it is in that situation where I think the Vice President would not act, the Cabinet would not support him, and they would want to know that they had the support, whether or not, whatever system it [was] done under, they would surely want to know they had the overwhelming support of both Houses of Congress if they were determined to act in this totally unprecedented way.[9]

Bayh then added that congressional action was the closest substitute for action by the people:

The final determination, we feel, must be made by the representatives of the people. If there were some way we could get the people themselves to make this decision, I would say more power to this. But we have found no practical way of doing this.

Katzenbach also pointed out that a Vice President acting as President had the power to remove a Cabinet officer to gain support or even to change a member in the event of a Cabinet evenly divided on the question of the President's recovery. Said Katzenbach:

Certainly, if [the Vice President] were discharging the powers of the Presidency, he could remove a Cabinet officer. There is no question about that, Senator. He could only effectively appoint one if Congress happened to be out of session at that time.[10]

These possibilities, he argued, represented a further reason for allowing Congress to make the final determination.

On the vice presidential vacancy feature of the proposed amendment, Katzenbach rejected the suggestion that the President's choice be limited to certain public officials because it would alter the long tradition that the President can choose his running mate. He added that a requirement of a two-thirds vote for confirmation would give too much power to the opposition party in the selection of a Vice President, and possibly delay the filling of the vacancy.[11]

Following Katzenbach's testimony, Senator Hruska testified in favor of his S. J. Res. 28 and strongly urged that Congress be prohibited from substituting for the Cabinet a procedure for determining a President's inability which involved either the judicial or the legislative branch of government. He urged:

The determination of presidential inability and its termination is obviously a factual matter. No policy is involved. The issue is simply whether a specific individual with certain physical, mental, or emotional impairments possesses the ability to continue as the Chief Executive or whether his infirmity is so serious and severe as to render him incapable of executing the duties of his office.

To inject Congress into the factual question of inability would be to create a secondary impeachment procedure in which the conduct of the President would not be the test.[12]

The involvement of Congress, he said, would also delay the process, and he added:

> Obviously, such a decision must rest on the relevant and reliable facts regarding the President's physical or mental faculties. It must be divorced from any thoughts of political advantage, personal prejudice, or other extraneous factors. Those possessing such firsthand information about the Chief Executive, or most accessible to it on a personal basis, are found within the executive branch and not elsewhere.[13]

Hruska further noted that difficulties would be encountered in construing the term "immediately" in Section 5. It could be interpreted, he said, so as to limit debate in Congress, as well as to preclude hearings seeking evidence with regard to a disagreement issue. Earlier Katzenbach had testified that he felt the expression was broad enough to permit reasonable debate, and to enable Congress to inquire of psychiatrists and physicians and of members of the President's family and of the Cabinet.[14]

Speaking on behalf of the Committee for Economic Development (CED), Marion B. Folsom, who had served as Secretary of Health, Education and Welfare under Eisenhower, urged that a vice presidential nominee be subject to confirmation by a joint session of Congress. He said that such a procedure would correspond to the voting strength of each state in the electoral college, would be more expeditious, and would avoid the difficulties which would arise if the House and Senate disagreed.[15] He also suggested that the Cabinet initiate the question of inability, and that the Vice President's role be limited to one of concurrence. Folsom's reasoning was that a Vice President would be most reluctant to initiate such a question, "no matter how urgent or obvious the necessity." Folsom stated that the Vice President should "never be forced to accept authority under conditions permitting unfair charges of usurpation against him, nor should his natural feelings of deference and loyalty to a disabled Chief Executive be allowed to absolve him from his proper responsibility." [16] Folsom also expressed CED's opposition to the "such other body" provision of Section 5 on the ground of separation of powers, and said that the Cabinet, through its knowledge of major issues and association with the President, was best situated to judge a case of presidential inability. Accordingly, in the view of CED the issue of termination of an inability should be decided by the Cabinet alone, subject only to presidential concurrence. Folsom noted that S. J. Res. 1 allowed for the possibility of a President's terminating his inability despite the contrary judgment of the Vice President, the entire Cabinet, and the unanimous vote of the Senate, since all he needed was a one-third vote of either House.[17] In his concluding remarks, Folsom quoted the following paragraph from CED's policy statement concerning the disadvantage of bringing Congress into the picture:

. . . a Congress with a hostile two-thirds majority such as existed during
the Presidency of Andrew Johnson . . . could be used to deprive the
President of his powers and duties, without resorting to the circumscribed
impeachment procedures.[18]

CED concluded therefore that Congress should play no role in the area
of presidential inability.

In his testimony before the subcommittee, Brownell expressed the
view that public opinion and the patriotism of our public officials would
assure the proper and speedy application of the amendment. "I think
our public officials always rise to their best heights at a time of crisis
. . . ," he said, and "with the overwhelming backing of public opinion
for a solution of any crisis to having an orderly government, the Congress
could be counted upon . . . to do its part." [19] He added that "the men
who are involved here, both in the executive branch and the congressional
branch, in time of crisis will act not as rogues and rascals, but as patriotic
Americans, as they always do and have done in time of crisis. . . ." [20]
Specifically, Brownell said that the use of separate sessions of each House
would speed consideration and eliminate the procedural difficulties which
might arise with a joint session. He also regarded the term "immediately"
as sufficient, since, if the extraordinary case of a disagreement occurred,
there would be an overwhelming opinion on one side or the other which
would demand immediate action. He expressed the view that a case of
disagreement would be one in which the President "was mentally un-
balanced," which "would be very obvious to everyone when you consider
the white heat of publicity that beats upon the White House." [21] Congressional involvement, he said, would promote "greater confidence on
the part of the public that the right solution had been reached . . ."
and would provide "safeguards against cabals, against charges, however
ridiculous they might be, that certain public officials within the executive
branch were acting for personal selfish gains rather than for the public
interest." [22]

Among other witnesses who testified was Martin Taylor, who continued to oppose S. J. Res. 1 and to support the broad, inability language
of S. J. Res. 35.* "Everyone," he said, approved of the vice presidential
vacancy provision of S. J. Res. 1, but other features of the amendment

---

* Others who testified were Representative Willard S. Curtin of Pennsylvania, who
favored a presidential inability commission headed by the Chief Justice; Justice Michael
Musmanno of the Pennsylvania Supreme Court, who suggested that the term "forthwith"
be substituted for "immediately" in Section 5 and that the Vice President be transferred
from the legislative to the executive branch; Professor Robert Deasy, who favored the
ad hoc letter arrangement of Eisenhower and the election of a second Vice President;
and Senator Jack Miller of Iowa, who recommended that the President be required to
nominate a person of his own party for Vice President and that the nomination be confirmed by a joint session.

were objectionable. Criticizing the machinery for resolving a disagreement issue, Taylor said:

> First, the President has to transmit his own conviction that he is well. Then the Vice President has to say, "No, I do not agree with you, you are not well." Then the Vice President has to have a talk with a majority of the members of the Cabinet. They do not agree. Then he has to agree with this other body created by statute, and they do not agree. Meanwhile, airplanes are flying over the Potomac.
>
> Then Congress, with no other guide as to urgency, imminence, or time, has to meet and make this executive decision that three other tribunals and individuals have been unable to make.[23]

Taylor also raised questions about the effect of the "such other body" provision. His so doing established the important legislative history that if Congress created another body, that body would replace the Cabinet in the determination of a President's inability.[24] Prophetically, Taylor, who was the last witness to testify at the one-day hearing, concluded: "Instead of arguing your questions, let me congratulate you [Bayh] on your success to this point and hope that you have further success." [25]

Three days later the subcommittee unanimously approved S. J. Res. 1 and reported it to the full Judiciary Committee, where it was approved on February 10, 1965, with amendments.[26] In individual views accompanying the committee's report, Senator Hruska suggested that Section 5 be amended by the full Senate to enlarge the two-day period in which to challenge a President's declaration of recovery. He said that the two-day period did not take into account the fact that Cabinet members often travel and that there may be long periods of time in which they do not observe and meet with the President.

Among the amendments made by the full Judiciary Committee was the specification in Section 3 of a requirement that a declaration of inability be sent to the Speaker of the House and the President of the Senate. S. J. Res. 139 as passed by the Senate, and S. J. Res. 1 as introduced, had included no public notice to Congress in Section 3, simply stating that "if the President declares in writing that he is unable to discharge the powers and duties of his office, such powers and duties shall be discharged by the Vice President as Acting President." Concern was expressed in committee over the absence of a provision for the transmittal of a declaration of inability. As Hruska speculated, a Vice President might produce a letter from the President at a critical point in history, and a question could be raised whether the letter actually was genuine.[27]

Similarly, while Sections 4 and 5 provided that declarations of inability and recovery be sent to "Congress," the committee decided instead that the transmittal should be to the Speaker and the President of the Senate. It felt that notice to these officials, even if they were not in their "offices" at the time of transmittal, would guaranty "notice to the entire country," and would provide a basis for Congress' being called into session, if then out of session, to consider a disagreement issue. With that change, the committee believed that Congress would be empowered to reconvene in special session and that the presiding officers would then be required to call a special session to consider a Section 5 issue, if Congress were also in recess. The committee noted, however, that nothing would limit the President's power under Article II, section 3 of the Constitution to call a special session.

Another change made by the committee was to substitute the expression "principal officers of the executive departments" for "heads of the executive departments." This change was meant to clarify that only those who are members of the Cabinet would be permitted to participate in any decision regarding inability, as well as conform the terminology to that used in Article II, section 2, clause 1 of the Constitution.* In response to the concern expressed by Senator Robert Kennedy of New York over a possible Cabinet coup, Judiciary Committee Chairman James Eastland of Mississippi moved unsuccessfully to require a vote of two-thirds of the Cabinet.[28]

Finally, the "immediately decide" language of Section 5 was changed to "immediately proceed to decide." The committee stated that the new expression would connote great urgency while at the same time allowing Congress "to collect all necessary evidence and to participate in the debate needed to make a considered judgment."[29] The committee opposed a specific time limitation "because of the complexities involved in determining different types of disability," but noted that "the proceedings in the Congress prescribed in section 5 would be pursued under rules prescribed, or to be prescribed, by the Congress itself."[30]

A little more than a week later, on February 19, 1965, S. J. Res. 1 was debated in the Senate. There was almost unanimous agreement on the need for a constitutional amendment to solve the inability and vice presidential vacancy problems, but Senator Allen J. Ellender of Louisiana expressed the view that Article II gave Congress the power to legislate all the procedures of S. J. Res. 1 except the method of selecting a new Vice President.[31] Disagreeing, Bayh reflected the dominant view when he said: "Dealing with the problem in statutory form alone would create all the uncertainty of a court test of the constitutionality of the statute. That, we believe, should be avoided, if at all possible."[32]

One area in which there was substantial disagreement during the debate was whether the amendment should set forth specific procedures for handling a case of inability, as did S. J. Res. 1, or merely empower

---

* "[The President] may require the Opinion, in writing, of the principal Officer in each of the executive Departments. . . ."

Congress to enact procedures by legislation, as S. J. Res. 35 had done. Senator Everett Dirksen of Illinois, a leading proponent of the latter approach, argued that "it has been pretty much of a rule in our constitutional history that we do not legislate in the Constitution. We try to keep the language simple. We . . . offer some latitude for statutory implementation thereafter, depending upon the events and circumstances that might arise." [33]

Therefore, Dirksen offered a substitute amendment providing: " 'The commencement and termination of any inability shall be determined by such method as Congress may by law provide.' " [34] He noted that, under his proposal, Congress could deal with such situations as the simultaneous inabilities of both the President and the Vice President as well as the inability of either of them. Dirksen observed that S. J. Res. 1 did not treat the inability of a Vice President or an Acting President, and if there were no Vice President, the inability procedures for a President could not be invoked. He also raised questions about a situation when Congress was not in session. He further stated that S. J. Res. 1 was not clear on whether the recovery mechanism of Section 5 applied to instances in which the President had declared his own inability under Section 3; whether under Section 5 the President had to wait two days to see if the Vice President and Cabinet challenged his declaration of recovery; and how a President who was physically unable to write or sign his name would make a declaration of inability under Section 3. "My interest," concluded Dirksen, "is that there be no ambiguities and no rigidities written into the Constitution that could be modified only by another constitutional amendment." [35]

Senator Ervin opposed Dirksen's substitute amendment, declaring that it "totally ignores one of the crucial questions which has brought this matter to the floor of the Senate. That is the fact that vacancies occur in the office of Vice President." He added that the Dirksen proposal "would place dangerous power in the hands of Congress," since it would give Congress a new power over the President by which "any time that power-hungry men in Congress were willing to go to the extremes that men were willing to go to in those days [i.e., when radical Republicans sought to remove President Andrew Johnson], they could take charge of the Presidency." [36] Only if specifics were set out in the Constitution, said Ervin, would the presidency be sufficiently protected. Ervin observed: "[W]hen we try to protect somebody, we had better write specifics into the Constitution if we do not want to run the risk of converting the United States into what I would call a banana republic." [37] Senator Bayh, agreeing with Ervin, pointed out that the Constitution was quite specific in its provisions for the election and impeachment of the President. If this specificity were not maintained for the case of inability, Bayh argued, there would be a violation of the principle of separation of powers, and the state legislatures might hesitate to ratify a general amendment. Finally, unless the amendment were specific Congress might never settle on procedures for determining inability, since interest in the subject would wane once the amendment had been ratified. In answer to Dirksen's technical objections to S. J. Res. 1, Bayh observed that the legislative history was quite clear on the meaning and intent of Sections 3, 4, and 5,[38] and that Section 5 applied only to declarations of inability by a Vice President and Cabinet under Section 4. At the conclusion of this debate, a vote was taken on the Dirksen substitute amendment, and it was defeated 60 to 12.

Senator Strom Thurmond of South Carolina then proposed an amendment to empower the last electoral college to fill a vacancy in the vice presidency. He argued that the college had the advantage of retaining the general election process, and that it would generate "a greater degree of public confidence and a broader base of support for the individual chosen." In response to the objections that this method would be time-consuming and would not allow for hearings on the qualifications of a candidate, Thurmond said that the college could act within a month and that formal hearings were not necessary since the views of any serious candidate would be well known. Thurmond added that the electors most likely would select the person desired by the President.[39] In reply, Bayh argued that the people of the country "would wonder what in the world was being perpetrated upon them if we brought in members of the electoral college whom they did not know from Adam." [40] He said that the people would accept a judgment made by Congress. Thurmond's proposal was rejected by voice vote.

Senator Hruska then offered his promised amendment to change from two to seven the number of days which the President might be required to wait before resuming his powers and duties after his declaration of recovery. Said Hruska:

> In these days when much traveling is done by members of our Cabinet, and when on occasion the Vice President also travels frequently, if there would be . . . a declaration by the President in the absence of these parties the 48-hour period would obviously prove to be much too small. . . .
> I feel that 7 days would be an appropriate and adequate time for the members of the Cabinet to . . . inform themselves of the actual condition of the President, perhaps visit with him, perhaps visit with his personal physician.[41]

The amendment was accepted.[42]

Senator John O. Pastore of Rhode Island moved to amend Section 5 of S. J. Res. 1 to require Congress to decide an inability disagreement without transacting any other business in the interim. "[W]e ought to stay here," said Pastore, "until we decide that question, even if we must sit around the clock, or around the calendar, because this problem involves the Presidency of the United States." [43] Pastore noted that a filibuster or hearings could unduly delay a decision. Senators Bayh, Hruska, and Ervin opposed Pastore's suggestion, arguing that such a restriction would be unwise as evidence might have to be taken in committee or the President examined before a decision could be reached. Said Hruska:

> Suppose the question should relate to the mental ability of the President. An examination would be necessary. Psychiatrists would not be able to go into the President's office, look him over, and say, "The man is insane," or, "the man is not insane." They would need time in which to observe and conduct tests. Congress would need time to hear the reasons why the members of the Cabinet had said, "Mr. President, you are not able to resume the duties and powers of your office." [44]

Bayh and Hruska argued that the use of the word "immediately," which also appeared in the Twelfth Amendment, would connote the needed urgency, and Hruska added that while hearings were proceeding, Congress would and should be free to deal with any other urgent situation. Unpersuaded, Pastore retorted: "I can conceive of nothing more important to the people of our country and the peace of the world than to determine the question as to who is the President of the United States." [45] In the course of the debate Senator Hart suggested that a time limit such as three days might be appropriate, to which Ervin replied: "If we cannot trust Members of the Senate and House to exercise intelligence and patriotism in a time of national crisis, we might as well not do anything." He then declared: "This is essentially a subject . . . which will require the taking of testimony. We cannot put a time limit on the search for truth, especially when it concerns the intelligence of the President." [46]

As the Senate debated Pastore's proposal, Senator Ross Bass of Tennessee offered an amendment adding the word "immediately" to Section 2 so that whenever a vacancy arose in the vice presidency and the President nominated a replacement, Congress would be required to act with dispatch.[47] Without such a direction, Bass feared, Congress might delay filling a vacancy to keep the Speaker first in line of succession. Said Bass: "If Vice President Nixon had succeeded to the Office of the Presidency, his nomination [of a new Vice President], from my own experience in the House, would have been delayed and stalled, because Members of the House had a deep respect for Sam Rayburn." [48] The possibility of delay would be especially real, said Bass, when Congress was controlled by the opposition party. Bayh responded: "I have more faith in the Congress acting in an emergency in the white heat of publicity, with the American people looking on. The last thing Congress would dare to do would be to become involved in a purely political move." [49]

And Ervin, referring to the possibility that Congress might stall to keep the Speaker first, remarked: "God help this Nation if we ever get a House of Representatives, or a Senate, which will wait for a President to die so someone whom they love more than their country will succeed to the Presidency." [50]

Bayh and Hruska argued that under Bass's proposal Congress might be required to act more quickly than the circumstances required. Said Bayh: "I do not believe we need to grind everything to a halt to decide who the Vice President is." [51] Both senators felt that the urgency was greater when the President's recovery from an inability was at issue; hence, the use of the word "immediately" in Section 5 and not in Section 2. Hruska remarked that the use of "immediately" in Section 2 would raise such questions as: "Does it mean that there will be no hearings? Does it mean that there will be no debate? Does it mean that there will be no consideration of any kind to determine what kind of person the nominee is?" [52]

Following the discussion, both the Bass and Pastore proposals were rejected by voice votes. Initially, Bayh had been willing to accept Pastore's amendment, but rejected the change when he realized that if it should be accepted, the entire proposed amendment would likely be sent back to committee for further study.* As Bayh said: "Later, thinking it over, I was to see that point as a turning point. If I had given ground on the Pastore amendment, all would have been lost: the resolution would have gone back to committee and might never have seen the light of the Senate Chamber again." [53]

After the rejection of these proposals, Bayh proceeded to clarify the legislative intent behind various provisions of the amendment. As for definitions of the words "inability" and "unable" as used in Sections 4 and 5, he said: "[They] refer to an impairment of the President's faculties, [and] mean that he is unable either to make or communicate his decisions as to his own competency to execute the powers and duties of his office." Added Bayh: "[We] are not dealing with an unpopular decision that must be made in time of trial and which might render the President unpopular." [54] Bayh also stated his interpretation of the meaning of the expression "heads of the executive departments," used in Sections 3, 4, and 5, and discussed the effect of a Cabinet vacancy. It also was made clear that the Vice President would continue to serve as Acting President during the seven-day challenge period in Section 5, since there likely would be a serious question about the President's mental capacity; however, the Vice President could agree to the President's resuming his powers and duties immediately upon his declaration of recovery. Bayh also stated that a Vice President acting as President could replace a Cabinet

* Because of the view that each provision of a constitutional amendment should first be considered in committee.

member who died or resigned. A usurping Vice President, Bayh said, would be checked by Section 5, which enabled the President to refer the issue to Congress.

At the conclusion of this legislative history-making, the Senate unanimously approved S. J. Res. 1, as amended, by a vote of 72 to 0.[55]

ACTION IN THE HOUSE

As the Senate was preparing to debate S. J. Res. 1, the full House Judiciary Committee, on February 9, 1965, commenced hearings on H. R. J. Res. 1 and the more than thirty proposals dealing with presidential inability and vice presidential vacancy. At the outset, Representative William M. McCulloch, the ranking Republican committee member, expressed his strong support for a provision requiring congressional action within a period of ten days on a challenge to a President's declaration of recovery, stating: "For, right or wrong, we are providing a means for taking away the President's office. The burden should thereby be placed upon the Vice President and, indirectly, the Congress to have the issue decided without unnecessary delay." [56] McCulloch said that he was influenced by the fact that Congress at times has been hostile to the President, and at times the Vice President and President have not been on friendly terms. Without a time limitation, he feared, Congress might delay reaching a decision or a Vice President acting as President might fail to reconvene an adjourned Congress.

Considerable discussion followed at these hearings on the advisability of a time provision. Brownell, Powell, Katzenbach, and Bayh all expressed their preference for no such provision, believing that Congress would act quickly if a disagreement occurred. Brownell thought that the possibility of a disagreement was remote, but felt that if such a situation should arise "public opinion would force speedy action, as speedy as was wise under the circumstances, assuming that Congress was obviously filibustering or delaying for some non-public reason. . . ." [57] He added: "I have always found in my experience that men under the pressure of national or international crises do act responsibly, but if the occasion arose when they didn't, I think public opinion would force them to do it, or [they would] destroy their usefulness as public officials thereafter." [58] However, Brownell and Powell indicated that the adoption of a time provision would do no violence to the ABA consensus. Said Katzenbach: "It is almost impossible for me to envision circumstances where there would, in fact, be delay. For a Vice President to take those steps, [he] would really have to be assured of quick and overwhelming support in the Congress." [59] Bayh noted that "[i]t might well take longer for Congress to make a determination in one type of illness than another type of illness. The type of testimony that would be involved to fully disclose to the Members of Congress the condition of the President might take longer in one type of illness than another. . . ." [60] Representative Poff added later in the hearings that he and other proponents of the time provision were "concerned primarily that a filibuster might develop in the other body which might not be altogether pure in its motivation." [61]

In addition to focusing on the recovery procedures of Section 5, the hearings before the House Judiciary Committee are particularly significant for the record made on the meaning and intent of the amendment.* At the hearings Katzenbach again urged that there be "a provision which would clearly enable the President to terminate immediately any period of inability he has voluntarily declared." [62] He said that a President might be hesitant to declare his own inability if the procedures of Section 5 applied to a voluntary declaration. Bayh initially opposed such a provision, stating:

> Suppose, if you will, that such language were added. A President voluntarily divests himself of his powers and duties. Then, when he believes he is fit, he immediately resumes them. Then, pursuant to section 4 of the proposal, the Vice President and majority of the Cabinet declare the President really isn't fit at all. The Vice President immediately resumes the powers and duties of the Presidency. Then, under section 5, the President again declares no inability exists. The Vice President and Cabinet, under section 5, challenge the President's declaration again. Then Congress decides in favor of the President, who immediately resumes the powers and duties again. Here, in the space of a few days, the Nation would have the powers and duties of the Presidency change hands three times. The turmoil this would create is almost unimaginable. As now written, Senate Joint Resolution 1 and House Joint Resolution 1 would keep the transfer of these awesome powers and duties to an irreducible minimum, thereby enabling as smooth a transition of executive power as possible in difficult circumstances. [63]

A number of witnesses suggested that the amendment also deal with such cases as the simultaneous inabilities of the President and Vice President, the inability of a President when there is no Vice President, the inability of an Acting President, and dual vacancies. [64] With respect to these suggestions, Brownell expressed the dominant view when he said of the amendment: "I believe it covers, in consonance with the basic constitutional principles, at least 90 percent of the cases we could reasonably foresee." [65]

Representative Charles M. Mathias, Jr., of Maryland was particularly strong in his opposition to granting the President power to nominate a Vice President. He felt such a power was undemocratic and autocratic

---

* In that connection, the testimony of Bayh and Brownell sheds significant light on the legislative history. See pp. 198–203, *infra*.

in nature, and would be used to select men of weak caliber for the office. Contrasting the presidential candidate's role at the nominating convention, Mathias said: "The man he chooses to run with him will be chosen from motives which may be substantially different from those of the incumbent President who is picking his official heir and successor." [66] "A man who sat in the White House," said Mathias, "might well feel he would appear greater on the pages of history if his Vice President were a weak and pallid kind of an individual. . . ." [67] The presidential candidate, on the other hand, has to be concerned about his ticket's winning in the election. Mathias also questioned whether Congress would be even reasonably critical of a President's choice which followed in the shadow of a tragedy. [68]

In response to Mathias' position, Bayh argued that a President acting in the spotlight of public opinion would be motivated by the desire "to get the very best possible man he could get for the job. . . ." If a "namby-pamby person" were sent to Congress, he said, "Congress wouldn't go along." [69] On the question of time limits for congressional action on the nominee, Bayh said that it would be better to omit them and "trust the President and Congress to use their good judgment as to what would be reasonable." He added: "There would be some times . . . when a name would be submitted for which there would be patent reasons for a tremendous amount of debate. Other times a name might be submitted and would be readily acceptable and there would be little reason for a prolonged debate and everyone would recognize this." [70]

With respect to Mathias' preference for congressional selection of the Vice President, Bayh remarked that "we [are] going to proliferate further the executive branch and try to set up someone who would be competing with the President unless we gave the President primary responsibility of picking the man with whom he could work." [71] Poff suggested that, under a system of congressional selection, the leadership of the majority party would actually decide in caucus, so that this approach would not be more democratic. [72]

Following the conclusion of these hearings, H. R. J. Res. 1 was approved on March 24, 1965,* with the following changes. [73] Omitted language is enclosed in brackets and new matter is italicized.

SECTION 1. In case of the removal of the President from office or of his death or resignation, the Vice President shall become President.

SEC. 2. Whenever there is a vacancy in the office of the Vice President, the President shall nominate a Vice President who shall take office upon confirmation by a majority vote of both Houses of Congress.

* Dissenting views were expressed by Representatives Edward Hutchinson of Michigan and Mathias of Maryland. House Comm. on the Judiciary, Report on Presidential Inability and Vacancies in the Office of Vice President, H. R. Rep. No. 203, 89th Cong., 1st Sess. 17–23 (1965).

SEC. 3. [If the President declares in writing] *Whenever the President transmits to the President pro tempore of the Senate and the Speaker of the House of Representatives his written declaration* that he is unable to discharge the powers and duties of his office, *and until he transmits a written declaration to the contrary*, such powers and duties shall be discharged by the Vice President as Acting President.

SEC. 4. [If the President does not so declare, and the Vice President with the written concurrence of a majority of the heads of the executive departments or such other body as Congress may by law provide, transmits to the Congress his] *Whenever the Vice President and a majority of the principal officers of the executive departments, or such other body as Congress may by law provide, transmit to the President pro tempore of the Senate and the Speaker of the House of Representatives their* written declaration that the President is unable to discharge the powers and duties of his office, the Vice President shall immediately assume the powers and duties of the office as Acting President.

[SEC. 5.] *Thereafter,* when[ever] the President transmits to the [Congress] *President pro tempore of the Senate and the Speaker of the House of Representatives* his written declaration that no inability exists, he shall resume the powers and duties of his office unless the Vice President, [with the written concurrence of a majority of the heads of the executive departments or such other body as Congress may by law provide, transmits within two days to the Congress his] *and a majority of the principal officers of the executive departments, or such other body as Congress may by law provide, transmit within two days to the President pro tempore of the Senate and the Speaker of the House of Representatives their* written declaration that the President is unable to discharge the powers and duties of his office. Thereupon Congress shall [immediately] decide the issue, *immediately assembling for that purpose if not in session.* If the Congress, *within ten days after the receipt of the written declaration of the Vice President and a majority of the principal officers of the executive departments, or such other body as Congress may by law provide,* determines by two-thirds vote of both Houses that the President is unable to discharge the powers and duties of the office, the Vice President shall continue to discharge the same as Acting President; otherwise the President shall resume the powers and duties of his office.

Thus, the ten-day time limitation advocated by Poff and McCulloch was adopted, and language was added requiring Congress to assemble immediately, if not already in session, to pass on a disagreement issue. The committee refused to change the two-day provision of Section 5 relating to the President's resumption of his powers and duties after a declaration of recovery. Section 3 was clarified, as Katzenbach had suggested, to permit the President, in a case when he had voluntarily declared his own inability, to resume his powers and duties upon his declaration of recovery without having that declaration subject to the challenge procedures of Section 5. In order to emphasize this intent, the substance of Section 5 was placed in Section 4, which related solely to cases in which presidential inability had been declared by the Vice President and Cabinet (or such other body established by law). Certain other changes made earlier by the Senate Judiciary Committee also were adopted.[74]

Despite its approval by the House Judiciary Committee, H. R. J. Res. 1 faced criticism in the House Rules Committee.[75] Among the critics were Representative William Colmer of Mississippi, who expressed his dislike of the method of declaring a President disabled because it might encourage a coup headed by the Vice President; and Representative James J. Delaney of New York, who preferred the elective process to fill a vacancy in the vice presidency. Supporters of the amendment prevailed, however, and on March 31, by a vote of 6 to 4, the Rules Committee cleared the proposal for consideration by the full House.

That consideration came on April 13, 1965. In his opening remarks, Representative Emanuel Celler, Chairman of the House Judiciary Committee, observed that "[e]veryone will agree that amending . . . the charter . . . of our Nation is not a task to be undertaken lightly. Today, however, we are faced with filling a gap which has existed since our beginnings [i.e., presidential inability], and this gap becomes more threatening as the complexity of the domestic and foreign policy grows." [76] Celler noted that the proposal did not meet every conceivable contingency but rather "[f]oreseen contingencies," especially the "practical human problems with reference to Presidential inability." [77]

During the House debates Representatives Celler, McCulloch, Poff, and others forcefully urged the adoption of H. R. J. Res. 1, as amended. They repeatedly underscored the need for the constitutional amendment and argued that the proposal represented as good a solution as could be found to the problems of presidential inability and vice presidential vacancy. Said Celler:

> This is by no means . . . a perfect bill. No bill can be perfect. . . . The world of actuality permits us to attain no perfection. . . . But nonetheless, this bill has a minimum of drawbacks. It is [a] well-rounded, sensible, and efficient approach toward a solution of a perplexing problem—a problem that has baffled us for over 100 years.[78]

Quoting Walter Lippmann, Celler added:

> "It is a great deal better than an endless search for the absolutely perfect solution, which will never be found and, indeed, is not necessary." [79]

Representative McCulloch stated:

> We must provide the means for an orderly transition of Executive power in a manner that respects the separation of powers doctrine, and

maintains the safeguards of our traditional checks and balances. I believe that House Joint Resolution 1, as amended . . . answers these needs, and will undoubtedly correct the shortcomings of the Constitution with respect to presidential inability and succession.[80]

Poff observed that to proceed by way of statute rather than constitutional amendment would invite a court test of the constitutionality of the legislation at the worst possible time—namely, when the President became disabled or asserted his recovery from an inability.[81]

House Minority Leader Gerald R. Ford of Michigan also gave his support for the proposal, noting that the nation had been without a Vice President sixteen times and that the proposal would assure "a clear-cut method of action to result in proper succession." [82] Also supporting the proposal was Representative Peter Rodino of New Jersey, who observed that it assures an orderly presidential succession and that the "requirement of congressional confirmation [in Section 2] is an added safeguard that only fully qualified persons of the highest character and national stature would ever be nominated by the President." [83]

As for the specific provisions of H. R. J. Res. 1, Celler, McCulloch, and Poff asserted that, throughout it, all doubts were resolved in favor of the President.[84] Thus, in a case of disagreement, "[t]he burden . . . is placed upon the Vice President and the Cabinet to prove the continuance of the disability and not on the President who has the primary claim to the office." [85] The Vice President and Cabinet, reasoned Poff, were the proper people to be entrusted with the power of decision:

> The Vice President, a man of the same political party, a man originally chosen by the President, a man familiar with the President's health, a man who knows what great decisions of state are waiting to be made, and a man intended by the authors of the Constitution to be the President's heir at death or upon disability, surely should participate in a decision involving the transfer of presidential powers. The same is true of the Cabinet whose members were appointed by the President and are closest to him physically and most loyal to him politically.[86]

If future experience should dictate the naming of another body, Poff said, Section 4 would authorize Congress to designate another body "to act with the Vice President."

Poff also noted that the so-called involuntary inability procedures of Section 4 covered such cases as when "the President by reason of some physical ailment or some sudden accident is unconscious or paralyzed and therefore unable to make or to communicate the decision to relinquish the powers of his Office," or when "the President, by reason of mental debility, is unable or unwilling to make any rational decision, including particularly the decision to stand aside." [87]

There was opposition, however, to H. R. J. Res. 1. Representatives

Hutchinson and Basil Lee Whitener of North Carolina argued that Article II, section 1, clause 6 of the Constitution gave Congress the power to legislate on inability so that a constitutional amendment was unnecessary.[88] Representatives Clarence J. Brown of Ohio, John D. Dingell of Michigan, James G. O'Hara of Michigan, and others felt that Section 2 was demeaning to the House of Representatives because it minimized the chances of the Speaker's succeeding to the presidency. Said Dingell:

> [T]he legislation . . . is in real effect a slap at the Members of the House of Representatives, a slap at our elected leadership, and it in effect says that the Membership of the House of Representatives and our elected leadership are not capable to succeed to the high Office of Presidency.[89]

Brown contended that the amendment would take away "from the House a constitutional right it now has to select a President" by virtue of selecting the Speaker who would be the heir apparent when there was no Vice President, and that "the man named Vice President could be an individual who was never elected to any public office." [90] He conjectured that:

> Under certain conditions and certain circumstances, a vacancy could exist in the Vice-Presidency and a President could name a billy goat as Vice President and some Congresses would approve of that nomination and that selection.[91]

Following Lyndon Johnson's succession, he said, it would have been difficult for Congress to reject anyone he chose for Vice President.

Representative Roman C. Pucinski of Illinois shared Brown's misgivings about the vice presidential vacancy provision of Section 2, stating that it opens "the door at some future time . . . to a phenomenon which has not bothered or plagued our country heretofore; namely, the problem of palace intrigue." [92] "[I]f we permit a President to name his own Vice President," said Pucinski, "you are in effect setting up a form of dynasty where your Vice President will run for President." [93] Representative Dingell stated that Section 2 was bad legislation, since it would "permit a President to begin an orderly chain of successors through an appointive device, and to effectively deny the citizens of the Nation [the power] to decide who will serve in the highest office in the land." [94] Representative Hutchinson urged that a vice presidential vacancy be filled automatically by some other officer of the government such as the Speaker of the House.[95]

Despite these opposing views, a motion by Pucinski to strike Section 2 was defeated by a vote of 140 to 44,[96] and a related motion by Representative Mathias was rejected by voice vote. He had moved to substitute a new Section 2, as follows:

> "SEC. 2. The Congress may by law provide for the case of a vacancy in the office of Vice President and for the case of removal, death, resigna-

tion or inability both of the President and the Vice President, declare what official would then act as President and such official would act accordingly until disability be removed or a President would be elected." [97]

Repeating his criticisms from the committee hearings, Mathias said that if Section 2 remains "we shall have changed the nature of the presidency for the first time in the history of the Republic, and it will be no longer a purely elective office." [98] He asserted:

> . . . I am opposed to an appointive Vice President. The Presidency since the history of this Republic began has been an elective office and I think it should continue to be an elective office. I believe that we should not have an appointive Vice President who would become the heir apparent of the Presidency and potentially the President.[99]

Mathias also suggested that the analogy to the nominating conventions was inapposite, because "a presidential nominee choosing his running mate is merely presenting a running mate to the people and the electability of the vice presidential candidate is a measure of the accountability of the presidential candidate." [100] He added that the presidential candidate, unlike an occupant of the White House, "will choose a man who has the strength to complement his own candidacy." [101]

Following the rejection of the Mathias proposal, Representative Arch A. Moore, Jr. of West Virginia sought to amend that part of Section 4 under which the Vice President would continue to act as President during the period Congress considered a challenge to a presidential declaration of recovery.[102] Moore, John V. Lindsay of New York, and several other representatives argued that the President should resume the discharge of his powers and duties during that period. "[A]ll presumptions," Moore said, "should be in favor of the President of the United States." If the Vice President is permitted to act during this period, declared Moore, "he could resort to many manipulations that would never permit the President of the United States . . . to present his case to the Congress of the United States." [103] He added that "[t]his could be a very indirect way to impeach a President . . . if you did not want to try him here in the Congress of the United States." [104] Moore pointed out that the President would be placed in the "position of coming here to the Congress and trying to lobby himself back into the job to which the people have elected him." [105] Representative Richard C. White of Texas agreed, stating:

> I do not believe the scepter of power should ever be removed from the President until the Congress itself . . . should so remove this power. This is consistent with our present Constitution and the proper separation of officers.[106]

In reply, Celler, McCulloch, Poff, and others argued that, since the capacity of the President would have been seriously challenged by the Vice President and a majority of the Cabinet, it was the wiser and less hazardous course to have the Vice President act during that ten-day period. "The President," said Celler, "may be as nutty as a fruitcake. He may be utterly insane." [107] Unless the Vice President served, said Representative Rodino, the issue might never get to Congress since, if the President immediately resumed his powers and duties, he might immediately discharge his Cabinet before a declaration of challenge could be filed with Congress.[108] Celler said that the impeachment power could be used if the Vice President acted irresponsibly under the circumstances. "We can impeach for high crimes and misdemeanors," he said, "and these high crimes and misdemeanors can mean anything that this Congress wants it to mean." [109] Thereupon, Moore's amendment was rejected by a vote of 122 to 58.[110]

Representative H. R. Gross of Iowa then proposed an amendment requiring a roll call vote whenever Congress voted on a President's nominee for Vice President, indicating that he also would make the same proposal regarding a vote on a disagreement in the case of inability.[111] The amendment was opposed by Celler, who argued that the House and Senate could demand such a vote under their rules, and that therefore the amendment was unnecessary. Gross's amendment was defeated on two votes, 102 to 92 and 130 to 115.[112]

One change successfully made on the floor of the House was an amendment offered by Representative Poff, but actually suggested by Speaker John W. McCormack of Massachusetts, which required Congress, if not in session, to assemble automatically within forty-eight hours after receiving a challenge from the Vice President and Cabinet to a presidential declaration of recovery.[113]

The debate concluded with Speaker McCormack's giving his full support to the measure, stating:

> I have lived for 14 months in the position of the man who, in the event of an unfortunate event happening to the occupant of the White House, under the law then would have assumed the Office of Chief Executive of our country. I can assure you, my friends and colleagues, that a matter of great concern to me was the vacuum which existed in the subject of determining inability of the occupant of the White House, if and when that should arise.
>
> I have in my safe in my office a written agreement.* As has been well said, it is outside the law. It is an agreement between individuals. But it was the only thing that could be done under the circumstances,

---

* See pp. 55–56, *supra*.

when we do not have a disability law in relation to the President in existence.

We have made a marked contribution by this resolution, and particularly by section 3 and section 4.[114]

He added:

We cannot legislate for every human consideration that might occur in the future. All we can do is the best that we can under the circumstances. The considerations of the committee and the deliberations of the members of both parties have resolved the problem confronting us in the best manner possible, having in mind the fact that with all our strengths we have weaknesses as human beings.[115]

A vote was then taken and H. R. J. Res. 1, as amended, was approved 368 to 29.[116]

CONFERENCE COMMITTEE

In order to resolve the differences between the House and Senate versions of the amendment, a Conference Committee was appointed.† It met several times during the following weeks and was divided along House and Senate lines on whether a time limitation should be placed upon Congress in deciding a disagreement issue. The House conferees insisted on a ten-day limitation, while the Senate conferees preferred no limitation at all.

On June 23, 1965, after a two-month deadlock,‡ agreement was reached on a twenty-one–day limitation.[117] The committee accepted the language of the House version that the recipients of all inability notifications be the Speaker and President pro tempore, instead of the Speaker and "President of the Senate" who, at the time of the notice, would be the Vice President himself. In addition, the committee accepted the House version of Section 3 permitting the President, in the event of a voluntary declaration of inability, to resume his powers and duties immediately upon transmittal of his declaration of recovery to the President pro tempore and the Speaker. The committee compromised on four days as the period within which the Vice President and Cabinet could challenge a President's declaration of recovery, when they had made the original inability determination. It also agreed to accept the provision in the House version requiring Congress to convene within forty-eight hours, if not then in session, to settle a disagreement.

† The conferees on behalf of the House were Celler, McCulloch, Poff, Byron G. Rogers of Colorado, and James C. Corman of California; and on behalf of the Senate, Bayh, Eastland, Ervin, Dirksen, and Hruska.
‡ Bayh's *One Heartbeat Away* 279–304 presents a fascinating account of the attempts at a resolution during that period and the key role played by Lewis F. Powell, Jr.

The expression "the Vice President and a majority of the principal officers of the executive departments, or such other body as Congress may by law provide" was changed to "the Vice President and a majority of either the principal officers of the executive departments or of such other body as Congress may by law provide." This change was made at the suggestion of Senator Hruska to ensure that if Congress in the future designated another body to replace the Cabinet, that body would be required to act with the Vice President.[118]

The conference report was passed by voice vote in the House of Representatives on June 30, 1965, after Poff explained its principal recommendations. He gave this explanation for the time limitation insisted upon by the House of Representatives:

> No one should assume that House insistence upon a time limit was a criticism of the Senate. It is true that the rules of the other body permit unlimited debate and a small minority of Senators hostile to the President and loyal to the Vice President as Acting President could, in the absence of a time limit, make a great deal of public mischief at a most critical time in the life of the Nation. It is no less true that such mischief could be wrought by a small dedicated band of enemies of the President in the House. By tedious invocation of the technical rules of procedure, that little band could frustrate action on the Vice President's challenge for a protracted period of time, during which the Vice President would continue to serve as Acting President and the President, knocking on his own door for readmission, would be kept standing outside. If this little band happened to be one more than half the membership of the House, their task would be much easier, because they could simply meet and adjourn every third day without any action at all. Thus, more than half but less than two-thirds could effectively accomplish by inaction the same thing it would take two-thirds to accomplish by vote if there is no time limit in the Constitution. The conference committee understood this danger, and that is why the 21-day provision is in the conference report.[119]

The report was considered in the Senate later that same day. Senators Robert F. Kennedy and Eugene J. McCarthy expressed reservations about the method prescribed for determining inability. Senator Kennedy said a President might discharge his Cabinet. A conflict could arise, he said, on

> . . . whether the President had, in fact, fired the Cabinet at the time they had met and decided to put in a new President. What we could end up with, in effect, would be the spectacle of having two Presidents both claiming the right to exercise the powers and duties of the Presidency, and perhaps two sets of Cabinet officers both claiming the right to act.[120]

Kennedy elaborated:

> A Cabinet decides that a President was disabled. The President fires the Cabinet. The members of the Cabinet say they did not receive notice that

they were fired until after they had declared the President disabled. The President says he fired them first. If the Congress is in recess, the President appoints another Cabinet, or else he says the Deputies and Under Secretaries are now the Cabinet. There would be two Presidents and two Cabinets. There would be a conflict as to which ones were the members of the Cabinet and as to whether the members of the first Cabinet had made the decision before or after they were fired by the President.[121]

Senator McCarthy added that the amendment was unclear on whether the members of the Cabinet had to be confirmed by the Senate before they could pass on a question of inability. He said that, if it were not for the fact that under Section 4 Congress could designate a body other than the Cabinet, he could not support the amendment.[122] This grant of power to Congress also lessened Kennedy's concern about a coup, which he felt to be a distinct possibility with the Cabinet in the picture.

Senator Albert Gore of Tennessee, however, objected to the wording of Section 4, arguing that it would permit the Vice President to choose between the Cabinet and the other body created by Congress. He said that the use of the expression "either/or" put the two groups on a par.[123] * Senator Bayh, pointing to the abundance of legislative history on the point, said that, under the proposed amendment, the Cabinet would have the responsibility unless Congress passed a law appointing another body. In that event, the "newly created body and not the Cabinet would act with the Vice President." [124] Bayh noted that if a Vice President believed that the President were disabled but the Cabinet refused to concur in that judgment, Congress could, if it agreed with the Vice President, establish another body to function with the Vice President. Senator Javits remarked that if the power to establish another body were exercised, he would interpret it "to give exclusivity to the other body," since it would be "completely contrary to the purpose of Congress to create two bodies which could compete with one another." [125] Senator John Sherman Cooper of Kentucky said that "it would be unreasonable to follow any other position." [126] "[T]he intent of the amendment," said Gore, "is not supported by the language of the amendment." [127] Gore then sought and obtained postponement of further discussion in order to study the question in greater detail.

On Tuesday, July 6, 1965, the measure again came up for consideration in the Senate. Senator Gore reiterated his objection to the proposed amendment because of the "either/or" expression and urged that the proposal be returned to committee. By virtue of this wording in Section 4, argued Gore, "a Vice President would be in a position to 'shop around'

---

* This writer called this unintended, possible construction to the attention of staff members of the House and Senate Judiciary Committees shortly after the conference report was issued; but it was too late then for any additional language changes to be made.

for support of his view that the President is not able to discharge the duties of his office." He added that

> . . . if the identity of the determining authority should be subject to conflicting interpretations, this Nation could undergo the potentially disastrous spectacle of competing claims to the power of the Presidency of the United States.[128]

As for Javits' point about exclusivity, Gore stated that he knew of no rule "which provides or could provide that a legislative enactment would take precedence over an express provision of the U. S. Constitution. . . ." [129] Senator McCarthy remarked that

> the word "either" appears to have been dropped into the amendment almost by inadvertence. It was not used as a result of carefully considered judgment. It is not a word that was weighed or was subject to any prolonged discussion in conference.[130]

Senator Bayh observed that:

> As a result of the insight and the perseverence of the Senator from Tennessee, we have now written a record of legislative intent, as long as our arms, to the effect that we desire only one body to act on the subject.[131]

Senator Bayh said that the language was clear—that if Congress designated another body, that body would supersede the Cabinet. Senator Dirksen agreed and said that, although he could not imagine a Vice President shopping around, if a Vice President did so, the people would not tolerate it and his political future would be ruined.[132] Dirksen noted:

> [L]anguage is not absolute. . . . [I]nterpretations of all kinds can be placed upon language. . . .
> Fashioning language to do what we have in mind, particularly when we are subject to the requirement of compression for constitutional amendment purposes, is certainly not an easy undertaking.[133]

He added: "I believe we have done a reasonably worthwhile job insofar as the feeble attributes of the language can accomplish it." [134] Senator Ervin expressed the view that, even if Senator Gore's interpretation were correct, it "would improve, instead of hurt, the amendment by making it more flexible," [135] and he observed that "the conference report . . . would submit to the States the very best possible resolution on the subject obtainable in the Congress of the United States as it is now constituted." [136]

At the conclusion of the debate on July 6, 1965, the Senate approved the measure by a vote of 68 to 5,* and a few days later the legislation

* The five were Senators Gore and McCarthy, Walter Mondale of Minnesota, John Tower of Texas, and Frank J. Lausche of Ohio.

was on its way to the state legislatures for ratification as the Twenty-Fifth Amendment to the Constitution.[137]

NOTES

1. Hearings on Presidential Inability and Vacancies in the Office of Vice President Before the Subcomm. on Constitutional Amendments of the Senate Comm. on the Judiciary, 89th Cong., 1st Sess. 13 (1965).
2. 111 Cong. Rec. 30 (1965).
3. 1965 Senate Hearings 14.
4. *Id.* 11–12.
5. *Id.* 11.
6. *Id.* 10.
7. *Id.* 29.
8. *Id.* 26.
9. *Id.* 27.
10. *Id.* 28.
11. *Id.* 18–19.
12. *Id.* 33.
13. *Id.* 34.
14. *Id.* 22–23, 29.
15. *Id.* 48.
16. *Id.* 48–49.
17. *Id.* 49.
18. *Id.* 50.
19. *Id.* 64.
20. *Id.* 66.
21. *Id.* 67.
22. *Id.* 73.
23. *Id.* 99.
24. *Id.* 98.
25. *Id.* 101.
26. Senate Comm. on the Judiciary, Report on Presidential Inability and Vacancies in the Office of Vice President, S. Rep. No. 66, 89th Cong., 1st Sess. (1965).
27. Bayh, *One Heartbeat Away* 210.
28. *Id.* 211–12.
29. S. Rep. No. 66 at 3 (1965).
30. *Id.*
31. 111 Cong. Rec. 3253 (1965).
32. *Id.* 3255.
33. *Id.* 3265.
34. *Id.* 3257.
35. *Id.* 3268–69.
36. *Id.* 3269.
37. *Id.* 3270.
38. *Id.* 3271.
39. *Id.* 3273.
40. *Id.* 3274.
41. *Id.*
42. *Id.* 3276.
43. *Id.*

44. *Id.* 3278.
45. *Id.*
46. *Id.* 3279.
47. *Id.* 3281.
48. *Id.* 3275.
49. *Id.*
50. *Id.* 3281.
51. *Id.* 3279.
52. *Id.* 3282.
53. Bayh 269.
54. 111 Cong. Rec. 3283 (1965).
55. *Id.* 3286.
56. Hearings on Presidential Inability and Vice Presidential Vacancy Before the House Comm. on the Judiciary, 89th Cong., 1st Sess. 4 (1965).
57. *Id.* 245.
58. *Id.* 243.
59. *Id.* 104.
60. *Id.* 67.
61. *Id.* 236.
62. *Id.* 96.
63. *Id.* 41–42.
64. *Id.* 5, 56–57, 77–78, 86–87.
65. *Id.* 242.
66. *Id.* 205.
67. *Id.* 91.
68. *Id.* 190.
69. *Id.* 90–91.
70. *Id.* 66.
71. *Id.* 91.
72. *Id.* 206.
73. House Committee on the Judiciary, Report on Presidential Inability and Vacancies in the Office of Vice President, H. R. Rep. No. 203, 89th Cong., 1st Sess. (1965).
74. See text at pp. 89–90, *supra.* "President pro tempore of the Senate," however, was used instead of "President of the Senate," so as to make clear that the Vice President would not be the recipient of any presidential inability notices to Congress.
75. *N. Y. Times,* April 1, 1965 at 20.
76. 111 Cong. Rec. 7936–37 (1965).
77. *Id.* 7937.
78. *Id.* 7936.
79. *Id.*
80. *Id.* 7942.
81. *Id.* 7940.
82. *Id.* 7967.
83. *Id.* 7955.
84. *Id.* 7938.
85. *Id.* 7943.
86. *Id.* 7941.
87. *Id.*
88. *Id.* 7944–46.
89. *Id.* 7961.
90. *Id.* 7932–33.

91. *Id.* 7932.
92. *Id.* 7960.
93. *Id.* 7961.
94. *Id.*
95. *Id.* 7946.
96. *Id.* 7963.
97. *Id.*
98. *Id.* 7950.
99. *Id.* 7963.
100. *Id.* 7950.
101. *Id.*
102. *Id.* 7963–64.
103. *Id.* 7964.
104. *Id.*
105. *Id.* 7949.
106. *Id.* 7958.
107. *Id.* 7965.
108. *Id.*
109. *Id.*
110. *Id.* 7966.
111. *Id.*
112. *Id.*
113. *Id.* 7967.
114. *Id.*
115. *Id.*
116. *Id.* 7968–69.
117. Conference Committee, Report on Presidential Inability and Vacancies in the Office of Vice President, H. R. Rep. No. 564, 89th Cong., 1st Sess. (1965).
118. 1965 conversation between the author and Larry Conrad, then chief counsel to the Senate Subcommittee on Constitutional Amendments.
119. 111 Cong. Rec. 15214 (1965).
120. *Id.* 15380.
121. *Id.* 15382.
122. *Id.* 15381–82.
123. *Id.* 15382–83.
124. *Id.* 15384.
125. *Id.* 15386.
126. *Id.*
127. *Id.* 15387.
128. *Id.* 15587.
129. *Id.* 15588.
130. *Id.* 15585.
131. *Id.* 15594.
132. *Id.* 15592.
133. *Id.* 15591.
134. *Id.* 15593.
135. *Id.* 15589.
136. *Id.* 15595.
137. *Id.* 15596.

7

Ratification

Once, perhaps, we could pay the price of inaction. But today in this crisis-ridden era there is no margin for delay, no possible justification for ever permitting a vacuum in our national leadership. Now, at last, through the 25th amendment, we have the means of responding to these crises of responsibility.

LYNDON B. JOHNSON
February 23, 1967 [1]

THE AMENDMENT WAS RATIFIED by the necessary thirty-eight state legislatures on February 10, 1967, and formally proclaimed the Twenty-Fifth Amendment to the Constitution at a White House ceremony held on February 23, 1967.[2] During the ratification period no serious opposition to the proposed amendment developed.* By the end of 1965, thirteen states had ratified it, and one year after its submission thirty states had done so. In several states confusion about the meaning of the amendment briefly delayed the ratification efforts. A *South Carolina Law Review* article,† which criticized certain features of the amendment, particularly Section 2, was distributed to members of the Arkansas legislature and temporarily led its Speaker to defer a vote on ratification. Arkansas eventually ratified on November 4, 1965. West Virginia initially sought to ratify the amendment without the provisions on presidential inability. In Colorado, a snarl developed over whether the amendment was properly before a special session of the legislature, in July 1965. It nonetheless was voted on, receiving slightly less than the two-thirds vote required by the state's constitution.‡ The following February Colorado ratified

---

* As the amendment was being ratified, the need for it was underscored twice when President Johnson underwent surgery, first in 1965 for the removal of a gall bladder and then in 1966 to repair a hernia and remove a polyp from his throat. On both occasions, Johnson was under anesthesia.

† See Haimbaugh, Vice Presidential Succession: A Criticism of the Bayh–Celler Plan, 17 South Carolina L. Rev. 315 (1965), which contended that there was no urgency for machinery to fill a vice presidential vacancy; that giving the President the power to nominate so as to assure continuity of executive policies is not supported by the reasons for which a presidential candidate actually selects a running mate; and that the confirmation role of Congress would be little more than a formality. This writer responded in Vice Presidential Succession: In Support of the Bayh–Celler Plan, 18 South Carolina L. Rev. 226 (1966).

‡ Whether such an extraordinary vote requirement is constitutional is a point of contention. Since the Constitution prescribes no vote for ratification, it has been argued that a simple majority is all that is required. See *Hawke* v. *Smith*, No. 1, 253 U. S. 221 (1920), and *Leser* v. *Garnett*, 258 U. S. 130 (1922).

by more than a two-thirds vote, but only after an effective campaign in response to an attack against the amendment by the *Denver Post* and a few members of the Colorado legislature. Senator L. T. Skiffington objected to Section 2 on the ground that it failed to include some qualification, such as a specified number of years of congressional service, as a requirement for appointment as a replacement Vice President. With respect to the inability provisions, he contended that the President could have an unnecessarily difficult time resuming his powers and duties after his recovery. In the Colorado General Assembly, Representative John Carroll led an attack on the amendment, arguing that it left unclear exactly who would participate with the Vice President in an inability decision and that it set the stage for a constitutional coup d'état. He also criticized the twenty-one–day provision of Section 4, stating: "During this time, no one would know who is president, and one president could be countermanding orders given by the other." He added: ". . . Who would order the armed forces into combat? Which president would the armed forces obey?" §

In Alabama the amendment's proponents did not press it to a vote in 1965, fearing that it might not be ratified and that such a failure could become a states' rights issue and hurt legislative efforts elsewhere. Alabama later ratified the Amendment—on March 14, 1967, a few weeks after it had been added to the Constitution.

It is unclear which state became the first, and which the thirty-eighth, to ratify. Nebraska's unicameral legislature ratified the amendment on July 12, 1965, but because of a question concerning the need for the governor's signature, the ratifying resolution was not signed by the Acting Governor until the next day. On July 13, before such signing, the Wisconsin legislature also ratified the amendment. As a consequence, both states claim to be first to have ratified. The claim of Nebraska would seem to be the better one, since there is substantial authority for the principle that Article V contemplates ratification by the state legislatures only.[3] On February 9, 1967, North Dakota ratified the amendment, believing that it was the thirty-eighth state to do so. When it learned that it was the thirty-seventh, the state's legislative leaders declared the ratification illegal on the ground that there was a voice vote in one house. They hoped that once another state ratified, North Dakota would ratify again, making it the thirty-eighth state. However, before North Dakota could act, Minnesota and Nevada ratified the Amendment on February 10. It is interesting that North Dakota never took any further steps toward ratification. Since that time, nine other states have ratified the Amendment. The only states not to ratify are Georgia, South Carolina, and North Dakota.[4] *

§ *Denver Post,* Jan. 23, 1966 at 26.

* In a letter dated March 20, 1967 to the Archivist of the United States, Robert Bahmer, North Dakota Secretary of State Ben Meier wrote that North Dakota did not ratify the Twenty-Fifth Amendment.

The relatively smooth and rapid ratification accorded the Amendment was the result in large measure of the efforts of lawyer groups throughout the country, working in conjunction with the ABA. Young lawyers, in particular, made substantial contributions to the Amendment's success in their states.

NOTES

1. 1 *Public Papers of the Presidents of the United States, Lyndon B. Johnson —1967* 217–18 (1968).

2. See generally Bayh, *One Heartbeat Away* 335–42, and the state ratification files in the office of the General Services Administration.

3. See Amendment of the Constitution by the Convention Method Under Article V, American Bar Association Special Constitutional Convention Study Committee 28–30 (1974).

4. See *id*. 32–33.

III

First Implementations of the Solution

8

The Resignation of Spiro T. Agnew

> It is unthinkable that this nation should have been required to endure the anguish and uncertainty of a prolonged period in which the man next in line of succession to the Presidency was fighting the charges brought against him by his own government.
>
> ELLIOT RICHARDSON
> October 10, 1973 [1]

ON NOVEMBER 7, 1972, Richard M. Nixon and Spiro T. Agnew received more popular votes for President and Vice President than any other candidates in American history. Less than two years later both had resigned their offices, and Gerald R. Ford and Nelson A. Rockefeller had become President and Vice President by virtue of the Twenty-Fifth Amendment. Although it is beyond the scope of this book to detail the unique and unprecedented events leading to the fall of Nixon and Agnew,* a summary of certain of these events is necessarily set forth in order to place in context the accessions of Ford and Rockefeller.

In January 1973, shortly before the second inauguration of Nixon and Agnew, the United States District Court for the District of Columbia began hearing the first Watergate break-in case, which was to become a two-year untangling process. This criminal trial of the Watergate burglars resulted in guilty verdicts for G. Gordon Liddy and James McCord of the Committee for the Re-election of the President and in guilty pleas by E. Howard Hunt and four others. That month the Pentagon Papers trial also began, and in February the United States Senate created a select committee of four Democrats and three Republicans, chaired by Senator Sam Ervin, to investigate 1972 campaign abuses.

An indication that higher Republicans had been involved in the Watergate break-in came on March 19, 1973 when McCord wrote to federal judge John J. Sirica that he was under political pressure to plead guilty and remain silent and that perjury had been committed at the trial. Sirica disclosed the letter in open court and deferred final sentencing of the defendants, urging their cooperation with the ongoing Watergate in-

---

* See generally, C. Bernstein & B. Woodward, *All the President's Men* (1974); T. White, *Breach of Faith: The Fall of Richard Nixon* (1975); and R. Cohen & J. Witcover, *A Heartbeat Away: The Investigation and Resignation of Vice President Spiro T. Agnew* (1974).

vestigation. McCord met with the investigators and appeared before the Ervin committee in closed session. By late April 1973 allegations had been made to the government prosecutors which implicated a number of close aides to the President in prior knowledge and the cover-up of the Watergate break-in. On April 30 the White House announced the resignations of Attorney General Richard Kleindienst and presidential aides John Ehrlichman, H. R. Haldeman, and John Dean. In a televised address the President accepted responsibility for the Watergate incident but denied any personal involvement in the break-in or the cover-up. In May federal judge W. Matthew Byrne, Jr. dismissed the Pentagon Papers case because of government misconduct and revealed that Ehrlichman had offered him the directorship of the FBI during the course of the trial. At about the same time the Ervin committee began its televised hearings, and Elliot Richardson and Archibald Cox were sworn in as Attorney General and Special Prosecutor, respectively.

As criticism of the Nixon administration increased, former Secretary of Defense Clark Clifford wrote a provocative article for *The New York Times* in which he expressed the opinion that the public loss of confidence in Nixon was so widespread that the executive branch could no longer function effectively.[2] He suggested that the President employ the provisions of the Twenty-Fifth Amendment and announce that both he and Vice President Agnew would resign, the Vice President resigning first. Then Nixon could nominate a Vice President whom Congress would approve and, after his confirmation, Nixon could resign leaving a new successor as President. President Nixon, seemingly determined to remain in office, never commented on this proposal.

Throughout June and July 1973 the Ervin committee and Special Prosecutor Cox requested White House files for their investigations, but Nixon rejected these requests on the ground of executive privilege. On July 16 a bombshell struck when Alexander Butterfield, Nixon's former appointments secretary, revealed to the Ervin committee that tape recordings had been made of all conversations and telephone calls in the President's office since 1970. With this revelation, the historic legal battles for the tapes began, which one year later would culminate in Nixon's resignation. Nixon, who had been hospitalized with viral pneumonia for a week, labeled rumors that he would resign as "poppycock." Both the Ervin committee and Cox issued subpoenas for certain tapes and filed suit in federal court to obtain them. Thus, by August 1973 the stage had been set for the ultimate legal confrontation.

As these events unfolded, others unknown to the public were occurring which eventually would cause Agnew to resign as Vice President.[3] In December 1972, the United States Attorney's office in Maryland had begun an investigation of political corruption in Baltimore County. In early February 1973, rumors swept Baltimore that Agnew had been implicated in the investigation. George White, the Vice President's personal attorney, visited United States Attorney George Beall to inquire whether Agnew was under investigation. Beall assured White that only the current Baltimore County leadership was under investigation, and that the prosecutors would do everything possible to protect Agnew's name.[4]

On February 6, 1973, Beall visited Attorney General Richard Kleindienst to inform him that the rumors about Agnew's involvement in the investigation were false. In April Agnew retained as his counsel Washington attorney Judah Best, a law partner of former White House special counsel Charles W. Colson. On April 19 Best met with Beall and described Agnew's willingness to cooperate with the investigation and his concern about adverse publicity. Beall reaffirmed that the investigation did not involve Agnew. By June, however, the United States Attorney's office had uncovered information that Agnew allegedly had received bribes for awards of public works contracts during the period of his service as County Executive of Baltimore County and as Governor of Maryland. On July 3 this information was brought to the attention of Attorney General Elliot Richardson. Richardson is said to have remarked that " 'the continuing capacity of the nation to govern itself' " was at stake, and referred to the fact that Agnew was a heartbeat away from the presidency. " 'The President's plane could go down tomorrow,' " he said. " 'There could be an assassin's bullet. He could die tomorrow.' "[5] The President's possible impeachment for participating in the Watergate cover-up might have been in Richardson's mind as well. Richardson wanted to confront Agnew immediately with the evidence of corruption in the hope that he would resign, but he was persuaded by the prosecutors to wait until the investigation had progressed further. Richardson also decided not to inform the President about the allegations at that time.[6] For the rest of the month, the United States Attorney's office in Baltimore developed the evidence against Agnew. On July 27 Richardson and the prosecutors agreed that President Nixon should be informed about the case and that Agnew should be sent a formal letter advising him that he was under investigation for possible violations of federal criminal statutes. Richardson then visited White House Chief of Staff Alexander Haig to schedule an appointment with the President, and learned that Agnew already had spoken with General Haig and the President about the investigation and had asserted his innocence.[7]

On August 1 Agnew's attorney was given a letter from George Beall stating that Agnew was under investigation for conspiracy, extortion, bribery, and tax fraud, and it requested certain documents. On August 6 Richardson met in the White House with the President, Haig, and special presidential counsel J. Fred Buzhardt, and detailed the case against the Vice President. According to Richardson, Nixon's " 'reaction was remarkably objective and deliberate.' " [8] It was agreed that Henry Peterson, an assistant attorney general, should make an independent evaluation of the evidence against Agnew and report to Richardson and Nixon. While it seemed to Richardson that the White House favored Agnew's resignation, Nixon did not wish to alienate Agnew's constituency, whose support he clearly needed in the unfolding impeachment drama.

At Haig's suggestion, Richardson met that afternoon with Agnew and his attorneys * and summarized the status of the Baltimore investigation. Agnew denied the charges, attacked the integrity of the prosecution and its witnesses, and agreed that Henry Peterson should review the case. Late that night, as the *Wall Street Journal* and *Washington Post* published the first accounts of the investigation, Agnew publicly announced that he had been informed about the investigation and that he was innocent of any wrongdoing. For the next sixty-five days, as evidence of President Nixon's involvement in the Watergate scandals developed, the nation watched the demise of the Vice President's public career.

On August 7 Agnew conferred privately with Nixon and was told by the President that he had complete confidence in him. But when Agnew returned to his office, he was visited by General Haig, who suggested that if the allegations against him were sustainable, Agnew should consider taking some action prior to indictment.[9] On the following day Agnew held a press conference, labeled the rumors about his conduct in Maryland politics "damned lies," and stated unequivocally that he would not resign. He said that he would cooperate with the prosecutors and had "absolutely nothing to hide."

Almost daily thereafter the press printed new stories about the investigation. Some of the articles cited Justice Department or government sources, leading Agnew's staff to conclude that the administration intended to destroy the Vice President through the device of news leaks.[10] On August 15 Agnew released to the prosecutors his personal financial records, and in a public relations counterattack published the covering letter which promised his full cooperation in the investigation. As the news leaks continued, Agnew called his second news conference to charge that officials of the Justice Department "have decided to indict me in the press," and demanded an inquiry into the source of the leaks. Nixon telephoned Agnew to tell him that he would support his call for an investigation, and in a televised news conference on August 22 the President directed Richardson to conduct a full investigation.[11] Nixon carefully praised Agnew's performance and integrity as Vice President while refusing to comment on his prior activities. The following day the White House revealed to reporters that the President's lawyers refused to formulate a joint strategy on the issues of executive privilege and in-

* In addition to Best, Agnew had engaged Jay H. Topkis and Martin London of the New York firm of Paul, Weiss, Rifkind, Wharton & Garrison.

dictability because they saw no common interest with the Vice President.[12]

On September 1 Nixon and Agnew met privately for two hours, prompting rumors that Agnew's resignation was being planned. Speculation was increased because Nixon had cut short a Labor Day weekend holiday at San Clemente to return to Washington for the meeting. It is reported that Nixon wanted Agnew to resign but could not bring himself to make a direct request for his resignation.[13] After the meeting, it was reported that they had held a thorough discussion of the investigation and that the subject of resignation was not even mentioned. At some point during the next few days Bryce N. Harlow, a confidant of Nixon's and a good friend of Agnew's, visited the Vice President on behalf of the President and suggested that a resignation would be in the best interest of the country. While Agnew appeared to entertain the proposition, he demanded assurances that he would not go to prison.[14]

On September 3 Richardson authorized the prosecutors to proceed with the grand jury investigation of the charges against Agnew. As the prosecutors readied their case for presentation to the grand jury, Agnew threatened to ask the House of Representatives to begin impeachment proceedings. Perhaps because of the ominous parallel to the President himself, the White House opposed such a move, fearing that it would resolve the question of whether a President or Vice President must be impeached before he can be indicted.[15] Thereupon, the White House asked Richardson to postpone submitting evidence to the grand jury in the hope of persuading Agnew to abandon the impeachment plan.

On September 10 Haig and Buzhardt met with Agnew and Best. Buzhardt reviewed the case against Agnew, and Haig demanded that he resign. Best protested, and Agnew left the room without replying to the demand. The next day the White House informed Richardson that Agnew's attorneys wanted to discuss the procedural options available to the Vice President. On September 12 Richardson, Peterson, and Beall met with Agnew's attorneys and told them that the Justice Department was prepared to press for an indictment. The next day Best met with Richardson and Peterson and, in effect, opened plea-bargaining negotiations. At this meeting it was indicated that Agnew would resign as Vice President and plead no contest to a single tax charge in return for the government's recommendation that no jail sentence be imposed.[16] The government subsequently insisted on a settlement provision that all the evidence collected against Agnew be disclosed to the public.

Meanwhile, on September 14 Agnew met with Senator Barry Goldwater of Arizona to discuss the situation, and Goldwater subsequently complained to Harlow about the pressure being exerted on Agnew to resign. On September 18 the *Washington Post* printed an article by David Broder which quoted an unnamed senior Republican as stating that Agnew would resign within the week. The White House refusal to comment on the report or even to affirm the President's support of Agnew added further momentum to the rumors about his future.

The plea bargaining continued with disagreements over an admission of guilt by Agnew and the plea to a felony charge. It is reported that throughout these discussions Richardson expressed his worry that Nixon "might be impeached, assassinated, he was not in the best psychological condition." [17] On September 20 Agnew met secretly with Nixon and complained that the Justice Department was making it too difficult for him to make a deal.[18] That evening Richardson was summoned to the White House to meet with Haig and Buzhardt. They insisted that Agnew's resignation was the primary goal and that Richardson must not frustrate this result by demanding too much. Richardson, however, refused to alter his conditions.[19]

On September 22 the *Washington Post* printed a story describing the negotiations and Agnew's possible resignation. Convinced that the Justice Department had leaked the story to embarrass him and weaken his bargaining position, Agnew broke off negotiations and disclosed that he was establishing a legal defense fund. The Columbia Broadcasting System that day also quoted Henry Peterson as saying " 'We've got the evidence. We've got it cold.' "

On September 25 Richardson and Peterson spent two hours with the President and told him that, since the plea bargaining had failed, an indictment of the Vice President should be sought. Nixon appears to have been concerned that such a course would weaken his current argument that an incumbent President must be impeached before indictment, and therefore he favored resort to the House of Representatives for an impeachment proceeding.[20] Shortly after Richardson and Peterson left the White House, Agnew arrived and stated that he would seek a House investigation. Nixon then released a statement to the press reporting on his meeting with Agnew. Nixon said that the Vice President had denied the charges made against him and that he was entitled to the presumption of innocence. Richardson also issued a statement in which he said that evidence regarding the Vice President would be presented to the grand jury when it reconvened on September 27.

In the morning of September 25 House Minority Leader Gerald Ford and Leslie C. Arends of Illinois, the House Republican Whip, relayed to House Speaker Carl Albert of Oklahoma a request from Agnew for a meeting prior to Albert's taking a call from Richardson. It appears that Ford and Arends had been to the White House earlier in the morning and had seen both Nixon and Agnew.[21] That afternoon, about 3:30, Agnew met personally with Albert and gave him a letter which formally requested that the House of Representatives investigate the charges against him. During this meeting Agnew criticized the Justice Department and expressed his feeling that the White House was going to let him down.

The meeting with Albert, to which the legislative leaders of both parties were called in, lasted about an hour. Following it, Agnew's letter was read to the approximately fifty members present on the floor of the House of Representatives. In his letter Agnew cited a precedent involving Vice President John C. Calhoun and declared that the leaks and newspaper reports had made it impossible for a grand jury to consider the charges against him on the merits. House Minority Leader Ford, Senate Minority Leader Hugh Scott of Pennsylvania, and other Republican leaders urged that Agnew be given an impeachment hearing.[22] On September 26, Albert, who, like Ford, had been alerted by Richardson to Agnew's forthcoming indictment, refused Agnew's request on the ground that the House should not interfere with a matter before the courts.* Ford called the decision unfortunate and political, stating: " 'They made a Democratic decision. I don't think there's anything we can do since we are in the minority.' " [23] Another Republican leader remarked that the Democrats " 'won't bail the Vice President out of his predicament.' " [24] Supporting the decision, Democratic Representative John Conyers, Jr. of Michigan reportedly said: " 'We should not interrupt the legal process. I would trust 12 honest citizens of Maryland rather than 435 members of Congress.' " [25]

On September 27 the grand jury began to hear evidence against Agnew which caused him to institute court proceedings the next day in an effort to stop the grand jury. Agnew urged that the Constitution prohibits criminal proceedings against an incumbent Vice President and, further, that leaks had deprived him of the possibility of a fair trial on the merits. Agnew then began a public relations offensive.

A New York Times article on September 28 by James Reston quoted Agnew as saying that he would not resign but would fight through the courts and keep appealing to the House of Representatives. He also criticized Henry Peterson and certain members of the President's staff. On September 29, in a Los Angeles speech before more than 2,000 women, Agnew emotionally stated: " 'I will not resign if indicted.' " He again criticized the Justice Department, saying that its members were " 'severely stunned by their ineptness in the Watergate case. . . . They are trying to recoup their reputations at my expense. I am a big trophy.' " [26] On October 2 Agnew's news secretary predicted that the Vice

---

* For an interesting account of Democratic Majority Leader Thomas P. ("Tip") O'Neill's efforts to persuade Speaker Albert and Chairman Rodino of the Judiciary Committee to decline Agnew's request, see J. Breslin, How the Good Guys Finally Won 57–65 (1975). According to Breslin, O'Neill feared that if Agnew's request was granted, the House would be left with insufficient time and resources to deal with the question of Nixon's impeachment. Of Agnew's request for a House investigation, Albert has stated: "I don't know to this date whether the White House contrived this situation to get this matter before the House of Representatives, or whether the Vice President and the President were really at odds." Albert, The Most Dramatic Events of My Life, Oklahoma State University Outreach 5 (March 1974).

President's next speech would contain additional attacks. Haig almost immediately telephoned Agnew's top assistant, stating that the President wanted no more attacks on Peterson, the Justice Department, or the Administration, and indicating that unless such attacks ceased there would be no plea bargaining and Agnew would end up behind bars. Haig demanded that Agnew's press secretary be dismissed, and he was in fact relieved of duty.[27]

Agnew's repeated protestations of innocence and his criticisms of the press for leaking secret grand jury information won him sympathy throughout the country. On October 3 federal district judge Walter E. Hoffman granted Agnew's request to conduct an investigation of Justice Department leaks, including the right to serve subpoenas and to begin taking depositions as soon as possible. That same day Nixon held an informal press conference. While calling Agnew's decision not to resign " 'an altogether proper one,' " he characterized the charges against Agnew as " 'serious and not frivolous' " and defended Henry Peterson.[28] The President also stated that he had not asked Agnew to resign, or developed a list of possible vice presidential replacements. On the following night at a speech in Chicago, Agnew stated : " 'A candle is only so long, and eventually it burns out.' "

One day later, on October 5, the Justice Department expressed the view that Agnew could be indicted without first being impeached and that, upon an indictment, the Congress had the power to proceed by way of impeachment.[29] This report further isolated Agnew from the President. Then, the same day, Agnew abruptly indicated his interest in working out a settlement, which was secretly concluded in the following days. Present at some of the critical negotiations was Judge Hoffman. The settlement embodied the terms discussed at the first meeting, as well as a full disclosure by the government of the evidence developed against him. At a meeting in the White House on the evening of October 9, Agnew informed Nixon of his decision to resign.[30]

Shortly after 2:00 P.M. on Wednesday, October 10, Agnew, his attorneys, Richardson, and other representatives of the Justice Department appeared before Judge Hoffman in Baltimore's federal district court and implemented the terms of the settlement, to wit: Agnew pleaded nolo contendere to the felony of tax evasion for the year 1967, the Attorney General announced the dismissal of all further prosecution of Agnew and the release of a forty-page summary of the evidence against him, and Agnew announced his decision to resign. Said Hoffman: " 'You are submitting your resignation as Vice President of the United States. I want you to know that no Federal Court could require you to take this action.' " [31]

In explaining the settlement, Richardson told the court that a prosecution or impeachment of Agnew would have consumed years, " 'with

potentially disastrous consequences to vital interests of the United States.' "
He concluded by urging that the court not confine Agnew, basing his request on compassion, respect for the office of Vice President, and the fact that Agnew had spared the nation protracted agony by his resignation.

Agnew admitted that he had received certain unreported taxable income in 1967 but denied any other wrong-doing, stating:

> In all the circumstances, I have concluded that protracted proceedings before the Grand Jury, the Congress and the courts, with the speculation and controversy surrounding them, would seriously prejudice the national interest.

His plea was accepted, and he was fined $10,000 and placed on three years' probation.

Concurrently with the court proceedings, Agnew's staff in Washington was informed of the resignation and a formal letter of resignation was delivered to the Secretary of State. In an exchange of letters with the President that day, Agnew stated that "it is in the best interest of the Nation that I relinquish the Vice Presidency." Nixon replied:

> The most difficult decisions are often those that are the most personal, and I know your decision to resign as Vice President has been as difficult as any facing a man in public life could be. Your departure from the Administration leaves me with a great sense of personal loss. You have been a valued associate throughout these nearly five years that we have served together. However, I respect your decision, and I also respect the concern for the national interest that led you to conclude that a resolution of the matter in this way, rather than through an extended battle in the courts and the Congress, was advisable in order to prevent a protracted period of national division and uncertainty.
>
> As Vice President, you have addressed the great issues of our times with courage and candor. Your strong patriotism, and your profound dedication to the welfare of the nation, have been an inspiration to all who have served with you as well as to millions of others throughout the country.
>
> I have been deeply saddened by this whole course of events, and I hope that you and your family will be sustained in the days ahead by a well-justified pride in all that you have contributed to the nation by your years of service as Vice President.[32]

Gerald Ford was listening to a debate in the House of Representatives on home rule for the District of Columbia when he was informed by a colleague of Agnew's resignation. " 'You're kidding,' " he replied. Ford, who said that he had had no prior knowledge of Agnew's decision to resign, described his first reaction as " 'one of disbelief, his second . . . one of great sadness.' " [33] It was reported that Ford was relieved that Agnew had resigned, since the Republican Party was having enough trouble defending Nixon. " 'How much could the country take?' " Ford reportedly said to a friend on the day Agnew resigned. " 'It's the best thing that he's now out.' " [34]

According to White House press secretary Ronald L. Ziegler, President Nixon " 'played no direct role in the arrangement that was worked out or the decision which has been announced today.' " He added that " '[t]he President and the White House and the Vice President have made the point that this is a . . . personal decision which only the Vice President could make. The President, of course, respected that.' " [35]

Obviously, President Nixon had played an important part in the resignation drama. According to Richardson, " '[t]he President was kept . . . fully informed at all times. He fully approved each of the major steps that were taken in the course of these negotiations.' " [36] Once the White House recognized the gravity of the charges against Agnew, it sought to compel his resignation. For, of the three solutions available to Agnew—resignation, indictment, or impeachment—either indictment or impeachment would have set a potentially dangerous precedent for a President facing a similar situation. It was to Nixon's advantage to avoid a legal confrontation which might impair his own ability to defend himself against the inevitable Watergate attacks, and to re-establish credibility for his administration by the selection of a new Vice President. Attorney General Richardson seems to have realized that the nation could not bear possible simultaneous criminal prosecutions of both the President and the Vice President and, therefore, he sought Agnew's resignation in the national interest, knowing that a procedure existed for selecting a new and untarnished Vice President.

NOTES

1. *N. Y. Times*, Oct. 11, 1973 at 35.
2. Clifford, A Government of National Unity, *id.*, June 4, 1973 at 35.
3. The facts set forth in this section are taken largely from issues of the *N. Y. Times* and *Wash. Post* and from R. Cohen and J. Witcover, *A Heartbeat Away: The Investigation and Resignation of Vice President Spiro T. Agnew* (1974). For an excellent summary of the events leading to the resignation, see, in particular, Naughton, How Agnew Bartered his Office to Keep From Going to Prison, *N. Y. Times*, Oct. 23, 1973 at 1, 36.
4. Cohen & Witcover 15.
5. Naughton 36.
6. Cohen & Witcover 110–11.
7. *Id.* 133–34.
8. *Id.* 145–46.
9. *Id.* 159.
10. *Id.* 192.
11. *N. Y. Times*, Aug. 23, 1973 at 1.
12. Cohen & Witcover 203–04.
13. *N. Y. Times*, Sept. 2, 1973 at 1, 34.

14. Naughton 36.

15. Cohen & Witcover 218–19.

16. *Id.* 223–24.

17. Naughton 36.

18. Cohen & Witcover 243.

19. *Id.* 244.

20. *Id.* 252–53.

21. Albert, The Most Dramatic Events of My Life, Oklahoma State University Outreach 4–5 (March 1974).

22. *N. Y. Times,* Sept. 27, 1973 at 28; *id.,* Sept. 26, 1973 at 1, 23; terHorst, *Gerald Ford and the Future of the Presidency* 154.

23. *N. Y. Times,* Sept. 27, 1973 at 1.

24. *Id.* 28.

25. *Id.*

26. *Id.,* Sept. 30, 1973 at 60.

27. Cohen & Witcover 277–78.

28. *N. Y. Times,* Oct. 4, 1973 at 30.

29. *Id.,* Oct. 6, 1973 at 1, 9.

30. Cohen & Witcover 328.

31. *N. Y. Times,* Oct. 11, 1973 at 35.

32. *Id.* 1.

33. *Id.* 34.

34. terHorst 154.

35. *N. Y. Times,* Oct. 11, 1973 at 34.

36. *Id.,* Oct. 12, 1973 at 26.

9

The Substitution of Gerald R. Ford

> Together we have made history here today. For the first time
> we have carried out the command of the 25th amendment. In
> exactly 8 weeks, we have demonstrated to the world that our
> great republic stands solid, stands strong upon the bedrock of
> the Constitution.
>
> GERALD R. FORD
> December 6, 1973 [1]

NOMINATION

SPECULATION ABOUT A NEW VICE PRESIDENT to replace Agnew began weeks before his resignation. In September 1973, in anticipation of Agnew's resignation, three major congressional committees began to study secretly the process by which a vice presidential vacancy would be filled.[2] It is not surprising that, at about the same time, various names were mentioned in the press as possible replacements. Those who figured most prominently in the September speculation were former Texas Governor John B. Connally,* who had recently joined the Republican Party; former New York Governor Nelson A. Rockefeller; Governor Ronald Reagan of California; Senators Goldwater and Scott, and Howard H. Baker of Tennessee, and Attorney General Richardson.

On September 20, at a meeting with Democratic freshmen members of the House, the House Democratic leaders indicated that they would insist that the President nominate a caretaker Vice President who would pledge not to run for President in 1976.[3] One of the leaders reportedly said: " 'We're not going to be a party to picking somebody who is going to run against us three years from now.' " [4] Robert Strauss, the chairman of the Democratic National Committee, said that Nixon should avoid a " 'tricky, treacherous situation' " by choosing a " 'nonpresidential' " person.[5] Among those mentioned for such a stand-in role were former Secretary of State William P. Rogers and former Senator John Sherman Cooper of Kentucky.

---

* Nixon's interest in Connally seems to have had a long history. It is reported that, prior to the 1972 Republican convention and because of Agnew's disenchantment with the vice presidency, Nixon explored the possibility that Agnew could resign and be replaced by Connally under the Twenty-Fifth Amendment. Newsweek, April 7, 1975 at 32–33.

On September 21, Senator Edward M. Kennedy of Massachusetts suggested that, if Agnew resigned, Congress should confirm no successor until the issue raised by President Nixon's refusal to turn over the Watergate tapes was settled. " 'So long as the President himself is so clearly under the cloud of the possible disclosures on the tapes, grave questions exist as to the propriety of the President's choosing his own successor,' " Kennedy said.[6]

On October 10, immediately following Agnew's resignation, Press Secretary Ziegler announced: " 'President Nixon intends to move expeditiously in selecting a nominee and he trusts the Congress will then act promptly to consider the nomination.' "[7] Ziegler also stated that the President would confer over the next few days with a wide range of national leaders to ascertain their views on the kind of person to be named as the nominee. Nixon met in the afternoon of October 10 with the congressional leaders of both Houses. He met first with the Republican leaders: Senators Scott and Robert P. Griffin of Michigan and Representatives Ford and Arends; and then with Democratic leaders: House Speaker Albert and Senate Majority Leader Mansfield.† At the latter meeting Albert reportedly told Nixon that " 'we have a man in the House' who could win confirmation without difficulty," that is, Gerald Ford.[8] Mansfield opined that former Secretary Rogers and former Senator Cooper would be confirmed quickly.[9] Nixon also spoke on October 10 with George Bush, chairman of the Republican National Committee, and Senator Eastland, the President pro tempore of the Senate. Bush then sent telegrams to the members of the Republican National Committee asking for their suggestions.

Reports immediately began to circulate about likely nominees. Those who were mentioned most frequently were Connally, Reagan, and Rockefeller. Connally was said to be Nixon's first choice. Other possibilities mentioned in the press of October 11 included Senator Goldwater, former Secretary of State Rogers, former Pennsylvania Governor William W. Scranton, former Senator Cooper, Treasury Secretary George P. Shultz, presidential counselor Melvin R. Laird, Chief Justice Warren Burger, Richardson,‡ and Deputy Attorney General William D. Ruckelshaus. The name of Gerald R. Ford did not appear prominently in the early post-resignation public speculation.§

---

† At these meetings Nixon reportedly said that his Vice President must meet the criteria of being qualified to be President, have a reasonable chance of being confirmed by a simple majority of Congress, and be in tune with his foreign policy. *N. Y. Times*, Oct. 12, 1973 at 1.

‡ On October 11, Richardson ruled himself out as a potential nominee, stating that " 'it would be highly inappropriate for me as the Government accuser of the Vice President' " to be considered " 'for one moment . . . as a potential successor to him.' " *N. Y. Times*, Oct. 12, 1973 at 26.

§ However, within minutes of the news of Agnew's resignation, Representatives Jack Kemp of New York and Dan Kuykendall of Tennessee were circulating petitions on the House floor urging Nixon to appoint Ford. R. Reeves, *A Ford Not a Lincoln* 32 (1975).

At a meeting of the Democratic leaders on October 11, strong opposition to Connally surfaced. He was described by some at the meeting as a " 'traitor and a doublecrosser' " to the Democratic Party.[10] Said Senator Ervin of Connally: " 'A lot of Democrats think he should have stayed in our party and helped those who express similar views. I think some Republicans think they ought not to give such a high position to a recent convert who has not borne the burden and felt the heat of the day.' " [11] Declared Republican Governor Daniel Evans of Washington: " 'I frankly think in a party as big and as varied as ours, I'd hate to have to see us turn to someone who has so recently discovered its virtues. There are many others of equal capacity who ought to get prior consideration.' " [12]

Although not a favorite of the conservative wing of the Republican Party, Rockfeller was to many the ideal nominee for the position. Oregon Governor Tom McCall called Rockefeller " 'the equivalent of a President in administrative experience and in his command of the respect of the people.' " [13] Governor Winfield Dunn of Tennessee said Rockefeller is " 'without peer as a prospective appointee for this position.' " [14] Strong support was also expressed for Ronald Reagan, especially in the South.

The Democratic leaders of both Houses indicated to Nixon, however, that there would be substantial resistance in Congress to any nominee who might be a strong contender for the Republican Party presidential nomination in 1976.[15] Neither the Democrats nor potential 1976 Republican candidates for President wanted to approve a person against whom they might campaign. The suggestions made in September reappeared—namely, that Nixon should nominate a caretaker Vice President and that no Vice President should be confirmed until the President released the tapes sought by Special Prosecutor Cox. House Speaker Albert, now first in line of succession, denied a report that he was in favor of a caretaker Vice President. However, House Majority Leader Thomas P. O'Neill of Massachusetts and House Democratic Whip John McFall of California both indicated that they would oppose a potential 1976 Republican presidential nominee.[16]

The idea of a caretaker Vice President was soundly denounced in the press, and an Oliver Quayle poll revealed that 93 per cent of the people were opposed to the proposal.[17] Senator Bayh declared that the Twenty-Fifth Amendment did not contemplate a caretaker Vice President. " 'If a man happens to be in the running in 1976,' " said Bayh, " 'that's just a fact of political life.' " " 'From the practical standpoint,' " he added, " 'we should find someone who's going to be a good Vice President and a good President.' " He concluded by saying that the consideration " 'has to be out of the partisan arena.' " [18] Governor McCall put it sharply: " 'This idea that you can have some doddering nincompoop caretaker in there when America is on her death bed, when the President could fall in a day, is nonsense.' " [19]

It was reported that following Agnew's resignation Nixon drew up two lists of names—a list of "high risk" candidates who were potential candidates for the Republican Party presidential nomination in 1976 and whose nomination would encounter opposition in Congress, such as Connally, Reagan, and Rockefeller, and a list of persons believed certain to be confirmed swiftly, such as Goldwater, Griffin, Scott, Laird, and Ford.

While at Camp David during the night of October 11–12, Nixon reportedly reduced to five the number under consideration, and decided on Ford in the morning.[20] By that time, little support had developed for Connally, and Reagan's strength was not great outside the South. While Rockefeller had received significant expressions of support, particularly from party professionals, it seemed likely that his nomination would alienate the conservative wing of the party, which had not forgotten his refusal to endorse Barry Goldwater's candidacy for President in 1964. Ford, on the other hand, had emerged as a favorite-son type of candidate among the members of Congress and of the Republican National Committee. Yet, declared John Herbers of *The New York Times* in its issue of October 12: "The boom for Representative Ford was considered more an expression of loyalty by his friends in the Congress than a serious effort to make him Vice President."

Without indicating his choice, President Nixon scheduled a nationwide television and radio address from the White House for October 12 at 9:00 P.M. He advised Ford of his selection as the vice presidential nominee around 7:30 P.M.[21] * Shortly after 9:00, in a brief speech from the East Room of the White House before scores of congressional and other governmental leaders, Nixon announced his choice to the nation.† He said that Ford met the criteria he had set—that he was qualified to be President, shared the same views on foreign policy and national defense, and had the ability to work with members of both parties in Congress in advancing administration programs. Ford then delivered a brief acceptance speech.

Ford's nomination was received favorably throughout the country and especially by members of both parties in Congress. Democratic Senator Kennedy summed up the general reaction when he said that Ford had had " 'an outstanding career and I foresee no difficulty whatever in his confirmation by the Senate.' "[22] Said House Democratic Majority Whip McFall: " 'He should have no trouble at all.' "[23]

Confirmation

THE ASSIGNMENT TO COMMITTEE · With the imminence of a vice presidential nomination under the Twenty-Fifth Amendment, questions im-

---

* It is reported that Ford learned of his nomination earlier that day from Melvin Laird. Reeves, *A Ford Not a Lincoln* 33.

† A number of news reporters mistakenly thought that Nixon was going to nominate

mediately were raised about the appropriate congressional committees to consider the nomination. At an informal meeting of the joint leadership of the Senate held on the afternoon of October 10, which was attended by representatives of the Senate Rules and Judiciary Committees and other interested senators, a number of suggestions were advanced and debated,[24] but no agreement was reached that afternoon or at another informal meeting held the next day. Some senators, including Bayh, advocated the creation of a select Senate committee. Other suggestions were to use a joint committee of both Houses, the Senate Rules and Administration Committee, the Senate Committee on the Judiciary, the Senate Government Operations Committee, or a Committee of the Whole Senate.‡ The claim of the Rules Committee was based on a rule which brought within its jurisdiction matters relating to presidential succession and the election of a President and Vice President. The Judiciary Committee based its claim on a rule giving it jurisdiction over constitutional amendments as well as its expertise in passing on presidential nominations generally. The claim of the Senate Government Operations Committee derived from its general supervisory responsibilities of government departments.

Two alternatives mentioned most prominently at the October 11 meeting were a referral to the Rules Committee, and the creation of a special committee consisting of representatives of the Senate Rules and Judiciary Committees and from the Senate at large, but "the prevailing view," said Mansfield, was "that to avoid duplication and accommodate expedition, the idea of conducting joint hearings with the House on the nomination be explored with the Speaker." [25] Both Albert and Mansfield personally seemed to favor joint hearings. Albert, however, yielded to the feelings of a number of representatives who wanted the House to hold its own hearings. Some House members reportedly were of the view that its members are upstaged when they participate in joint activities with the Senate.[26] There was no question that the House Judiciary Committee was the appropriate House committee for any separate hearing.

On October 11, Democratic Senator Lawton Chiles of Florida asked immediate consideration of a resolution that any nomination bypass committee action and be considered directly by the entire Senate. He said that senators with whom he had spoken wanted to participate in the selection process in order to find the best qualified person for the position of Vice President. Nothing could be more representative, said Chiles, than 100 senators sitting as the committee, especially at a time when public

---

Governor Lenwood Holton of Virginia and accordingly prepared news stories to that effect. For an interesting account of those unpublished stories, see J. F. terHorst, *Gerald Ford and the Future of the Presidency* 146–47 (1974).

‡ Underlying the question of which committee should consider the nomination was the ideological complexion of the committees. Thus, the Senate Rules and Administration Committee was of a conservative orientation whereas the Judiciary Committee had a significant number of senators of a liberal persuasion.

opinion of government was low.[27] His request for unanimous consent was denied, with the result that the resolution automatically was continued to the following day.[28] During the Senate discussion of October 11, Senator Humphrey suggested that a joint committee of both Houses be established, stating that it would lift the nomination "out of normal legislative procedures" and put "it on a higher plane of constitutional prerogative." He asserted that the nation would be better served by "one set of hearings, one inquiry, one investigation so to speak, in the sense of the qualifications and credentials of the nominee." [29]

On the morning of October 12 the subject was discussed at a Democratic Policy Committee meeting and then at a meeting of the Democratic Conference which, by a vote of 24 to 20, decided that the nomination should be referred to the Senate Rules Committee and that the committee should be expanded by six members—three appointed by the majority leader and three by the minority leader, with the majority leader being one of the six.[30] At a meeting of the Republican Conference that day it was decided unanimously that the nomination should be referred to the existing Rules Committee without additional members.

That afternoon the question was debated extensively in the Senate, the House already having decided to send the nomination to its Judiciary Committee.[31] Senator Chiles objected to a unanimous consent request by Majority Leader Mansfield for immediate consideration of a resolution embodying the action taken at the Democratic Conference. His objection was interpreted as a ploy to delay a decision on the committee question until after the President had announced his choice for Vice President, which was scheduled for nine o'clock that evening. Senators Pastore, Scott, Mansfield, Edward Brooke of Massachusetts, and others urged Chiles to let the matter come to a decision before the nominee was named. Said Brooke: "He [Chiles] wants to get into the politics of the nominee. But it is not important for us to consider who the nominee is when we are considering the procedural question. We should resolve the procedural question first. . . ." [32]

Pastore said that it would be "next to folly" to delay the matter to the next day. Chiles strongly disagreed, stating: "This is the appointment of a man who will be a heartbeat away from the Presidency at a time when the country is wondering whether there is an honest man to hold office. Is there someone we can put our trust and confidence in?" [33] He added: "[M]y feeling is that if we can sit to impeach a Vice President, we ought to have sense enough to act on the name of one who has been nominated and determine his qualifications." Toward the end of the debate Senator Kennedy argued that "the unique and unprecedented nature of the question before us is ample warrant for action by the Senate to name a select ad hoc committee. . . ." [34] He said that the Committees on Judiciary and Government Operations had as much claim to jurisdiction as the

Rules Committee, adding: "There has never been an instance in the history of this country in which the Rules Committee has considered a nomination." [35]

Senator Joseph R. Biden, Jr. of Delaware added: "[T]he one thing I think we must impress upon the American people is that we do not think this is business as usual, that the man whom we are going to confirm as the Vice President of the United States may very well be the next President within the next 3 years." [36] Senator Marlow W. Cook of Kentucky noted:

> So I can only say that I have a notion and a terrible suspicion that the House . . . will send the nomination to . . . committee, . . . have its hearings, . . . move that nomination to the floor, . . . have its up and down vote, and this distinguished body will still be sitting here making a determination of how it is even going to consider the nomination in the first place.[37]

"[I]f we find ourselves in that position," said Cook, "then we have proven to the country that we are the kind of body that, in many of their minds, they think we are." The eloquence notwithstanding, the resolutions offered by Chiles and Mansfield were put over to October 13, with Chiles's the first to be considered.

On October 13, with Ford's nomination now known, Chiles withdrew his resolution and the nomination was referred smoothly to the nine-member Rules Committee.[38] Since Gerald Ford did not fall in the category of a potential 1976 presidential candidate and since his confirmation seemed certain, the opportunity for members of the Senate to participate in the hearing process no longer appeared as politically significant as it had before the name of the nominee was known. Had the nominee then been considered a potential Republican presidential candidate for 1976, it is likely that considerable additional debate on the committee question would have ensued in the Senate.

ACTION BY THE SENATE · Following his nomination, Ford became the subject of the most extensive investigation accorded any candidate for national office.[39] The Federal Bureau of Investigation dispatched more than 350 agents from thirty-three field offices to inquire into every aspect of his life. The Library of Congress concurrently undertook to make available to the committees of Congress all the information it could assemble on his life and public career. Staff personnel from the General Accounting Office and the Government Operations Permanent Investigations Subcommittee were made available to assist in the investigation. Ford's tax returns for the past seven years were examined, and those for the previous five were audited by the Internal Revenue Service and analyzed by the staffs of the House Judiciary Committee, the Senate Rules Committee, and the Joint Congressional Committee on Taxation.

Ford's medical records were examined and persons who might have treated him questioned. Campaign reports, records, and statements on file with the House of Representatives and in Michigan were studied. His bank accounts, correspondence with government agencies, speeches, and office printing and payroll records were scrutinized; bar association and police records were examined for references to him.

As a result of this investigation, which included interviews with more than 1,000 persons, the FBI collected over 1700 pages of raw data which were inspected by the chairman and the ranking minority member of the Senate Rules Committee and the chairman and seven other members of the House Judiciary Committee.

Ford's confirmation hearings took place under the most ominous of circumstances. Less than two weeks before the start of the hearings, over the weekend of October 20, President Nixon had dismissed Special Prosecutor Archibald Cox and abolished his office—an action which led to the immediate resignations of Attorney General Richardson and Deputy Attorney General Ruckelshaus. These events prompted demands throughout the nation for the President's resignation and impeachment.* Western Union reported that more than 150,000 telegrams flooded Washington in the following three days, "the heaviest concentrated volume on record." More than twenty proposals were introduced in the House of Representatives calling either for Nixon's impeachment or for an impeachment investigation. A number of these resolutions were referred to the House Judiciary Committee, which was instructed to begin an impeachment inquiry. Chairman Peter Rodino declared on October 24 that his committee would "proceed full steam ahead," despite the President's decision earlier that week to turn certain Watergate tapes over to the federal district court. On October 25 Ford said that the House should "carry on" its impeachment inquiry. Several days later the nation again was startled, this time by the disclosure that certain of the tapes to be turned over did not exist. On November 1, the day Ford's confirmation hearings opened before the Senate Rules and Administration Committee, the office of Special Prosecutor was re-established, the appointment of Leon Jaworski as Special Prosecutor was announced, and the President indicated that he would cooperate with the ongoing investigation.

At the outset of the televised Senate hearings, Chairman Howard Cannon of Nevada stated that the "committee should view its obligations as no less important than the selection of a potential President of the

* In mid-November 1973, as demands for Nixon's impeachment increased, White House counsel Leonard Garment and Fred Buzhardt concluded that the President should resign. In weekend discussions with Alexander Haig and Ronald Ziegler they urged his resignation, but since Ford had not yet been confirmed as Vice President they did not act further. The President himself seemed determined not to resign. White, *Breach of Faith* 271–72.

United States." [40] He expressed his view that under the Twenty-Fifth Amendment the President has the right to choose a person "whose philosophy and politics are virtually identical to his own," and that it is not proper to withhold confirmation based on a nominee's voting record in Congress. Rather, said Cannon, the committee's function was to examine a nominee's qualifications for Vice President—his morals, integrity, financial history, and the like. He concluded:

> It is for the members of this committee to establish a precedent—a solid, constitutional precedent—by pursuing an orderly, logical, thorough, and honest inquiry into the nominee's qualifications. This is being done in the public interest, because the citizens of the United States who normally choose the President and Vice President are participating only vicariously in this confirmation proceeding by following each action taken by the respective branches of the Congress.[41]

Ford was the first witness to testify before the committee. In his opening remarks he made clear his intention not to be a candidate for public office in 1976: "I have no intention to run, and I can foresee no circumstances where I would change my mind." [42] He acknowledged the committee's responsibilities under the Twenty-Fifth Amendment and said that it would receive his full cooperation. During the course of his two days of testimony Ford was interrogated on his personal and campaign finances, real estate holdings, directorships, stock holdings, his role in the award of certain government contracts and in the impeachment investigation of Supreme Court Associate Justice William O. Douglas.

A great deal of the committee's attention in its questioning of Ford focused on charges made against him by a Washington lobbyist that he had received money for political favors, that his staff had received gifts from the lobbyist, and that he had been a patient of a New York psychiatrist. Ford's views on such issues as inflation, education, NATO, foreign relations, busing, and tax reform were elicited. His views on Watergate-related issues were also explored, including the subject of presidential immunity, impoundment of funds by the President, executive privilege, the independence of the special prosecutor, the missing Watergate tapes, the role of the FBI, and ways to improve President Nixon's credibility. It is interesting that, when Cannon asked Ford whether a successor President would have the power to prevent or terminate a criminal prosecution against his predecessor, Ford responded: "I do not think the public would stand for it. I think—and whether he has the technical authority or not, I cannot give you a categorical answer. The Attorney General, in my opinion, with the help and support of the American people, would be the controlling factor." [43]

In his answers to Watergate-related questions, Ford was careful not to undermine the positions taken by Nixon. For example, Ford indicated his support for a special prosecutor appointed by the executive branch rather than by the Judiciary or by Congress.[44] On executive privilege, he expressed the view that documents and tapes bearing upon the possible commission of crimes should not be withheld, but those bearing on national security and foreign relations were within the umbrella of the privilege.[45]

Ford's role in halting an early Watergate investigation by the House Banking and Currency Committee was also examined by the Rules Committee. His political philosophy was probed, as were his views on impeachment and the nature of impeachable offenses, the public financing of elections, the role of the Vice President, the relationship between the executive branch and Congress, and the role of the Attorney General.

In the course of his testimony, Ford said of his qualifications to be Vice President:

I believe I can be a ready conciliator and calm communicator between the White House and Capitol Hill, between the reelection mandate of the Republican President and the equally emphatic mandate of the Democratic 93d Congress.[46]

He said that, if confirmed, he would adopt Eisenhower's precept of doing "what I believe is best for America," and Lincoln's of doing it " 'with firmness in the right, as God gives us to see the right.' " He observed that "[t]ruth is the glue on the bond that holds government together, and not only government, but civilization itself." [47]

Upon the conclusion of Ford's testimony, Senator Bayh testified on the meaning and intent of the Twenty-Fifth Amendment, stating that the fundamental question was whether Ford could "serve our country as President." Bayh said that the intent of the Twenty-Fifth Amendment "was to get a Vice President who would be compatible and could work harmoniously with the President." Bayh suggested that the following criteria be considered: "Honesty, integrity, no skeletons in the closet that do not exacerbate the confidence problem as we have it right now, and appropriate respect for and dedication to reasonable interpretation of the Constitution." [48] He indicated that on the bases of such criteria he would support Ford, even though he and Ford had voted differently on a number of issues.

Ten members of the House of Representatives, representing both parties and different points of view and parts of the country, then testified in support of Ford's nomination. One of the ten presented a poll of his constituents which showed that 79.1 per cent favored Ford's confirmation.[49] Underscored throughout the testimony of these members of Congress were the respect and the esteem Ford had earned as a result of his twenty-five years in Congress. They described Ford as "honest," "reasonable," "absolutely fair," a person of "calm judgment," "straightforward," and "humble." They said he possessed "integrity" and "an ability to draw people together," to "rise above partisanship," and to inspire "mutual respect and good will." Said Representative Martha W. Griffiths of Michigan:

> Some people appear to believe that the Congress should not confirm as a Vice President a person who is not committed to the philosophy of the person writing or speaking. In my judgment, Congress cannot take such an attitude. We are not here to say that unless the choice of the President agrees with us on ecology or defense or some other popular issue, that Congress should not vote to confirm him. This is not the purpose of the 25th amendment, and it is not within the province of this body to say, because we do not agree with him on the issues, we will not support him. We are here to check Jerry Ford's integrity, his ability, his leadership ability, and with any confirmation, to give the stamp of approval upon those items.[50]

Testimony also was received against the nomination. Representative Bella S. Abzug of New York testified that the Twenty-Fifth Amendment did not envision a situation in which the elected President and Vice President both left office, and urged that a special election should be held under such circumstances.[51] She suggested that action on the Ford nomination be deferred until the House decided whether to impeach Nixon and hold a special election. Abzug added that she would vote against Ford's confirmation since she disagreed with his policies. Clarence Mitchell of the NAACP testified that Ford had shown a narrow approach to civil rights, but he hoped that if Ford became Vice President he would improve in this area, as Lyndon Johnson had after he succeeded to the presidency. Another black witness, Maurice Dawkins of Opportunities Industrialization Centers, however, praised Ford for his work for and support of minority enterprise programs throughout the nation.

Joseph L. Rauh, Jr., national vice-chairman of Americans for Democratic Action, argued that the Twenty-Fifth Amendment contemplated an active role for Congress, and that it reflected no presumption in favor of confirmation. He said that Congress was to be a surrogate for the voters, obligated to use the tests applied by the voters, such as stature, competence, experience, and philosophy. "[T]he appropriate standard," said Rauh, "is whether Mr. Ford is qualified to be President of the United States, and whether he is among the group of persons that a majority of the Members of both Houses of Congress want to see as President of the United States." [52] Basing his position on, among other things, Ford's voting record and his lack of experience in foreign affairs, Rauh urged that he not be confirmed. Rauh noted that many in the liberal community favored Ford's confirmation on the ground that it was a necessary precondition for impeachment of Nixon. Such a view, he said, was short-sighted because once people realized "more and more that Mr. Ford is not qualified for the job, . . . he is going to give President Nixon job insurance." [53]

Another witness, John F. Banzhaf III, a George Washington University law professor, stated that the Twenty-Fifth Amendment did not allow a President to force a Vice President out of office and then nominate his successor. Banzhaf requested that Congress determine whether Agnew had been driven from office before it consider the Ford nomination.

Besides holding public hearings on November 1, 5, and 14, the committee met in executive session on November 7 to receive testimony regarding the charges made against Ford. At this session the lobbyist, Robert N. Winter-Berger, was unable to document his charges, and the psychiatrist, Dr. Arnold Hutschnecker, labeled the reports that Ford had been his patient as "lies" and "fantasies." At the end of the hearing the committee decided to make public the transcript of its proceedings. On November 15 the committee made a number of other decisions, including one not to disclose Ford's tax returns, since no other official was required to do so. A statement of Ford's net worth as of September 30, 1973 was placed in the record, together with a statement from his accountant of his earnings and taxes over the past five years. The committee also decided to have the transcript of its November 7 executive session reviewed by the Department of Justice for possible violations of law by the lobbyist, including perjury.

On November 20, thirty-eight days after beginning its inquiry, the Senate Rules and Administration Committee approved Ford's nomination, 9 to 0. In its report the committee said that not every member agreed with Ford's voting record, philosophy of government, personal and political views, and public actions during his twenty-five years in Congress, but judging him on his total record it saw no impediment which would disqualify him. The report stated that under the Twenty-Fifth Amendment a President would be expected to nominate a person of his own party and perhaps his own political philosophy, and added that some members of the committee and electorate might not agree that Ford was the best choice the President could have made from available Republicans. In conclusion, the committee stated that in the critical areas of philosophy, character, and integrity, Ford "fully met reasonable tests." [54]

Ford's nomination came to the floor of the Senate on November 27. The debate which followed was not extensive and reflected widespread support for Ford and little opposition. Democratic and Republican senators alike praised Ford's openness, candor, and integrity. A number of senators indicated that they would vote for confirmation despite their disagreement with his political philosophy. Democratic Senator Kennedy's remarks were typical:

> [T]he nature of the 25th amendment is such that it intends not for the Senate to choose on its own a candidate for the Vice-Presidency who reflects the political beliefs of each Senator or of the body as a whole, but to "advise and consent" to the nomination of an individual.[55]

Democratic Senator Church said:

> Mr. President, some have argued that Gerald Ford is not the man of their choice for Vice President. Neither is he mine. But the Constitution leaves it with the President—not with Congress—to do the choosing. Our duty is either to ratify or reject the President's choice. If the hearings had revealed any basis on which to conclude that Mr. Ford were ineligible to serve as Vice President, I would, without hesitation, vote against him. The record, however, reveals nothing in Mr. Ford's background that would disqualify him from holding this office.[56]

Democratic Senator John Tunney of California added:

> I do not always share his political views, but I believe that while Congress may impeach a President, it should not repeal the platform that elected him.[57]

Senator Hart declared that Ford met the Twenty-Fifth Amendment tests articulated by Bayh during the confirmation hearings, and that, "should he be called to the Presidency, he would be a steady, decent, and believable Chief Executive. And those attributes, I believe, are what this Nation needs most at this particular moment in history." [58] One senator, Gaylord Nelson of Wisconsin, said that his philosophical differences with Ford were so fundamental that he could not compromise his principles by voting for him. Senator William D. Hathaway of Maine inquired whether the emoluments of the vice presidency had been increased recently and thereby raised a question about the applicability of Article 1, section 6 of the Constitution.* Cannon replied that they had not been increased during the period of Ford's current term, and also added that he had been advised that a Vice President was not a "civil officer" within the meaning of that provision.[59]

Throughout the debate senators acknowledged the possibility that Ford might become President. Thus, immediately after his nomination was approved, by a vote of 92 to 3,† Senator Tunney stated:

> Mr. Ford, within the next year, may, indeed, be President. So today's action not only initiates the 25th amendment of our Constitution, but may, in fact, ordain the 38th President of our Nation.[60]

ACTION BY THE HOUSE · On November 15, the day after the Senate Rules Committee closed its public hearings, the thirty-eight-member House

---

* Which provides, in part: "No Senator or Representative shall, during the Time for which he was elected, be appointed to any civil Office under the Authority of the United States, which shall have been created, or the Emoluments whereof shall have been encreased during such time. . . ." The focus of attention was on an act passed by Congress on October 24, 1973 which increased the retirement annuities of certain federal employees, including possibly the Vice President.

† Voting against were Democratic Senators Hathaway, Nelson, and Thomas Eagleton of Missouri. Absent on official business was, among others, former Democratic presidential candidate George McGovern of South Dakota.

Judiciary Committee opened its televised hearings, with Gerald Ford as the first witness. Almost half the witnesses who testified before the Senate Rules Committee also testified or submitted statements to the House Judiciary Committee. Prior to the commencement of the hearings, the House leadership made clear its determination that Ford's confirmation should not be delayed, as advocated by several members of the House, pending the outcome of the impeachment investigation; and that the confirmation hearings should be thorough so as to avoid charges of cronyism being leveled against the House.[61]

In opening the House hearings, Chairman Rodino emphasized the need for both expeditious action and a thorough examination of Ford's qualifications and fitness for the vice presidency. He stated that under the Twenty-Fifth Amendment Congress "must act as the surrogate for the electorate in evaluating this nomination" and recognize "that the President has the right to nominate a man with whom he can work in concert, ideologically, and politically." "I am hopeful," said Rodino, "that these hearings can produce a new sense of trust in the essential decency of our Nation and in its ability to meet the challenges to its Government's integrity." [62]

Throughout the hearings the prediction was repeated that Ford might soon be President. Said Representative George E. Danielson of California on the second day of the hearings: "I am thinking you are going to be President within a year. . . ." [63] Another committee member, Representative Edward Mezvinsky of Iowa, observed that "[w]e could face it again [i.e., another nomination under the Amendment], as some said, within a year. . . ." [64] In his testimony before the committee, Representative Edward P. Boland of Massachusetts remarked that "[t]his is the first time in the history of this Nation that a Vice-Presidential nominee has sought confirmation under the provisions of the 25th Amendment. It is also one of the few times when it seems possible that a Vice-Presidential nominee has a more than average chance of succeeding a President." [65] Toward the end of the hearings Representative Jerome Waldie of California said: "I am quite convinced you will, despite my own personal opposition and reservations, become President of the United States. . . ." [66]

Perhaps with this possible succession in mind, Chairman Rodino made plain at the outset that Ford would be accorded no special privileges as a member of Congress. Accordingly, Ford was intensively interrogated by the committee for four of its six days of hearings. Of the thirty-six hours of testimony heard by the committee, nineteen were devoted to questioning Ford, on many of the matters covered in his Senate testimony as well as on new issues.

Ford's role in the attempted impeachment of Justice Douglas came under closer scrutiny than it had in the Senate, and new information was developed about the political nature of that effort. Representative Waldie, in particular, closely questioned Ford about his relationship with the Justice Department at the time of the Douglas impeachment inquiry. At one point during Waldie's interrogation, Ford exhibited an issue of *Evergreen* magazine containing photographs of nudes near excerpts from a book written by Douglas. This prompted some members of the committee to criticize Ford, one member characterizing the display as "incredibly insensitive." [67]

Ford's testimony on the 1970 invasion of Cambodia and his justification for a President's withholding information from Congress also brought critical responses from several members of the committee.[68] As in his Senate testimony, Ford was careful not to undermine President Nixon's positions. Although he testified that the impeachment inquiry should go forward expeditiously, he also expressed the view that on the information available there were no grounds for impeachment.[69] He testified about the approach Nixon should take to restore confidence in his administration but at the same time defended Nixon's firing of Cox, the invasion of Cambodia, and the impoundment of funds.[70]

One area of controversy which arose during the hearings was the denial to most committee members of access to the raw data assembled by the FBI. Democratic Representatives Danielson, Mezvinsky, Conyers, William S. Cohen of Maine, Elizabeth Holtzman of New York, Charles B. Rangel of New York, and John F. Seiberling of Ohio criticized the Department of Justice's limitation of such access to the committee's chairman and its seven senior members.[71] * Rangel argued that the committee could not discharge its responsibilities properly without such information, and suggested that Ford's nomination be delayed pending its availability.[72] In response, Republican Representatives Thomas Railsback of Illinois, Robert McClory of Illinois, David Dennis of Indiana, and others contended that the hearings had already been delayed and that it was important to bring them to a close. The latter point of view prevailed with the close of the hearings on November 26, eleven days after their opening.

Another area of disagreement involved the role of Congress under the Twenty-Fifth Amendment. Many accepted the view that the Amendment gave the President the right to choose a person who would be ideologically compatible with him. According to Representative Hutchinson,

> the role of this committee is not to determine whether Gerald R. Ford's views on domestic and foreign policy are consonant with those of its members, but rather to determine whether he is qualified to assume the tensions and troubles of the Presidency if that office should for any reason

* This criticism undoubtedly prompted the Department of Justice a year later to turn over to the entire committee the raw data assembled in connection with Nelson Rockefeller's nomination for Vice President.

devolve upon him, as well as to determine whether he is the kind of person in whom the people can place their trust.[73]

Gerald Ford testified that

the person so nominated must have a record that has been thoroughly investigated, that would justify the Congress and the American people in having faith and trust in his honesty, his experience, and his judgment. I think that is the criteria.

The 25th amendment says nothing about the qualifications on a partisan basis or philosophical basis.[74]

Others disagreed, suggesting that Congress should take into account changes in public opinion since the last presidential election. The following exchange between Ford and Representative Robert Drinan of Massachusetts is illustrative:

MR. DRINAN. . . . But what are the rights of the people under the 25th amendment and, if I may, let me tell you a little bit about my district, and I am their surrogate or their Representative here.

Senator McGovern got more votes in my district than I did. They believe in new priorities and they were overwhelmingly against the war. There is almost a majority so far as we know who want the impeachment of the President and both Elliot Richardson and Mr. Cox are my constituents. . . .

MR. FORD. Mr. Drinan, obviously I couldn't get elected in that district.

MR. DRINAN. I don't know. After the last 2 days, I think you could.

But the people who are disillusioned with this administration, and I am just asking your assistance, what are their rights in this matter? What is the role of the voters, in other words.

If a reliable poll were taken should I, as Congressman, should I follow that? . . . To what extent am I the surrogate, so to speak, under the 25th amendment.

MR. FORD. Under these most unusual circumstances where we have never had any experience, where the Constitution is being newly tried, we almost have to play it by ear. But my feeling would be, if I were in your position, that they sent you here to exercise your good judgment, and that if you don't use judgment that coincides with theirs you may find some political difficulties a year from November or next November. . . .

MR. DRINAN. Well, would you say, Mr. Ford, that this is really an election by the House, that it doesn't really compare with the "advice and consent"? It is not an approval, it is really an election similar to what the House has under the 12th amendment in unusual cases. Assuming that is so, and I think the legislative history demonstrates that it is at least a mini-election, then political ideology is relevant and to some extent partisan concepts may be employed, and compatibility is not the sole consideration. But I suppose you have to come to priorities and your voting record, and the priorities that you have chosen from your convictions and your conscience are not the priorities of the vast majority of the people that I represent. . . .

Now, to what extent do all those priorities enter in. I am asking the question I think in a more difficult way, to what extent should I say that I am simply the surrogate, the representative, and I follow a Gallup poll?

MR. FORD. I would try to put myself in your position if I were in that position, and in the last election, the voters had chosen, we will say, a liberal Democrat, and as President, and Vice President, and the Vice Presidency was vacant and it then—and the then President recommended somebody with political philosophy compatible with his own, which would mean a nominated Vice President who was likewise liberal philosophically, I think I would act in those circumstances to confirm that individual, providing he passed the other tests of forthrightness, honesty, truth, et cetera.[75]

Witness James Larson of the National Lawyers Guild asserted that the last election was void, and that Nixon consequently did not have the right to nominate anyone under the Twenty-Fifth Amendment.[76] Representatives Conyers, Robert W. Kastenmeier of Wisconsin, and others thought it inappropriate for confirmation hearings to take place until the question of impeachment had been settled.[77] This led Representative McClory to declare: "To suggest that we must await with the expectation or hope on the part of some that perhaps the President might be removed from office before acting to fill the office . . . seems to me entirely erroneous and quite inappropriate. . . ."[78] The Amendment, said McClory, calls for an expeditious filling of the office of Vice President whenever it becomes vacant.

Ford's reputation in Congress and his conduct during the hearings provided a solid base for confirmation. As in the Senate hearings, members of both parties and witnesses constantly referred to his qualities of openness and honesty. While expressing his disapproval of Ford's civil rights record, Clarence Mitchell of the NAACP nevertheless stated that Ford was the "kind of person I would be glad to go on a hunting trip with; I know I would not get shot in the back."[79] But, said Representative Michael Harrington of Massachusetts, "honesty and decency are not enough. We also must look for proven qualities of leadership and an ability to serve as a focal point around which a country, a troubled country as I view it, can rally."[80] For Harrington, Rauh, and Mitchell, Ford did not possess these qualities. However, the image Ford presented at these televised hearings earned him accolades across the nation. Said Rodino: "With the question of candor before the public and so absolutely important and so much talked about, you certainly have displayed that kind of candor that has to be commended."[81]

On November 29, 1973, two days after the Senate had voted on Ford's confirmation, the House Judiciary Committee recommended Ford's confirmation by a vote of 29 to 8, with one member voting present.* In its report the committee said:

> Finally, not every member of the Committee subscribing to this Report finds himself in complete agreement with the totality of Mr. Ford's voting record, or even with all aspects of his general philosophy of government. Some, though by no means all, are disturbed with elements of his voting record in the area of civil rights and human rights.
>
> But looking at the total record, the Committee finds Mr. Ford fit and qualified to hold the high office for which he has been nominated pursuant to the Twenty-fifth Amendment.[82]

The eight dissenting members generally expressed the view that Ford had not demonstrated the ability to be a capable and effective President. His lack of executive experience and of background in international affairs, his role in the Douglas impeachment, and his voting record in the areas of civil and human rights were all cited as reasons why he should not be confirmed. Thus, Representative Edwards declared that Nixon should have provided a nominee who "would inspire and motivate the Nation . . . "; Kastenmeier, that Ford was too close to Nixon and that under existing circumstances the nominee should "harmonize more with the Congress and the public at large"; and Holtzman, that his twenty-five years in Congress "are barren of creative and independent legislative initiatives on matters of substantive policy." Exclaimed Waldie:

> When succession to the Nixon Presidency occurs, the person succeeding will confront a shambles that has never been equalled in any previous Presidential succession. Nixon will have left the Executive Branch machinery in complete chaos and disarray; the confidence of the people that normally is willingly and earnestly extended to a Presidential successor will be absent and not transferable with ease to Nixon's successor.[83]

Ford did not measure up to such "enormous" and "unique" responsibilities, Waldie said.

On December 6, 1973, the full House of Representatives took up Ford's nomination. During the almost six hours of debate, views were expressed similar to those aired at the hearings. A number of representatives said that they were voting in favor of confirmation on the basis of

---

* The eight dissenters were all Democrats: Representatives Kastenmeier, Conyers, Waldie, Drinan, Rangel, Holtzman, Don Edwards of California, and Barbara Jordan of Texas. Representative Seiberling, also a Democrat, voted present. Although he did not support the nomination, Seiberling believed that the House should consider it; consequently, he also refused to vote against approval, fearing such a vote could be construed as an effort to prevent the House from voting on the nomination. House Comm. on the Judiciary, Report on Confirmation of Gerald R. Ford as Vice President of the United States, H. R. Rep. No. 93–695, 93d Cong., 1st Sess. 27–68 (1973).

their understanding of the Twenty-Fifth Amendment even though they differed with Ford's philosophy and voting record. Representative James O'Hara of Michigan said:

> I fail to see, in my reading of the 25th amendment, any requirement that the Congress withhold its consent to the nomination of a Vice President because his views are at variance with those of the majority of the Congress. I submit that to allow ourselves to be caught up in measuring Mr. Ford's qualifications for office against the subjective yardstick of our own philosophies would be to disserve the American people who expect Congress, at this critical moment in history, to rise above partisanship.[84]

Numerous representatives expressed their admiration for Ford's candor, openness, integrity, and ability, and for his conduct during the most exhaustive and thorough investigation ever accorded a candidate for national office in American history. Experiences which members of Congress had shared with Ford during his twenty-five years as a member of the House were recited to show his qualifications for the vice presidency. "[A]t a time when many Americans are questioning the honesty of public officials and . . . have lost faith in those who serve in public office," said Robert E. Bauman of Maryland, "Gerald Ford's greatest attribute is his integrity." [85]

In supporting his confirmation, members of the House emphasized that Ford had the ability to work effectively with both parties in Congress, had a compassionate nature, kept his word, and respected opposing points of view. The results of Gallup and various congressional district polls were introduced to show that the people of the country supported his confirmation.[86] Said Representative Samuel L. Devine of Ohio: "If I have any ability to read the pulse of the folks back home, they desperately crave an era of peace, tranquility, calm and serenity. Jerry Ford is just the man to lead us in that direction." [87] In urging Ford's confirmation, Representative Bo Ginn of Georgia stated:

> These are troubled times in our Nation. We are faced with the recurring problems of the Watergate affair, we are confronted with a critical energy shortage, and with the problems of crime, drug abuse, and many other areas of grave concern to us all. This is a time, then, when we here in Washington must put aside political bickering and pull together to solve these great problems that face us all.[88]

Other representatives argued that Ford's confirmation satisfied the intent of the Twenty-Fifth Amendment. Since he held the same philosophy as President Nixon, his confirmation would continue the election mandate of 1972 in the event that anything should happen to the President.[89] Representative Andrew Young of Georgia said that he was voting for Ford's confirmation because "his accession to the Vice-Presidency will facilitate either the resignation or impeachment of the present occupant of the White House. . . ." [90]

But the nomination was opposed by some representatives. Representative Rodino, although praising Ford's integrity and ability and stating that the election mandate of 1972 must be maintained, registered his dissent to the nomination on the ground that the Nixon administration had been indifferent in the area of human rights and the cause of the working people.[91] Other representatives expressed their disapproval on the grounds that Ford had a poor record in civil rights, lacked executive experience, was too partisan, and did not possess the ability to move the country in the right direction. Some pointed to Ford's role in the attempted impeachment of Justice Douglas. Representative Abzug argued that there was a strong possibility that Ford was ineligible because of the emoluments clause of the Constitution. Consequently, she urged that the nomination be deferred pending congressional hearings on the subject.[92]

Some representatives registered their disapproval of Ford on the grounds that the people of the country or of their districts would not select him in an open election.[93] Representative Jonathan Bingham of New York, on the other hand, despite a poll which showed his constituents favoring Ford, voted against confirmation because of his opposition to Ford's voting record and his view that Nixon should have nominated a person with views half way between the President's and those of a majority of Congress.[94] Other representatives said that under existing circumstances Congress actually was selecting a President, and that Ford did not qualify for that position. "[I]t is my firm opinion," said Representative Danielson, "that he will soon become the President of the United States." [95] Representative Boland stated that there was a better than even chance of Ford's succeeding to the presidency.[96] Representative Edward R. Roybal of California stated that Ford was highly qualified for the office of Vice President but, since the surrounding circumstances indicated he might become President, he felt obliged to determine whether Ford would be acceptable to a majority of his constituency. After reviewing his voting record, Roybal concluded that it did not represent the views of his district and that his constituents would not have elected Ford as Vice President.[97]

In opposing Ford's nomination, Representative Waldie stated that in reality Congress was electing a President, adding:

> But I suggest to the Members that we do not fulfill our responsibility if we are just voting for Gerald Ford because it will make it easier, under whatever theory we approach it, to obtain the removal of the incumbent President of the United States.
>
> We know we hear that. We hear that all over the floor, and we see it on the wire services, and prominent members of the Republican Party and of the other House are suggesting that the moment Gerald Ford is

confirmed, the requirement that confronts the country of removing the President will be more easily and readily obtainable.[98]

Throughout the House debates on Ford's nomination, unlike the Senate debates, differences of opinion were expressed concerning the intent of the Twenty-Fifth Amendment. Some said that it embodied a presumption in favor of the President's choice, and that it was improper to reject a nominee because his political philosophy was the same as the President's.[99] Representative Conyers argued "that a Member of Congress should vote against . . . any nominee if in his judgment that nominee holds views or has a philosophy which when brought to that high office would in the judgment of the Congressman be unsatisfactory or harmful to the Nation as a whole." [100] In response, Representative Charles E. Wiggins of California stated that such a standard would permit a repudiation of the popular mandate from the previous election. Added Wiggins: "It is my point of view . . . that individual Members of Congress must rise against their personal notions of philosophy in order to maintain a continuity in the administration." [101] Representative Patricia Schroeder of Colorado asserted that, in voting on the nomination, the Congress, "acting as surrogates for the people, [has] the responsibility to weigh Mr. Ford's judgment, independence, and philosophical outlook, all in the context of whether he is a person we can conscientiously endorse as a potential President of the United States." [102] Said Representative M. Caldwell Butler of Virginia: "I am not impressed by the suggestion that we are but surrogates of our constituents. We were elected to bring our best judgment to bear on the questions that come before us." [103]

Several representatives argued that the Twenty-Fifth Amendment was never intended for the selection of a President, which they believed was occurring by virtue of the surrounding circumstances. Representative Abzug said that there should be a special presidential election in the event of dual vacancies. Declared Representative Wiley Mayne of Iowa: "[T]hey [i.e., the dissenting members of the House Judiciary Committee] want to substitute some other method of choice than that which is provided in the 25th amendment. The hangup is that they want to abandon the 25th amendment and substitute a new and different method of choosing a Vice President." [104]

During the debate of December 6, Representative Rangel referred to the arrangements already set for Ford's swearing-in and observed: "I feel somewhat superfluous in my role as a Member of the House debating and voting on this confirmation. It appears as if we do not hurry the ceremony will begin before we have a chance to vote." [105] After six hours of debate, Ford's nomination was favorably acted upon by a vote of 387 to 35. Among those voting against the nomination were the eight dissenting members of the House Judiciary Committee and a number of Democratic representatives of liberal persuasion. No Republican cast a negative vote. Immediately following his confirmation as the fortieth Vice President, Ford was administered the vice presidential oath by Chief Justice Warren Burger before a joint meeting of the Congress held in the chamber of the House of Representatives. Among those in attendance were the justices of the Supreme Court, the members of the Cabinet, ambassadors and ministers of foreign countries, and President Nixon.

NOTES

1. 119 Cong. Rec. 39926 (1973).
2. Anderson, Congress Is Ready If Agnew Quits, *Reporter Dispatch,* Sept. 21, 1973 at 7.
3. *N. Y. Times,* Sept. 21, 1973 at 20.
4. *Id.* 1.
5. *Id.*
6. *Id.,* Sept. 22, 1973 at 25.
7. *Id.,* Oct. 11, 1973 at 1.
8. *Wash. Post,* Oct. 12, 1973 at A15.
9. Albert, Most Dramatic Events of My Life 6.
10. *Wash. Post,* Oct. 12, 1973 at A12.
11. *Id.*
12. *Id.*
13. *Id.*
14. *Id.*
15. *N. Y. Times,* Oct. 11, 1973 at 1, 33.
16. *Id.,* Oct. 12, 1973 at 28; *Wash. Post,* Oct. 12, 1973 at A1, A15.
17. *N. Y. Times,* Oct. 12, 1973 at 28.
18. *Wash. Post,* Oct. 12, 1973 at A10.
19. *Id.* A12.
20. *N. Y. Times,* Oct. 13, 1973 at 19.
21. terHorst, *Gerald Ford and the Future of the Presidency* 155–56.
22. *N. Y. Times,* Oct. 13, 1973 at 19.
23. *Id.*
24. 119 Cong. Rec. 33993–94 (1973).
25. *Id.* 33994.
26. *N. Y. Times,* Oct. 12, 1973 at 28; *Wash. Post,* Oct. 12, 1973 at A1, A15.
27. 119 Cong. Rec. 33793 (1973).
28. *Id.* 33792–95.
29. *Id.* 33794.
30. *Id.* 33994.
31. *N. Y. Times,* Oct. 13, 1973 at 18.
32. 119 Cong. Rec. 33998 (1973).
33. *Id.* 33997.
34. *Id.* 34001.
35. *Id.*
36. *Id.* 34003.
37. *Id.*
38. *Id.* 34047.
39. The investigation is described in Senate Comm. on Rules and Administration, Report on Nomination of Gerald R. Ford of Michigan to be the Vice Presi-

dent of the United States, S. Exec. Rep. No. 93–26, 93d Cong., 1st Sess. (1973); House Comm. on the Judiciary, Report on Confirmation of Gerald R. Ford as Vice President of the United States, H. R. Rep. No. 93–695, 93d Cong., 1st Sess. (1973).

40. Hearings on Nomination of Gerald R. Ford of Michigan to be Vice President of the United States Before the Senate Comm. on Rules and Administration, 93d Cong., 1st Sess. 4 (1973).

41. *Id.* 8.
42. *Id.* 114.
43. *Id.* 124.
44. *Id.* 41–42, 70–73.
45. *Id.* 31, 40–41.
46. *Id.* 18.
47. *Id.*
48. *Id.* 148, 153, 159.
49. *Id.* 181.
50. *Id.* 171.
51. *Id.* 290–98.
52. *Id.* 317.
53. *Id.* 338.
54. S. Exec. Rep. No. 93–26 at 97 (1973).
55. 119 Cong. Rec. 38224 (1973).
56. *Id.* 38217.
57. *Id.* 38225.
58. *Id.* 38213.
59. *Id.* 38218.
60. *Id.* 38225.
61. Albert 8.
62. Hearings on Nomination of Gerald R. Ford to be Vice President of the United States Before the House Comm. on the Judiciary, 93d Cong., 1st Sess. 2 (1973).

63. *Id.* 87.
64. *Id.* 236.
65. *Id.* 251.
66. *Id.* 621.
67. *Id.* 618–19, 645, 660.
68. *Id.* 116–17, 136, 669–70.
69. *Id.* 147.
70. *Id.* 58, 131, 141, 586–91.
71. *Id.* 91–97, 570–82.
72. *Id.* 576–78.
73. *Id.* 5.
74. *Id.* 583–84.
75. *Id.* 129–30.
76. *Id.* 534–35.
77. *Id.* 6, 18.
78. *Id.* 70.
79. *Id.* 227.
80. *Id.* 179.
81. *Id.* 669.
82. H. Rep. 93–695 at 13 (1973).
83. *Id.* 43.
84. 119 Cong. Rec. 39882 (1973).

85. *Id.* 39888.
86. *Id.* 39834, 39869–70.
87. *Id.* 39838–39.
88. *Id.* 39862.
89. *Id.* 39825–26, 39829–30, 39833–34.
90. *Id.* 39878.
91. *Id.* 39817–18.
92. *Id.* 39865–66.
93. *Id.* 39870–71, 39875, 39885–86, 39888–89.
94. *Id.* 39878–79.
95. *Id.* 39856.
96. *Id.* 39862.
97. *Id.* 39885–86.
98. *Id.* 39820–21.
99. *Id.* 39825, 39826–27, 39829–30, 39833, 39840–41, 39882.
100. *Id.* 39830.
101. *Id.*
102. *Id.* 39842.
103. *Id.* 39837.
104. *Id.* 39840.
105. *Id.* 39834.

10

The Resignation of Richard M. Nixon and Succession of Gerald R. Ford

Fellow citizens: God reigns, and the Government at Washington still lives.

JAMES A. GARFIELD
April 15, 1865 [1]

THE CONFIRMATION OF GERALD FORD as Vice President suggested to some the solution to the tangle of Watergate.[2] While Agnew was next in line for the presidency it was difficult for many congressmen to consider removing Nixon. Moreover, during the period after Agnew's resignation when the vice presidency was vacant, Nixon remained secure, since it was unlikely that a Democratic Congress would risk the political consequences of appearing to "steal" the White House by installing Democratic Speaker Carl Albert in the presidency. With Ford's selection as Vice President, however, there now existed an attractive alternative to Nixon. It is not surprising, therefore, that during Ford's vice presidency the momentum for exposing the truth about Nixon's involvement in Watergate increased.

As the Watergate drama unfolded, Ford found himself in a difficult position because both critics and supporters of the Nixon presidency constantly looked to him for comments. In the months following his confirmation, Ford acquired a reputation for vacillation and inconsistency in dealing with the Watergate battles. Sometimes he spoke as a mediator between the congressional Watergate committees and President Nixon and urged Nixon to compromise with their requests for information.[3] Invariably, the White House failed to endorse these suggestions.[4] At other times, Ford defended Nixon as the victim of " 'a few extreme partisans' " bent on using Watergate to crush his policies.[5] Thus, speaking before the American Farm Bureau in January 1974, Ford delivered a speech, which he admitted had been written by the White House, and in which he charged that the attacks against Nixon were led by radicals, Nixon-haters, the press, and " 'super-welfare staters' " who sought to drive Nixon from office for their own political purposes.[6] Two hours later it was disclosed in federal court that an eighteen-minute gap on a crucial Watergate tape had been caused by five separate erasures.[7] As a consequence,

Ford received widespread criticism for acting as a Nixon apologist instead of maintaining his neutrality. A few days later Ford announced that the White House possessed information which would refute the testimony of former presidential counsel John Dean and exonerate the President, but that he had not had time to read the information.[8] President Nixon assured him, Ford said, that the release of key Watergate tapes was " 'being actively considered.' " [9] But the White House, citing executive privilege, refused to release those tapes.

In his first three months in office, Ford traveled nearly 30,000 miles, campaigning for Republican candidates and addressing party meetings. His popularity and self-confidence increased as the administration was weakened by daily Watergate revelations. Although he still defended Nixon, by March 1974 Ford was focusing on Republican Party achievements and occasionally criticizing Nixon for not cooperating with the investigations. He was disturbed that the Republicans had lost three out of four special congressional elections, including his former House seat in Michigan, and tried to enlist support for Republican candidates by forecasting a grave threat to the two-party system in overwhelming Democratic victories. So Ford walked "the fine line between loyalty to the President and loyalty to his fellow Republicans facing the electorate." [10] At a meeting of Middle Western Republican leaders in late March he blasted the Committee for the Re-election of the President as an " 'arrogant, elite guard of political adolescents' " which had bypassed the regular party organization and had dictated the terms of the national election.[11] Later that day he commented that he was not criticizing the President personally.[12]

Throughout the spring of 1974 Ford vacillated between defense of the President and subtle criticism of Nixon's failure to cooperate with the investigations. On April 14, he admitted that he had tried and failed to reach a compromise to avoid a subpoena by the House for certain Watergate tapes.[13] In California that month Ford advised Republicans to stress the individual merits of congressional candidates and the basic differences between the Republican and Democratic parties so that the fall elections would not become a referendum on President Nixon.[14] Yet several days later in Oklahoma he linked the fortunes of the Republican party with Nixon's and urged strong support for the President as a means of aiding Republican candidates for Congress.[15] On April 29, Nixon released to the House Judiciary Committee and made public edited transcripts of the Watergate tapes. When the committee voted to reject the transcripts as a substitute for the tapes, Ford suggested that the White House should be more flexible in permitting verification of the tapes by the committee.[16] He also said that he was " 'a little disappointed' " by the transcripts because they did not reflect the Richard Nixon he had known for twenty-five years.[17]

As the end of the Nixon presidency approached, criticism of Ford's speeches increased. He was variously described as a " 'rudderless tongue' " and a person without firm convictions who was adding to the climate of political confusion.[18] In answer to these criticisms, Ford said that he considered it his duty " 'to try to head off deadlock and seek a reasonable and prompt resolution of the nagging Watergate issue. . . .' "[19] In May 1974, *Newsweek* magazine reported that Nixon was considerably disenchanted with Ford and that, in a private meeting with Nelson Rockefeller, he had asked contemptuously whether Rockefeller could imagine Gerald Ford sitting in the presidential chair.[20] * Ford declined to comment on the report.

In June, Nixon traveled abroad, visiting the Middle East, Brussels, and Moscow,[21] as if seeking to quell the domestic turmoil with international successes. At about the same time it was revealed that Nixon was suffering from a mild case of phlebitis (inflammation of a vein) in his left leg, and that he was receiving medical treatment but was in "no danger."[22] The President's health had been a topic of discussion throughout the Watergate period, with attention focused on his actions under stress, his physical appearance, and his behavior.[23] There was even speculation that he might use the inability provision of Section 3 of the Twenty-Fifth Amendment to escape impeachment by declaring that he was physically unable to carry out his duties and thereby turning over his powers and duties to the Vice President as Acting President.[24]

Even apart from the possibility of Nixon's using the Twenty-Fifth Amendment because of a physical inability, the Amendment, it may be argued, offered him an opportunity to step aside temporarily during an impeachment inquiry. In fact, several members of Congress, including Senators Jacob Javits[25] and Milton R. Young of North Dakota[26] suggested that he consider standing aside under the Twenty-Fifth Amendment on the ground that he was unable to discharge the duties of his office because of the constitutional controversies attending Watergate. Such a move, it was reasoned, would ensure national stability under the leadership of Acting President Ford while freeing Nixon to concentrate on his Watergate defense.[27] However, the President himself continued to assert that he would never resign from office and, in an interview with James J. Kilpatrick, said that he would " 'rule out the rather fatuous suggestion that I take the 25th Amendment and just step out and have Vice President Ford step in for a while.' "[28]

During the month of July 1974, the fate of the Nixon presidency was sealed. On July 24, the Supreme Court ruled unanimously that the Presi-

* According to former presidential counsel Charles Colson, Nixon also supposedly said: " 'Maybe what this country needs is a nice, clean Jerry Ford. But the trouble with Jerry Ford is, it would take him two years just to get up to speed.' " Newsweek, February 17, 1975 at 21.

dent must turn over to Judge Sirica sixty-four tapes of conversations which might constitute evidence for the Watergate criminal cover-up trial.[29] It has been reported that Nixon considered defying the court and refusing to release the tapes on the ground that he had a constitutional right to withhold the tapes even from the judiciary. Special presidential counsel James St. Clair persuaded Nixon that impeachment by the House and conviction by the Senate would undoubtedly be the congressional reaction to such defiance.[30] Eight hours after the Supreme Court's decision, St. Clair announced that the President would " 'comply with that decision in all respects.' " [31]

Meanwhile, the House Judiciary Committee had begun hearing witnesses in its impeachment inquiry. By July 30, the committee had passed three articles of impeachment, charging, first, that Nixon had engaged in a course of conduct designed to obstruct justice; [32] second, that he had abused his presidential power; [33] and finally, that he had unconstitutionally defied the House subpoenas for Watergate tapes and documents.[34] In view of the committee's heavy, bipartisan vote, it seemed likely that the full House of Representatives would vote to impeach the President, but the outcome of a Senate trial, in which a two-thirds vote was needed for removal, was far from clear. On July 31, St. Clair learned why Nixon had tried so zealously to repress the tapes. Among those to be released to Judge Sirica were three tapes of conversations on June 23, 1972 between the President and presidential assistant H. R. Haldeman. These conversations revealed that Nixon had taken part in the cover-up by ordering the FBI not to investigate the burglary.

Against this background, the President's closest advisers began a campaign in early August to persuade him that resignation would serve the nation's and his own best interests. Although Nixon at first argued that the evidence was "inconsequential," he was finally convinced that impeachment and conviction were inevitable.[35]

As the pressure on Nixon to resign increased, Haig met with Ford on August 1 to inform him of the devastating tape evidence and the likelihood that Nixon would be impeached by the House of Representatives. Haig inquired of Ford whether he was prepared to assume the presidency and whether he had any recommendations as to what course of action Nixon should follow. Haig mentioned that various options were being considered by the White House, including Nixon's temporarily stepping aside under the Twenty-Fifth Amendment and resigning after granting himself a pardon. In response to a question by Ford about the President's pardoning power, Haig expressed the view that a President has the power to grant a pardon even before indictment. Ford concluded the meeting by saying that he needed time to consider what had been said. Early the next morning Ford met with James St. Clair and late that afternoon called

Haig to make clear that he would have no recommendations for Nixon on his resignation.*

On Saturday, August 3, Nixon retired to Camp David with his family and principal aides to draft a public statement to accompany the release of the tapes. It was reported that he still resisted resignation and thought he could survive the impeachment process.[36]

On August 4 Ford said in a speech: "I believe the President is innocent. I don't want any impression created that I've changed my mind about the President's innocence." † On August 5, the tapes were made public along with Nixon's statement acknowledging that the conversations are " 'at variance with certain of my previous statements,' " and admitting that he had not disclosed the evidence to his lawyers or supporters on the House Judiciary Committee.[37] Public and congressional reaction was devastating. The President's staunchest supporters on the House Judiciary Committee agreed now that he should be impeached and in public and private statements urged that he resign. Vice President Ford issued a statement that " 'the public interest is no longer served by repetition of my previously expressed belief that . . . the President is not guilty of an impeachable offense.' " [38]

On August 6, Nixon met with his Cabinet and declared that he would not resign but would let the constitutional process run its course.[39] Ford was present at the meeting and stated that he had no recommendations as to what Nixon should do in light of the new evidence. It is reported that Secretary of State Henry Kissinger stayed after that meeting to warn Nixon that the balance of international affairs might be upset if a powerless President continued in the White House.[40] Despite the counsel of his advisers, Nixon appeared determined to remain in office.

The next day Representative Robert McClory, a senior Republican member of the House Judiciary Committee, was informed by two key Democrats—Speaker Carl Albert and Judiciary Chairman Peter Rodino —that they were prepared to drop the impeachment proceedings against Nixon if he resigned. When McClory tried to pass the information along to the White House by way of the office of Vice President Ford, he was told by a Ford aide: " 'The Vice President is not taking part in the events

---

* Ford's version of the events of the first week in August is described in his testimony on Nixon's pardon. Hearings on the Pardon of Richard M. Nixon, and Related Matters, Before the Subcomm. on Criminal Justice of the House Comm. on the Judiciary, 93d Cong., 2d Sess. 90–111, 148–58 (1975).

† In his October 17, 1974 testimony about Nixon's pardon, Ford stated: "In the previous 8 months, I had repeatedly stated my opinion that the President would not be found guilty of any impeachable offense. Any change from my stated views, or even refusal to comment further, I feared, would lead in the press to conclusions that I now wanted to see the President resign to avoid an impeachment vote in the House and probable conviction in the Senate." 1974 Pardon Hearings 95.

occurring now. He would not want to have anything to do with it.'" ‡ Subsequently, the information was delivered by McClory to William E. Timmons, a White House aide, who gave the message to Nixon.

That same day Nixon was visited by Senator Goldwater, Senate Minority Leader Scott, and House Minority Leader John J. Rhodes of Arizona. Prior to this meeting, General Haig had privately told these members of Congress not to make a direct recommendation of resignation because Nixon was considering it and might balk if he felt pressured.⁴¹ At the meeting only Nixon himself mentioned resignation as an option, although the conversation indirectly centered on resignation. Nixon said he understood that only ten members of the House of Representatives would support him and asked about his chances in the Senate. Goldwater and Scott estimated that he might have up to fifteen votes. Then Goldwater listed lifelong Nixon admirers, both Republicans and Southern Democrats, who would vote for conviction. Nixon called the situation " 'damn gloomy,'" while Goldwater termed it " 'hopeless.'" As the meeting adjourned Nixon intimated that he understood that resignation was his only choice.⁴² That evening his speechwriters were told to prepare a resignation statement and Nixon informed Kissinger of his decision to resign.⁴³

On August 8, at about 11:00 A.M., President Nixon summoned Vice President Ford to the White House and informed him of his decision. They talked for about an hour and discussed the timing of events.⁴⁴ At eight that evening Nixon met with about forty of his most loyal congressional supporters and at nine announced to the nation on television that he would resign the next day at noon. He made no mention of his imminent impeachment but rather cited the erosion of his political base in Congress as the reason for his resignation. The speech was a recitation of the accomplishments of the Nixon administration with no reference to the matters which destroyed it.⁴⁵

On Friday morning, August 9, after a brief farewell to his staff, President and Mrs. Nixon boarded Air Force One for San Clemente. His letter of resignation was delivered to Secretary Kissinger at 11:30 and at noon Gerald R. Ford was sworn in as the thirty-eighth President of the United States. In an emotion-charged address, he declared that " 'our long national nightmare is over.'" He called upon the nation to " 'bind up the internal wounds of Watergate,'" adding: " 'Our Constitution works. Our great Republic is a government of laws and not of men. Here the people rule.'" While noting that he had not been elected President by the ballots of the people, he stated that he had been confirmed by members of " 'both parties, elected by all the people and acting under the Constitution in

‡ This incident was disclosed by the *Los Angeles Times* in its issue of December 16, 1975 at 1, 7.

their name.' " In his concluding remarks, Ford said: " 'May our former President, who brought peace to millions, find it for himself.' " [46]

What followed was an orderly transfer of power, with Ford acting quickly to open communications with Congress, reduce the White House staff, and shift some authority back to the Cabinet.

The smoothness of the transfer was not accidental. Transition planning for a Ford presidency had begun secretly in May 1974.[47] Philip Buchen, former law partner and close adviser to Ford, apparently concluded at that time that there was a good chance Ford might be suddenly thrust into the presidency. Without informing Ford, Buchen enlisted the help of Clay T. Whitehead, Nixon's adviser on telecommunications. Whitehead had served on the staff which guided the transition from the Johnson administration to the Nixon administration, and Buchen considered him a trustworthy ally. They acted in total secrecy so that Ford would not be embarrassed by appearing to lack confidence in the President. It is of interest that when on May 11 newsmen asked Ford if anyone on his staff was working on a possible transfer of power, Ford replied, " 'If they are, they are doing it without my knowledge and without my consent.' " Whitehead later said that he and Buchen regarded Ford's response as an implicit statement that he actually hoped someone was doing it but did not want to know about it.[48]

During the early summer of 1974 Buchen, Whitehead, and three unidentified acquaintances met several times at Whitehead's home to discuss a possible inauguration ceremony, transition team, and policy statements. As a result of these meetings, they developed a one-page checklist of issues * which would be initially important to Ford. When on August 6, at 10:30 P.M., Buchen told Whitehead that Nixon's resignation was probable, the final planning began. Ford was advised about the planning, and he gave Buchen the names of five friends whose views he wanted. On the night of August 7 the enlarged team met to discuss the essential elements of transition. Present in addition to Buchen and Whitehead were former Governor Scranton of Pennsylvania, Senator Robert Griffin, former Representative John W. Byrnes of Wisconsin, Bryce Harlow, and William Whyte, a vice president of United States Steel. Until about midnight they discussed the essential elements of transition. They agreed that Robert Hartmann, the Vice President's chief of staff, would draft a brief speech for Ford to deliver after he became President and that Jerald F. terHorst, then the Washington correspondent for *The Detroit News*, would be suggested for White House press secretary. Throughout

---

* The checklist included such topics as first principles, themes, objectives, the transition team, the "first week," nationwide address, the press and Congress, background policy papers, the organization of the presidency, and key personnel actions. Naughton, The Change in Presidents: Plans Began Months Ago, *N. Y. Times*, Aug. 26, 1974 at 1.

the meeting they expected a news bulletin of Nixon's resignation, but the meeting adjourned without any such announcement.[49] After Nixon informed Ford of his plans the next morning, the transition planners met to formalize their recommendations. Draft memoranda were prepared as well as formal notices of Ford's succession to the presidency. The men paused to watch Nixon's resignation address and finally completed their work at approximately 3:00 A.M. on Friday, August 9.[50]

The nation greeted the Ford presidency with a sense of profound relief.† During his first week in office Ford addressed a joint session of Congress, and met with governors, mayors, and county officials, members of the congressional black caucus, and representatives of several women's groups.[51] After ten days in the presidency, he addressed a meeting of the Veterans of Foreign Wars in Chicago and suggested a program of conditional amnesty for Vietnam war draft-dodgers and deserters, to the dismay of his audience and conservative followers. On August 20, with his popularity soaring, Ford nominated Nelson A. Rockefeller to be Vice President under the Twenty-Fifth Amendment.[52]

NOTES

1. Caldwell, *James A. Garfield* 155.
2. See terHorst, *Gerald Ford and the Future of the Presidency* 176; Riegle, The Ford Nomination as a Way Out, *N. Y. Times*, Nov. 29, 1973 at 43; Wicker, Nixon and Ford, *id.*, Dec. 7, 1973 at 41; *id.* 1.
3. *N. Y. Times*, Jan. 7, 1974 at 1, 12.
4. *Id.*, Jan. 8, 1974 at 15.
5. *Id.*, Jan. 18, 1974 at 33.
6. *Id.*
7. *Id.*
8. *Id.*, Jan. 23, 1974 at 18.
9. *Id.*, Feb. 8, 1974 at 29.
10. *Id.*, March 10, 1974 at 1.
11. *Id.*, March 31, 1974 at 1, 25.
12. *Id.* 25.
13. *Id.*, April 15, 1974 at 20.
14. *Id.*, April 21, 1974 at 26.
15. *Id.*, April 28, 1974 at 1, 26.
16. *Id.*, May 3, 1974 at 27.
17. *Id.*, May 4, 1974 at 24.
18. terHorst 178.
19. *N. Y. Times*, June 9, 1974 at 46.
20. *Id.*, May 29, 1974 at 24.
21. *Id.*, June 26, 1974 at 1.
22. *Id.* 16.
23. *Id.*, Dec. 4, 1973 at 36.

† Hugh Sidey declared in the August 26, 1974 issue of Time magazine: "Everywhere there was the feeling that the American presidency was back in the possession of the people" (p. 16).

24. *Id.*

25. *Id.*, April 4, 1974 at 34.

26. *N. Y. Post*, May 17, 1974 at 10.

27. Wilson, Nixon and the 25th, *Wash. Star–News*, April 8, 1974 at A10; Brzezinski, A "Leave of Absence" for Mr. Nixon?, *Wash. Post*, April 6, 1974 at 14.

28. Kilpatrick, Private Talk with Nixon, *San Francisco Chronicle*, May 17, 1974 at 14.

29. *N. Y. Times*, July 25, 1974 at 1.

30. *The End of a Presidency* 60 (*N. Y. Times* ed. 1974).

31. *Id.*

32. *N. Y. Times*, July 28, 1974 at 1.

33. *Id.*, July 30, 1974 at 1.

34. *Id.*, July 31, 1974 at 1.

35. *End of a Presidency* 63–64.

36. *Id.*

37. *N. Y. Times*, Aug. 6, 1974 at 1.

38. *Id.* 19.

39. *Id.*, Aug. 7, 1974 at 1.

40. *End of a Presidency* 69–70.

41. *Id.* 70.

42. *Id.* 71.

43. *N. Y. Times*, Aug. 9, 1974 at 3.

44. *Id.*

45. *Id.* 2.

46. *Id.*, Aug. 10, 1974 at 3.

47. Naughton, The Change in Presidents: Plans Began Months Ago, *N. Y. Times*, Aug. 26, 1974 at 1.

48. *Id.* 24.

49. *Id.*

50. *Id.*

51. *Id.*

52. terHorst 189.

11

The Installation of Nelson A. Rockefeller

> This situation is particularly unique . . . in that we have a
> nominee selected by a President who was himself placed on
> the Presidential succession ladder through the provisions of the
> 25th Amendment. We have learned through our first experi-
> ence with the 25th Amendment that Vice Presidential nominees
> must be judged as we would judge a prospective President.
>
> ROBERT W. KASTENMEIER
> December 17, 1974 [1]

NOMINATION

ON AUGUST 6, three days before Nixon's resignation, Melvin Laird, a close adviser to Ford, predicted flatly that Nelson Rockefeller would be Ford's choice as Vice President.[2] When questioned about Laird's statement on August 7, Ford replied that it was premature to discuss a vice presidential successor.[3] This did not stop political commentators from speculating, however, and Rockefeller, George Bush, Elliot Richardson, Melvin Laird, and Senators Howard Baker, Hugh Scott, and Barry Goldwater were all named as front-runners for the post.[4]

Following his swearing-in as President on August 9, Ford told congressional leaders that he would nominate a Vice President within ten days.[5] This would be his first and possibly most important decision, and the nation regarded it as the first test of the new President's judgment. Republican governors, Cabinet members, and political and congressional leaders were asked by Ford to submit preferential lists of their choices for Vice President.[6] Laird was quoted as saying that Nelson Rockefeller " 'would be the best choice to reassure foreign nations, heal the Republican Party and attract fresh talent to the depleted Federal establishment.' " [7] Conservative reaction to a possible Rockefeller nomination was mild. An aide to Senator Goldwater noted that the wounds from the Rockefeller–Goldwater battle for the presidential nomination in 1964 had healed, and that Goldwater would not object to the selection of Rockefeller.[8] Conservative Senators Strom Thurmond and John Tower also said that they would not oppose his selection, though he was not their first choice.[9]

Among congressional leaders, Rockefeller and Bush became the favorites. Senate Minority Leader Scott added his support for Rockefeller, while Senators Goldwater and Tower declared their preference for Bush, as did several Cabinet members who regarded Bush as an uncontroversial choice who might unite the party. Senator Jesse Helms of North Carolina sought to organize conservative support for Goldwater.[10]

As Ford continued his deliberations for over a week, "knowledgeable" Republicans concluded that the " 'front-runners' " had been rejected.[11] Ford himself brushed aside the delay and told a reporter, " 'I haven't been thinking about it.' " [12] Some Republican leaders complained that the President's indecision indicated a lack of enthusiasm for the candidates and was promoting division within the party. At about this time both Rockefeller and Bush ran into political troubles.

Columnist Jack Anderson reported that newly discovered files of E. Howard Hunt were believed to show that Rockefeller had financed a team of men assigned to disrupt the 1972 Democratic Convention.[13] The White House public response to this report on August 17 was confused. At first the White House said that it had received similar information about Rockefeller and that the President had ordered an investigation by the special prosecutor's office. Later in the day it was reported that the investigation had been completed and had turned up " 'nothing whatsoever.' " As for Rockefeller's continued candidacy, terHorst told reporters at the first news briefing on August 17 to draw their own conclusions. When this comment was interpreted as a statement that Rockefeller had been dumped, terHorst announced in a subsequent briefing that day that Rockefeller had been the victim of a smear campaign directed by right-wing extremists and that he remained under consideration for the vice presidency.[14] The handling of the reports about Rockefeller led *The New York Times* to declare editorially that "a chain of overresponse by government and press created a momentary sense that a nauseating new instance of political chicanery in the 1972 campaign had been uncovered." The *Times* concluded: "The astonishing thing still is how, given the unsubstantiality of its source, anyone chose to give the report currency before it had even been checked." [15]

Meanwhile, *Newsweek* magazine quoted unnamed sources as stating that Nixon had channeled $100,000 from a secret fund into Bush's 1970 senatorial campaign, and that $40,000 may not have been properly reported.[16] As in the case of the Rockefeller report, nothing further developed to substantiate this report, yet it damaged Bush's chances of securing the nomination.

On August 20 President Ford ended the speculation by announcing on television and radio from the White House the nomination of the sixty-six-year-old Rockefeller. While a few criticisms were voiced from the Democratic left and Republican right, predictions abounded that

Congress would confirm Rockefeller with due deliberation and speed.[17]
A feature article by R. W. Apple, Jr. in *The New York Times* stated:

President Ford's nomination of Nelson A. Rockefeller as Vice President completes a reversal of national political tides of potentially historic proportions. Ten days ago, politicians were asking whether the Republican party could survive; today, they were asking how the Democrats were going to mount a challenge in 1976.

Mr. Ford, as an admiring, if somewhat staggered, Democrat said this morning, "hasn't made a wrong move yet." [18]

In reviewing Ford's selection process, an aide reported that he sought to choose a person of presidential caliber. In Rockefeller were combined many attractive qualities—he was a person knowledgeable in administration, urban problems, corporate enterprises, and foreign affairs, and he was a politician from outside Congress who could be an effective campaigner in 1976. In hindsight a staff member said it had been " 'Rocky all the time.' " [19] However, it appears that there were two important elements in the decision: first, the mild reaction of conservative Republicans to Laird's early declaration for Rockefeller, and secondly Ford's own conviction that he would not be upstaged by a strong Vice President.[20]

In the afternoon of the day he was nominated, Rockefeller stated his belief that Ford had every intention of running in 1976.[21] The next day Jerry terHorst told reporters that the President had advised that he would seek election, thereby quieting speculation that Rockefeller would be the 1976 Republican candidate for President.[22] Later Rockefeller declared that he would not participate in any campaigns against incumbents until after his nomination had been acted upon by Congress.[23] This statement was viewed in some quarters as effectively assuring that Rockefeller would not be confirmed until after the November elections, since a Democratic Congress would not be anxious to have a new Republican Vice President appearing on behalf of Republican candidates. Other developments during the confirmation period made such delay inevitable.

In a news conference at his Maine summer home on August 23, Rockefeller indicated that he felt former President Nixon should not be prosecuted. Rockefeller quoted with approval Senator Scott's comment that Nixon had been hung and should not be drawn and quartered.[24] Several days later, at his first news conference, President Ford stated that, while he subscribed to Rockefeller's point of view, " 'until any legal process has been undertaken I think it's unwise and untimely for me to make any commitment.' " [25] Yet, on September 8, in a surprise announcement which shook the nation, Ford granted an unconditional pardon to Nixon for all criminal offenses against the United States which he may have committed during his term as President.[26] Ford said it was an act of compassion * designed to heal the wounds of Watergate. In accepting the pardon Nixon made no admission of deliberate wrongdoing but cited only " 'mistakes and misjudgments.' " Ford also released an agreement giving Nixon title to and control of all Watergate tapes and documents.

The pardon provoked an outpouring of public and congressional criticism which signaled the end of Ford's "honeymoon" period in the White House. A flood of critical telegrams and telephone calls inundated the White House. In the three days following the pardon about 110,000 telegrams, mailgrams, and personal opinion messages poured into Washington, according to Western Union.[27] Instead of marking the end of the Watergate era, the pardon left unanswered many questions relating to the crisis and succeeded in dividing the country. Two days after the Nixon pardon, the President indicated that he was considering pardons for all persons convicted or accused of crimes in the Watergate and related scandals. The suggestion was greeted with outrage by most commentators, and it was predicted that such an act would "perpetuate that scandal with far graver political, legal and moral consequences than those the country has already suffered." [28] A Gallup poll showed that support for Ford declined sharply after the pardon, and that over 60 per cent of those polled disapproved of the pardon.[29]

In addition to its impact on the popularity of the Ford administration, the pardon provoked suggestions that Ford might have made a deal with Nixon, a promise of a pardon in exchange for Nixon's resignation. Although there was no evidence of a deal, public suspicions remained even after Ford made an unprecedented appearance before a subcommittee of the House Judiciary Committee on October 17 to answer questions about the pardon.[30]

It was against this backdrop that the Rockefeller confirmation proceedings took place.

CONFIRMATION

As the congressional committees began their investigations prior to the formal hearings, Rockefeller submitted his tax returns for the previous seven years as well as a statement of his personal wealth, but he indicated

---

* In its issue of December 18, 1975, the *Washington Post* reported that General Haig discussed with Ford at some point on August 28, 1974 the subject of a pardon for Nixon. The *Post* also reported that former White House counsel Leonard Garment had given to Haig that day a memorandum urging that Nixon be pardoned. Among the points made in Garment's memorandum was that Nixon's mental and physical condition could not withstand a criminal prosecution and that, possibly, he might take his life unless he was pardoned. These disclosures are in apparent contradiction of Ford's testimony at the October 17, 1974 hearing that nobody had made any recommendation to him for a Nixon pardon or brought up on behalf of Nixon after August 9 the subject of a pardon. Following these disclosures, Rodino announced that the House

he would limit their public disclosure.[31] Rockefeller said that he would do whatever was appropriate to resolve any conflicts of interest arising from his vast financial holdings, and suggested that he might put his personal investments into a blind trust for the term of his vice presidency.[32]

On September 11 the Senate Rules Committee voted to ask Rockefeller to disclose publicly his financial holdings in lieu of any requirement that he divest himself of any investments or establish a blind trust. The committee concluded that a blind trust would be ineffective because of the breadth of his investments and that divestiture could adversely affect the economy. Under these circumstances it felt that full disclosure would best protect against conflicts of interest.[33] Rockefeller agreed to release a detailed disclosure of his assets, liabilities, and net worth at the start of the Senate public hearings on September 23.[34] But, on September 19, to counter what he described as misleading press leaks of information he had turned over to the committee, he reported that his net worth was $62.5-million plus the income from two trusts totaling $120-million.[35]

As the Senate hearings neared and the House hearings remained unscheduled, House Republicans began to complain that the Democrats were delaying the House investigation in an effort to prevent Rockefeller from campaigning in the fall elections.* Representative Railsback sent Chairman Rodino a letter on September 19 urging that the House Judiciary Committee, and the full House if necessary, stay in session through the November election until the confirmation was completed, stating that the nation " 'can ill afford to be without the services of a Vice President.' "[36] House Democrats, on the other hand, replied that the slow pace was caused by the need for a detailed financial investigation. Said Speaker Albert: " 'There is no inclination on the part of the leadership to delay the matter. We want to expedite it, but I don't want to dictate to the Judiciary Committee how much investigation is necessary.' "[37]

On September 23, the opening day of the Senate hearings, Rockefeller submitted a seventy-two–page autobiographical statement, including summaries of his tax returns for the previous ten years and of his financial position.[38] He said that he hoped the "myth or misconception" about the Rockefeller family fortune and its influence would be "exposed and

---

Judiciary Committee would review the matter to see whether the record of the subcommittee's hearing needed to be supplemented. Upon review, it was decided not to reopen the hearings. *N. Y. Times*, Feb. 20, 1976 at 12.

* The delay also gave rise to a number of legal questions not clearly answered by the legislative history of the Twenty-Fifth Amendment, such as what would happen if Rockefeller's nomination were not acted on until the new Congress met in January 1975. Would the nomination still be valid? Would favorable action by one House of Congress in 1974 have to be repeated by that House in 1975? Concern also was expressed about the status of the nomination in the event of President Ford's death. See *Hearing on the First Implementation of Section Two of the Twenty-Fifth Amendment Before the Subcomm. on Constitutional Amendments of the Senate Comm. on the Judiciary*, 94th Cong., 1st Sess. 55 (1975).

dissipated." However, the disclosure that his total holdings amounted to $218-million with an average annual income over the previous ten years of $4.6-million before taxes reinforced his image as a man of substantial wealth. To correct the widespread belief that his family dominated the oil industry, Rockefeller revealed that the total family holdings did not amount to more than 2.06 per cent of the stock of any oil company, and that no family member was on the board of any Standard Oil Company, or had any control over the management of these companies.

Committee members focused their questions on possible conflicts of interest between Rockefeller's economic concerns and the national interest if he were to succeed to the presidency. Rockefeller assured them that the public good would always be his prime consideration and relied on his record as governor of New York to demonstrate that his executive decisions had never been influenced by his private concerns. The committee inquired also about his views on taxation, welfare, abortion, and drug laws. A topic of considerable concern was his handling of the 1971 Attica prison revolt which resulted in the deaths of forty-three inmates and hostages. Rockefeller detailed the occurrences of the riot and admitted for the first time that the proper way to proceed would have been to stop the riot in the beginning without weapons.[39]

Throughout the questioning, Rockefeller was careful to give clear explanations of his views and policies. He refused to give an opinion on several of President Ford's actions, such as the Nixon pardon of September 8,[40] the Nixon tapes agreement,[41] or Ford's Senate testimony the previous year that the country would not stand for a pardon.[42] He also refused to commit himself on issues of executive privilege,[43] future pardons for Watergate defendants,[44] or pardons for a resigning President prior to criminal investigation or prosecution.[45]

Following Rockefeller's testimony, which lasted for two and one-half days, the committee for a half day heard testimonials in support of the nomination from ten members of Congress from both parties.[46] On the fourth day, testimony from outside interest groups was heard, including critics and supporters of his abortion stance, critics of the Attica problems, and conservatives who feared his internationalism.[47]

As the second day's hearings recessed, Senate Majority Whip Robert Byrd of West Virginia, who had been the most aggressive questioner of Rockefeller, agreed with committee Chairman Howard Cannon that nothing had emerged which would be a barrier to Rockefeller's confirmation,[48] and most commentators agreed that "Congress seems all but certain to approve overwhelmingly"[49] the Rockefeller nomination. The hearings were recessed on September 26, but no vote was taken pending receipt of an audit of Rockefeller's taxes by the staff of the Joint Committee on Internal Revenue Taxation.

On September 28, Mrs. Betty Ford underwent surgery for the removal of her cancerous right breast. This sudden development immediately gave rise to reports that Ford would not be a candidate for President in 1976. The President himself indicated that he was rethinking his plans to run in 1976, saying " '[w]e haven't thought beyond next week.' " [50] Thus, the congressional hearings became even more important.

In the next few weeks a number of political bombshells exploded which reversed the tide flowing toward confirmation, and by the end of October Rockefeller's nomination seemed destined for defeat. The absence of any congressional hearings during that month and a deluge of press leaks played a large part in this reversal. The first bombshell occurred on October 5 when Rockefeller disclosed that he had made gifts of $50,000 to Henry A. Kissinger; $86,000 to L. Judson Morhouse, former New York State Republican Party chairman; and an unspecified sum to Dr. William Ronan, Chairman of the Port Authority of New York and New Jersey and a senior adviser to the Rockefeller family. Hugh Murrow, Rockefeller's press secretary, explained the circumstances of each gift and noted that appropriate gift taxes had been paid. The gift to Kissinger was made in 1969 after he had ended a fifteen-year position as a Rockefeller adviser and before he became a national security adviser to former President Nixon. The gift, said Murrow, was an expression of Rockefeller's gratitude for Kissinger's long years of service.

The gift to Morhouse, in 1973, was in the form of the cancellation of an outstanding loan made to him in 1960 to invest in commercial real estate on Long Island. At that time the job of Republican State Chairman was unsalaried, and the loan was intended to provide Morhouse with income to help him resist " 'temptation to misuse political influence,' " according to Murrow. Morhouse resigned his party position in 1962, and in 1966 he was convicted of bribery and other charges arising from a State Liquor Authority scandal, and sentenced to prison. In 1970 Governor Rockefeller commuted his sentence because Morhouse was reported to be seriously ill with cancer and Parkinson's disease.[51] In response to these disclosures, Senator Byrd said on October 5 that he saw no need to recall Mr. Rockefeller and saw " 'nothing on the surface that appears to be sinister.' " [52]

On October 7, additional gifts and campaign contributions by Rockefeller were disclosed, including recent contributions to several Republican members of Congress who would be voting on Rockefeller's nomination. Senator Javits received a $15,000 contribution, and Representative Peter Peyser of New York had received $10,000 from Rockefeller family members, including $5,000 from Nelson. Other politicians who received " 'nominal contributions' " included Senators Peter Dominick of Colorado, Charles Mathias, and Milton Young, and Representative William S. Cohen. Murrow disclosed that Rockefeller had made him a gift of $100,000 by paying off a bank loan he had taken for medical and educational expenses for his family. It was also disclosed that in 1972 Nelson Rockefeller, his brothers Laurance and John, and his sister, Mrs. Abby Mauze, each gave $50,000 to President Nixon's re-election campaign.[53]

Murrow further disclosed that the gift to Ronan consisted of the cancellation of $550,000 in debts owed to Rockefeller. He said that the gift actually cost Rockefeller $880,000, including federal and state gift taxes. It was made during the interval between Ronan's resignation as head of the Metropolitan Transportation Authority (MTA), a job with a salary of $85,000 per year, and his assumption of the unsalaried chairmanship of the Port Authority. Murrow could not say how many separate loans there were or when they were made, whether they were interest-free or whether Ronan had paid back any money to Rockefeller.[54]

These gifts and contributions raised questions of both a political and a legal nature. Some commentators argued that the disclosure showed that Rockefeller was insensitive to the apparent impropriety of rewarding public figures. It was pointed out, for example, that shortly after the cancellation of his debts, Ronan became head of the Port Authority, which played a crucial role in planning the development of New York City in which the Rockefellers had vast financial interests. Others challenged the legality of the gifts under New York law. One section of the state penal law bars giving to a public official "unlawful gratuities"—that is, conferring a benefit upon a public servant for a duty he is required or authorized to perform. A second state law, Section 73 of the New York Public Officers Law, which became effective on January 1, 1966, forbids any state employee from accepting gifts or loans of $25 or more "under circumstances in which it could reasonably be inferred that the gift was intended to influence him, or could reasonably be expected to influence him, in the performance of his official duties or was intended as a reward for any official action on his part."

In a statement on the Senate floor on October 15, Senator Helms questioned whether the loans to Ronan occurred after Section 73 had become effective and while he was a state official. If the loans were made during that time, Helms suggested, then the law would apply if a reasonable inference could be drawn that the loans were intended to influence Ronan. Recognizing that Ronan as head of the MTA could affect the success of the Rockefeller governorship, Helms asked "whether an invidious inference is 'reasonable' under the circumstances." [55]

Senator Cannon responded to these disclosures with a request that Rockefeller supply detailed background information to the Senate Rules Committee. As rumors spread that the gifts disclosed were only the beginning, it appeared certain that the committee would reopen its hearings. Representative Waldie said that he found it " 'beyond comprehension' " that the Senate Rules Committee, with information on the gifts, had not questioned Rockefeller about the subject. Senator Helms called for the committee to reconvene, and labeled the gifts as raising " 'a grave question of propriety.' " [56] In addressing the Senate, Helms declared that "[u]ntil we, as U.S. Senators, know the full extent of the way in which Governor Rockefeller may have used the power of his fortune in building a network of political dependency, we will not be able to resolve the question of whether he ought to be confirmed as Vice President of the United States." [57]

Helms also observed that in the Rockefeller tax returns already made public was an enumeration of almost $4-million in gift taxes paid during the last ten years. Since it was acknowledged that a number of gifts were made to political figures, Helms called for a complete disclosure of the beneficiaries and demanded that Rockefeller and Ronan testify before the Rules Committee.[58] Helms also questioned the 1968 merger of the Triborough Bridge and Tunnel Authority and the Metropolitan Transportation Authority which was negotiated by David Rockefeller of The Chase Manhattan Bank representing the Triborough bondholders and Ronan on behalf of the MTA. The agreement increased the interest payments to the Triborough bondholders and permitted the Triborough profits to be applied to the MTA deficits. Helms called for full disclosure of the agreement.[59] There were news reports of other Rockefeller gifts and favors to aides and associates, including the use of Rockefeller properties, airplanes, and helicopters, appointments to high salaried positions, and financing of New York Republican campaigns. It also was reported that Rockefeller had assisted his brother David, president of The Chase Manhattan Bank, in numerous ways.[60]

On October 9, Senator Cannon announced that he would make public Rockefeller's response to the questions about his financial gifts. He also stated that no decision on reconvening the Senate hearings would be made until after the November 5 elections, when the tax report would be completed.[61] In a press conference that afternoon President Ford asserted that he had investigated the gift to Kissinger and found no impropriety.[62] But congressmen and political commentators began to question whether, in the words of a *New York Times* editorial, Rockefeller "may be insufficiently aware of the dangers to the democratic process that lie in even the most benevolent application of enormous concentrations of wealth and economic power." [63]

Meanwhile, Governor Brendan Byrne of New Jersey said that he would wait for more details about the gift to Ronan so that he could evaluate whether Ronan could serve the interests of New York and New Jersey impartially.[64] Later, on October 21, the New Jersey legislature ordered an investigation of the Rockefeller gift to Ronan, which was said to have " 'raised serious questions' " about Ronan's capacity to serve as Chairman of the Port Authority.[65] New York Attorney General Louis

Lefkowitz also said that he planned to investigate whether any state laws or ethical standards had been violated by the Ronan–Rockefeller arrangement,[66] and subsequently requested that his advisory committee on ethical standards explore the gifts and loans for possible violations.[67] *

In response to such criticisms, Ronan held a news conference on October 10. To counter charges of violations of the New York Public Officers Law, he stressed that the gift had been made during a two-week period when he was not on the state payroll. He stated that in his capacity as senior adviser to the Rockefellers, he had never given advice about Port Authority plans, and that The Chase Manhattan Bank had not received any special favors from the Port Authority. Several times during the news conference Ronan said that he saw no conflicts of interest in his roles as state official, Rockefeller adviser, corporate board member, and trustee of two small banks.[68] It was rumored that Rockefeller was unhappy that his motives were being questioned, since his lawyers had approved the gifts and reported them on his tax returns.[69]

On October 10 a second political bombshell exploded which further clouded Rockefeller's chances for confirmation. It was reported that the House Judiciary Committee had begun an investigation into the subject of an FBI report that Rockefeller, through intermediaries, might have been involved in underwriting a critical biography of Arthur Goldberg during the 1970 campaign for the governorship of New York. The book, *Arthur J. Goldberg: The Old and the New*, by Victor Lasky, claimed that Goldberg did not have the background and experience to be a successful governor.

When first asked about the book, press secretary Murrow replied that Nelson Rockefeller had nothing to do with it in any way. An hour later he released a statement by Rockefeller revealing that New York lawyer John A. Wells, a close Rockefeller associate, had told the governor early in the 1970 campaign that Victor Lasky was working on a Goldberg biography and some time after the book was published Rockefeller was shown a copy. The statement also revealed that when the FBI had interviewed Rockefeller in connection with his nomination, he was asked about the rumors that he had financed the Lasky book. Rockefeller replied that he had heard of the book but knew nothing of its preparation or financing. Subsequently, said Rockefeller, he was informed that his brother Laurance had invested $60,000 in a company set up to produce the book, and later lost $52,000 when the book proved a failure. Although the investment was said to be a business venture, Laurance Rockefeller did not take a tax deduction for a business loss. Nelson Rockefeller added: " 'Had he only told me about it at the time, I would have been totally opposed to it and would have strongly advised

---

* The committee later concluded that the Rockefeller gifts did not violate the State Code of Ethics but were " 'not in the public interest.' " *N. Y. Times*, Jan. 28, 1975 at 1.

against his participation in any form.' " [70] Upon being informed of Rockefeller's statement, Goldberg commented that he was shocked by the disclosure and demanded an apology for the financing of a " 'scandalous and libelous book.' " [71]

On October 11, the publishers of the book said that Wells had arranged for its publication and offered to purchase 100,000 copies for distribution in the 1970 campaign. It also was disclosed that the $60,000 from Laurance Rockefeller had paid for the entire publishing project, and that a total of 116,000 copies were published, of which 100,000 were given to the Rockefeller re-election campaign. Victor Lasky revealed that Wells had approached him about writing a campaign biography of Arthur Goldberg. It was also reported that the financing of the book was arranged through Literary Properties, Inc., a Delaware corporation organized to produce the book, and that funds were channeled to the corporation through Philadelphia. In light of these disclosures, Goldberg asked the House Judiciary Committee and the Senate Rules Committee to hold formal hearings into the circumstances surrounding the publication of the book.[72] Of Nelson Rockefeller, Goldberg stated that " 'he is not fit to be Vice President, based upon what occurred and the cover-up story.' " [73]

In response to the request of the Senate Rules Committee for detailed information about his gifts, Rockefeller released on October 11 a list of twenty present and former public officials and staff assistants to whom he had given $1.97-million over the previous seventeen years. The largest gift was to Ronan and was listed as $625,000. Other substantial gifts were made to Emmet J. Hughes, a former Rockefeller speechwriter, and to Edward J. Logue, Chairman of the New York Urban Development Corporation. Rockefeller explained that he had given money to help friends with such problems as medical expenses, marital difficulties, educational expenses, and relocation costs. He also complained that leaks from congressional committees checking his tax returns were creating an atmosphere of uncertainty and suspicion.[74] The House Judiciary Committee requested more gift tax information and was said to be interested in gifts of less than $3,000 which were not required to be reported to the IRS.[75]

The disclosure of the list of Rockefeller gifts generated widespread discussion in the press about the relationship of personal wealth and political power. Rockefeller argued that his loans and gifts had enabled some of the recipients to remain in public service when they might have been tempted to return to more lucrative private positions. On the other side, it was urged that when a person will engage in public service only if compensated by a third person, his loyalties necessarily become suspect. William Safire observed in *The New York Times* that in 1973 an elected Vice President was forced from office because he was "on the take," while in 1974 the vice presidential nominee was under fire for being "on the give." [76] Safire noted that although the gifts were well intentioned, they created an obvious conflict of interest, and that to assure his confirmation Rockefeller must admit that the practice is wrong and promise not to engage in it again.[77]

On October 12, Rockefeller sent a telegram to Goldberg offering his " 'sincere and unqualified apology.' " Rockefeller said that " '[i]t is quite clear that when the project was brought to my attention, I should have immediately taken steps to see to it that it was stopped as utterly alien to and incompatible with the standards I have always tried to observe in my political life. I take full responsibility for the whole regrettable episode.' " [78] Rockefeller also telephoned President Ford to read his apology and to discuss the congressional confirmation proceedings. An aide said that President Ford assured Rockefeller that " 'there is no problem.' " [79]

With the release of the Rockefeller gift list and the "dirty trick" charge about the Goldberg book, congressional support for Rockefeller waned. Senator Cannon said that in all probability he would recall Rockefeller to testify before the Senate Rules Committee, and suggested that as a result of the developments a vote on the nomination might be delayed until late December.[80] Meanwhile, the House Judiciary Committee was reported to be investigating whether there was any connection between the Rockefeller family contributions to President Nixon's 1972 campaign and the President's subsequent approval of the acquisition of Caribair, a Puerto Rico–based airline, by Eastern Airlines, in which the Rockefellers had large interests. The Rockefellers had contributed $200,000 to Nixon's campaign and, less than a year later, Nixon, citing foreign policy reasons, had reversed two Civil Aeronautics Board rulings which had denied the acquisition. The matter was included in the expansion of the House inquiry into the Rockefeller nomination to members of the Rockefeller family and their influence on governmental agencies and policy.[81]

On October 15, Rockefeller requested that both the Senate and the House conduct immediate hearings because of continuing leaks of financial information which, he said, were trying him in the press. Both committees refused the request because their investigations and the tax audit were not completed. Most Republicans on the committees supported Rockefeller's position, however, since the delays were weakening his chances of confirmation.[82]

On October 18 a third damaging blow struck. As a result of the IRS audit of Rockefeller's federal income and gift taxes, additional assessments were made of a total amount of $903,718: $820,718 in income taxes, and $83,000 in gift taxes. In a letter to the Senate and House Committees, Rockefeller disclosed that adjustments were made in his deductions for office and investment expenses and charitable contributions. No penalty charges were assessed, which suggested that no fraud or improper intent had been found. For the five-year period, the underpayment amounted to one-fifth of the taxes which had been paid.[83] President Ford, through his press secretary, reaffirmed his complete faith in Rockefeller's integrity and his belief that he would ultimately be confirmed.[84]

The day after this disclosure, Rockefeller released a list of his charitable donations over the previous seventeen years, which showed gifts totaling $24.7-million to 193 organizations. Political commentators pointed out, however, that since Rockefeller paid about two-thirds of his total income to the federal government, the cost to him of the contributions was closer to $8-million.[85] The press continued to request more detailed financial information until October 22 when Rockefeller announced that it had become impossible for him to fulfill the requests of the congressional committees while responding to press demands as well. Consequently, he determined to postpone answering further questions.[86]

On October 19 President Ford told newsmen that while some conservative Republicans had urged him to drop the Rockefeller nomination, he did not take the advice seriously. " 'I'm still convinced he would make a good Vice President,' " said Ford.[87] There was speculation that Rockefeller might withdraw, and many observers questioned whether any rich man could be confirmed, or even whether anyone at all could be confirmed when subjected to such intense scrutiny.[88] Senator Goldwater backed away from his initial support of Rockefeller, and was reported to be undecided. In a radio interview he said that there was a good chance that Rockefeller's name would be withdrawn to spare him additional questioning. Goldwater's views were considered significant to other congressional conservatives and were a bad sign to Rockefeller supporters.[89]

On October 28 Mr. Rockefeller released a list of loans revealing that a total of $507,800 had been advanced over the last seventeen years to friends, associates, and family members. The new loan list supplemented the previously released list of gifts which were often in the form of forgiven loans. The largest loan ($84,000) had been made in 1957 to Robert B. Anderson, former Secretary of the Navy and subsequently Secretary of the Treasury. The loan was made before President Eisenhower appointed Anderson to the Treasury position, and was repaid after his appointment. Anderson said that he used the loan to purchase stock in a Rockefeller-controlled corporation with extensive Latin American holdings, but that after his appointment as Treasury Secretary, he sold the stock back to Rockefeller because of the possibility of his participating in decisions which might affect the corporation.[90]

It is not surprising, then, that, while all these disclosures were being made, Rockefeller's nomination became an issue of discussion in congressional and state elections throughout the country. After the November elections, the timing of the hearings presented more potential troubles for the nominee. If the hearings were completed and Rockefeller were confirmed by a close vote in the "lame duck" Congress, in which many defeated or retiring Republicans would vote, his legitimacy as Vice President could be clouded. On the other hand, if the confirmation vote were delayed until the next session of Congress, it was possible that new hearings would be required, and the enlarged Democratic majorities might be less willing to confirm such a powerful political figure.[91] *

On November 12 Rockefeller arrived in Washington to appear for a second time before the Senate Rules Committee. He told reporters that he was " 'hopeful, not confident,' " that Congress would confirm him, and later met with President Ford to review his prepared testimony. As one indication of the change in the status of the nomination from certain to controversial, the major television networks agreed to broadcast the hearings live on a rotating basis.[92] House Speaker Albert told President Ford that he hoped to complete action on the nomination before Christmas.[93]

The Senate Rules Committee reopened the Rockefeller hearings on November 13. Rockefeller read from an opening statement which explained his political gifts and loans and his involvement in the publication of the Goldberg book. Regarding the Goldberg book, he described for the first time what he said was the full story "pieced together" from his memory and the recollections of others involved in the incident. He said that during the 1970 campaign John Wells had dropped into his office to discuss a Goldberg biography to be written by Victor Lasky. Rockefeller said that he referred Wells to Donal O'Brien, one of his attorneys, and "sent a message to my brother, Laurance, asking if he could help Jack Wells find some investors. That was the extent of my involvement with the project." [94] The complicated arrangement for financing the book through a dummy corporation was not an effort to launder the money, said Rockefeller, but an attempt to conceal the Rockefeller name from other potential investors.[95] He attributed to an "extremely sketchy" memory his failure to inform the FBI about his relationship to the biography and his conflicting reports to the press.[96]

Senator Byrd questioned Rockefeller closely about the Goldberg book, and complained about the "devious" way in which the book was financed and published and the slow revelation of Rockefeller's involvement with it.[97] Rockefeller replied that it was common for members of his family

---

* Decried Senator Hugh Scott on October 17: "Mr. President, as a member of the Senate Committee on Rules and Administration, I have personally urged that further hearings on the nomination of Nelson Rockefeller be held promptly in the cause of fairness to Governor Rockefeller and to the country. My urging has been for naught. The chairman (Mr. Cannon) and the majority members of the committee have decided to postpone further hearings until after the election. This is a great disservice to the Nation." 120 Cong. Rec. S. 19382 (daily ed. Oct. 17, 1974). See 120 Cong. Rec. S. 20148 (daily ed. Nov. 26, 1974).

to make investments through a nominee to conceal their identities so that other investors would not be affected.[98] He also defended his delay in making a full disclosure by reminding Senator Byrd that he had requested an opportunity to testify before the committee in October but was denied that chance.[99] Senator Claiborne Pell of Rhode Island asked why Laurance Rockefeller had not claimed a capital loss on the publication of the book if it were truly a business investment.[100] Rockefeller answered that his brother's tax lawyers thought the IRS would question such a deduction, and accordingly did not claim it to avoid controversy.[101]

Of the loans and gifts to his aides and political associates, Rockefeller stated that not one had been designed to corrupt or did in fact corrupt either the receiver or the giver, and that all had been motivated by affection, respect, and compelling need. He stressed that all the public officials or staff members who were listed as recipients of gifts had been appointed by him and were administratively responsible to him, so that they could not be of special use to him even if they could have been influenced by his gifts.[102]

The loans to Ronan, he said, were made between 1962 and 1969 to help him meet family responsibilities and assist him in meeting continuing financial burdens after his retirement. In 1974, he said, he forgave the loans and gave Ronan an additional $40,000 in appreciation of his friendship and eighteen-year association.[103]

Defending the merger of the Triborough Bridge and Tunnel Authority with the Metropolitan Transportation Authority, Rockefeller quoted a *New York Times* statement that the consolidation was " 'the greatest advance in the metropolitan transportation system in at least half a century.' "[104] Rockefeller explained his gifts to James W. Gaynor and Edward Logue as attempts to facilitate their moving to New York State from Colorado and Massachusetts and joining the public housing effort in New York.[105] To assist the unsalaried Republican State Chairman, L. Judson Morhouse, Rockefeller lent him $100,000 to enter a real estate business and requested further assistance from Laurance Rockefeller. Through Laurance a loan of $49,000 was arranged to purchase stock in two venture capital companies which Laurance had helped to finance. A year and a half later Morhouse sold some of the stock, which had appreciated in value, and repaid the loan.[106]

Along with his statement Rockefeller released a summary of his political contributions since 1957, which totalled $3,265,374 (including $1,000,228 to his own presidential campaigns, and $80,599 to his New York campaigns). He also revealed that his brothers and sister had contributed $2,850,000 to his campaigns and that his stepmother, Martha Baird Rockefeller, had contributed a total of ca. $11-million to his campaigns.[107]

The basic question presented by these disclosures of gifts, loans, political contributions, and involvement in financing the Goldberg biography was whether Rockefeller had used his money to buy political power. For the members of the Senate Rules Committee, the confirmation of Rockefeller would depend on their judgment of whether Rockefeller would use his wealth improperly as Vice President, or possibly as President, and whether his background would impair his ability to determine and promote the best interests of the American people. Many commentators argued that sizable gifts would necessarily place the recipients in positions of "psychological servitude," regardless of the donor's intent. Tom Wicker of *The New York Times* observed that Rockefeller's attitude toward use of his private wealth in public office gave the public no protection except his own promise to act for good purposes. And "in the long run it is the practice, not the purpose, of using private resources to supplement public office that is at issue." [108]

When the hearings continued on November 14, Rockefeller submitted a statement regarding gifts and loans to public officials. To avoid the misunderstandings which had arisen from the loans and gifts which he made while governor of New York, Rockefeller proposed that if confirmed as Vice President he would make no gifts or loans to any public official with the following exceptions: gifts of nominal amounts to friends at Christmas, weddings and birthdays, and, under exceptional circumstances, assistance to friends in the event of special hardship of a compelling human nature.[109]

Senator Byrd quoted the two sections of the New York statutes which prohibit gifts to public officials under certain circumstances, and intensely questioned Rockefeller about their applicability to his loans to Ronan.[110] Rockefeller responded that his lawyers had approved the transactions, and that he, as governor, had signed the statutes and was fully familiar with their intent.[111]

The second witness of the day, Arthur J. Goldberg, testified that Rockefeller's explanation of the financing of the Lasky book was "inherently noncredible." [112] Goldberg said that the public was entitled to candor and openness from those who hold or seek public office, and that "[c]arefully crafted public relations efforts, designed to forestall pursuit of relevant information and the entire truth, are simply unacceptable." [113]

That night at a news conference in Phoenix President Ford affirmed his support for Rockefeller, saying that he could imagine no circumstances under which he would withdraw Rockefeller's name. Ford complained that it was time for Congress to complete action on the Rockefeller nomination and " 'fish or cut bait.' " The President also suggested that the next Congress should consider changing the Twenty-Fifth Amendment to provide a specific deadline for the President to nominate and for the Congress to confirm a Vice President. The nation " 'need[s] a Vice President at all times' " and the delay in confirmation leaves no one prepared to assume the presidency on a moment's notice, explained Ford. However, he reaffirmed his intention to travel to Japan and the Soviet Union even though Rockefeller had not been confirmed as his successor.[114] The next day Ford said through his press secretary that he would definitely run for election in 1976.[115]

The third day of the resumed Senate hearings centered on the financing of the Goldberg biography, with witnesses who were involved in the 1970 campaign promotion. John Wells testified that he convinced Victor Lasky that a critical biography of Arthur Goldberg was needed and might be profitable. He later met with Nelson Rockefeller to explain the concept to him and seek suggestions from him of persons who might invest in the book. Rockefeller arranged for Wells to meet with several family lawyers and financial advisers, who agreed to name a nominee to hold stock in a corporation organized to finance the book.[116] Donal O'Brien, chief Rockefeller family counsel, recalled that after meeting with Wells he reported back to Nelson Rockefeller. He was told that Rockefeller would not participate in the venture but would contact his brother Laurance to see if he could locate investors.[117]

From the testimony of Donal O'Brien [118] and Laurance Rockefeller, it appeared that Mrs. Louise Boyer, an executive assistant and trusted adviser to both Rockefellers, described the idea to Laurance Rockefeller as a commercial venture and asked him to help organize a group of investors to finance the book.[119] Rockefeller replied that he did not have time to contact other investors but would agree to underwrite the venture himself. Laurance Rockefeller himself testified that he had no further conversation with anyone, including his brother Nelson, concerning the book, until a few months prior to his testimony when the FBI questioned his financial adviser about it.[120] When examined by the committee, Laurance Rockefeller agreed that he had acted more quickly and with less information on this investment than on most other venture capital proposals, but stated that he acted out of confidence in Mrs. Boyer's judgment and integrity.[121]

Laurance Rockefeller also provided details about his loan to L. Judson Morhouse and the Eastern Airlines acquisition of Caribair.[122] Following his testimony, Senator Byrd predicted that the Senate would probably confirm Nelson Rockefeller as Vice President, barring any unexpected development. Explaining that while it was his duty to ask difficult questions, Byrd said he intended to vote for confirmation.[123] The fact that Byrd had become the most persistent interrogator of Nelson Rockefeller was in sharp contrast to his early support for the nominee. It was reported that President Ford telephoned Byrd in August 1974 to solicit his advice on a choice for Vice President and that Byrd had told the President that he favored Nelson Rockefeller's selection because of his experience and ability. In the hindsight of November, Byrd reflected that " '[had] I known then what I know now, I'm not sure I would have reacted exactly as I did to Mr. Ford's question.' " [124]

The Senate Rules Committee completed its hearings on November 18 with testimony from four of the recipients of Rockefeller gifts and the vice president of Americans for Democratic Action. The principal witness was Ronan, who testified that to make adequate provision for his family in the future and for his retirement, he borrowed funds from Rockefeller for investment purposes. He said that "[t]he initiative, in this, was really mine" [125] and that "at no time did I consider the Governor was under any continuing obligation to loan me money." [126] Ronan also stated that the loans did not affect his willingness to stay in state service, and did not alter his outlook on any matter of public policy.[127] Senator Byrd questioned Ronan about whether prior to his resignation from the MTA he had discussed with Rockefeller the possibility that the outstanding loans might be forgiven. Ronan denied any such understanding. Senator Byrd again expressed concern that the two New York statutes prohibiting gifts to state employees might have been violated, but concluded that Rockefeller should be given the benefit of the doubt.[128]

Later in the day, the committee questioned Edward Logue, president of the New York State Urban Development Corporation (UDC), about the gifts and loans he had received from Rockefeller. When in 1968 Rockefeller asked Logue to become the first president of the new UDC, Logue said he told Rockefeller that it would be difficult for him to move from Boston to New York because of a debt of $30,000 incurred during his unsuccessful campaign for mayor of Boston in 1967, and because of the problem of locating comparable housing for his family in New York City without substantial financial sacrifice.[129] Rockefeller made a gift to Logue of an amount sufficient to liquidate his campaign debt, and in 1969 lent him $145,000 for the purchase of a cooperative apartment. Logue testified that without Rockefeller's assistance he "would not have been able to leave my private life in Boston to accept the appointment he offered." [130] Another former New York housing official, James W. Gaynor, also testified that Rockefeller's gift helped him to come to New York from Denver.[131]

The final committee witness was Joseph L. Rauh, Jr., of Americans for Democratic Action. Rauh urged, as he had done during the Ford confirmation hearings, that the committee establish as the standard for confirmation of a vice presidential nominee that he be among the group of persons whom a majority of the Congress would want as President of the United States.[132] The breadth of Rockefeller economic interests, Rauh asserted, should disqualify him from the presidency because of the inevitable conflicts of interest which would arise. As President, he would have to make decisions affecting business and financial interests, and would be unable to act without provoking suspicion that he was influenced by his own interests.[133]

On November 22 the Senate Rules Committee voted unanimously to recommend the confirmation of Nelson Rockefeller to the full Senate. But Senators Byrd and James Allen of Alabama said that they had not decided whether they would defend the nomination on the Senate floor. Committee Chairman Cannon said that it was undecided whether the Senate would vote before the conclusion of the House Judiciary Committee hearings.[134]

The House hearings had begun the day before with the suggestion by Chairman Rodino that the committee must measure "the network of Rockefeller wealth, family wealth, and place it into the perspective of both the American economy and the American political system." [135] * There were indications that other committee members would inquire about the family wealth, especially in light of its huge contributions to Rockefeller's political campaigns.

Representatives Mezvinsky and Kastenmeier requested that Rockefeller ask his brothers to disclose their holdings, securities, and trusts to dispel the suspicions that there was a pattern of economic control by the family.[136] Rockefeller agreed to discuss the request with members of his family.

In his opening statement, Rockefeller promised that if confirmed he would place his financial holdings in a blind trust and arrange to have the family trusts of which he was lifetime beneficiary administered in a "blind manner." [137] Many of the committee Democrats indicated that they regarded a blind trust as an empty gesture which would not resolve their worries about conflicts of interest.[138] The committee focused other questions on the 1971 Attica Prison revolt, the pardon of L. Judson Morhouse, and Rockefeller's loans to public officials which were forgiven when the officials retired from public service. Rockefeller admitted that he had made a "serious mistake" in handling the Attica uprising when he failed to order state police to retake the prison in the early stages of the rebellion.[139]

At the conclusion of Rockefeller's testimony, the committee heard two days of testimony from outside witnesses. The same groups which had appeared before the Senate committee gave testimony again, and in several instances the same individuals merely reread their Senate testimony. Abortion, Attica, and internationalism were the main issues addressed. Committee members were more critical of these witnesses than the senators had been. Support for Rockefeller's nomination was voiced by four members of the House of Representatives who previously had testified before the Senate committee. The only congressional critic was

---

* Although they had covered the Senate hearings, the major networks decided not to televise these hearings.

Representative Abzug, who stated that the immense economic holdings of the Rockefeller family would create intrinsic conflicts of interest which would further weaken public confidence in the executive.[140] She also suggested that members of the 94th Congress should pass on the nomination, since their recent election would best reflect the present views of the electorate.[141]

Following the Thanksgiving recess and after four more days of testimony, the House Judiciary Committee concluded its hearings on December 5. It received testimony from two professors about the collective Rockefeller financial network,[142] following which J. Richardson Dilworth, the Rockefeller family's senior financial adviser, sought to dispel the notion that the family acted in concert. He stressed that the investments of each family member were handled individually, without reference to those of other members. Dilworth released five tables showing the aggregate investments and stock holdings of the Rockefeller family, which totaled more than $1-billion in securities owned outright and in trusts, and stated the tables were the first attempt to aggregate the family holdings in this or any other way. The stock holdings were dispersed among more than two dozen companies and the percentages of outstanding shares were insignificant except for about 1 per cent of the stock of Exxon, 1.7 per cent of the Mobil Corporation, and 2 per cent of Standard Oil of California.[143] Committee members seemed so staggered by the vast amounts of money involved that it was difficult for them to question Dilworth.

Laurance Rockefeller and Ronan also testified before the House Judiciary Committee and essentially repeated their Senate statements. One surprise was the disclosure by Laurance Rockefeller of a loan of $30,000 in 1961 to William E. Miller, then chairman of the Republican National Committee and later a Republican vice presidential nominee. Rockefeller had told the Senate Rules Committee that he had made no loans to political figures except for the loan to L. Judson Morhouse in 1959. In reviewing his records since then, he said, he had found the loan to Miller. Rockefeller also testified that he assumed his brother Nelson had requested the loan because he did not know Miller. The loan was repaid in 1964.[144] The committee members questioned Rockefeller about the loan and about his political contributions, and to a lesser extent, about the Goldberg biography and the Caribair merger. Several committee Democrats were so angry that the Miller loan had not been revealed earlier that they demanded that Laurance Rockefeller supply a list of all loans and gifts he had ever made. Chairman Rodino restrained them by declaring that such a request was beyond the committee's authorization.[145]

Nelson Rockefeller returned as the final witness before the committee. He explained that he had asked Laurance to make the loan to Miller for an investment in venture capital, and stated that there was nothing "unusual, wrong immoral or questionable" about the loan.[146] He did not, however, explain his failure to disclose the loan earlier. Nevertheless, as the hearings concluded, confirmation of Rockefeller as Vice President seemed certain.

The formal debate on his confirmation began in the Senate on December 9. In opening the debate, Senator Cannon described the hearings of the Rules Committee and the investigations of the nominee by the FBI, IRS, and congressional committee staffs. He said that, after judging Rockefeller by his entire record, the committee found no bar or impediment to disqualify him from the vice presidency and therefore unanimously recommended his confirmation.[147] Numerous other senators, while expressing concern about the Goldberg biography and political gifts, added their support for the nominee.

The few critics of the confirmation voiced different reasons for their opposition. Senator William Scott of Virginia based his opposition on the lack of support for the nomination in his constituency and the suspicions engendered by the gifts and loans, the Goldberg book, and the family wealth and influence.[148] For Senator James Abourezk of South Dakota, Rockefeller's views on the use of nuclear weapons, antitrust policy, and covert CIA operations disqualified him from the vice presidency.[149] Reversing his initial support for Rockefeller, Senator Goldwater concluded that Rockefeller had used his personal wealth "to accomplish the purchase of political power" and that the nation would be better served by the selection of a younger man.[150] Senator Helms repeated many of his earlier criticisms of the nominee in announcing his opposition to confirmation.[151]

On December 10, one additional hour of debate was held before the confirmation vote. Two more senators spoke in opposition to Rockefeller. Gaylord Nelson complained that the nominee was insensitive to the threats to freedom posed by vast concentrations of wealth and power.[152] Senator Bayh viewed the restoration of public confidence in government as the most important consideration, and regarded Rockefeller's conflict of interest problems as insurmountable.[153] When the vote was called, Rockefeller was confirmed by a vote of 90 to 7,[154] and his assumption of the vice presidency awaited only approval by the House.

Later that week the House Judiciary Committee recommended that Rockefeller be confirmed by a vote of 26 to 12.[155] * All the committee Republicans voted in favor of confirmation, while the twelve Democrats who opposed the nominee cited the conflict of interest inherent in the

---

* Six of the eight members who had voted against Ford's nomination also voted against Rockefeller's. The exceptions were Representatives Rangel and Jordan. See note at p. 146, *supra*. The remaining six dissenters also were Democrats: Representatives Danielson, Edwards, Mezvinsky, Joshua Eilberg of Pennsylvania, Paul S. Sarbanes of Maryland, and Wayne Owens of Utah.

combination of high political office and massive wealth and economic power. Ten of the dissenters agreed that in a direct election the people might approve Rockefeller but that the Congress acting alone should not do so.[156]

The final debate and confirmation vote in the House occurred on December 19. During six hours of debate, sixty-six representatives argued for and against the confirmation.† The House confirmed Mr. Rockefeller by a vote of 287 to 128.[157]

The majority agreed with Congressman Rodino, who praised Rockefeller's experience, competence, and dedication to public service.[158] Others cited the intense scrutiny of the investigation and the nation's need for a Vice President.[159] If Rockefeller were defeated, some feared a less qualified nominee whose confirmation would be greatly delayed.[160] The negative votes were cast by conservative Republicans who criticized Rockefeller's "liberal ideology" and "big spender" reputation,[161] and by liberal Democrats who worried about his tremendous wealth and its political ramifications.[162] Many questioned his judgment regarding the Attica incident, political loans and gifts, and the Goldberg biography.[163] Although a sizable number of representatives opposed confirmation, there was never any doubt about the result. As Representative Otis G. Pike of New York observed, it was obvious that "the TV time has been ordered, the champagne is cooling in the bucket. . . ." [164]

Immediately after the House vote, President Ford traveled with Rockefeller to the Senate Chamber where Rockefeller was sworn in by Chief Justice Burger as the forty-first Vice President of the United States. In a short speech, the new Vice President expressed his "gratitude for the privilege of serving the country I love," and pledged himself to work with the President and Congress to solve the problems facing the nation.[165]

Rockefeller's vice presidency was never to realize the expectations which were expressed by many at the time of his confirmation hearings. Despite his capabilities and willingness to undertake assignments for the President, Rockefeller was unable to quiet the conservative critics who had opposed his nomination. Personal tours of the South and the Midwest and other advances toward conservative Republicans notwithstanding, he continued to be seen as a political liability throughout 1975 as Ford contemplated the 1976 election. By summer 1975 former Representative Howard H. Callaway of Georgia, Ford's campaign manager,

---

† As in the Ford confirmation debates, a number of representatives presented the results of polls they had taken of their constituents. As had not been the case with Ford, the results were adverse to Rockefeller in a number of instances. See, for example, 120 Cong. Rec. H. 12381 (Stratton), 12392 (Crane), 12393 (Ketchum), 12402 (Ichord), 12421 (Randall), 12424 (Carney), 12432 (Goldwater), 12442 (Bingham), 12443 (Bowen); but see 12383 (Studds), 12383 (Jones), 12423 (Paris) (daily ed. Dec. 19, 1974).

was publicly stating that Rockefeller would damage Ford's chances for the nomination, and the President himself was giving no assurances that Rockefeller would be his running mate.[166]

As the nation's economic ills continued and the concept of détente with the Soviet Union was increasingly questioned, Ronald Reagan began to mobilize a conservative challenge to President Ford. Ford seemed more vulnerable than the usual incumbent President. His frequent use of the veto power had cast his presidency in a negative light, and since he had never before waged a national campaign, he had no experienced political organization. To diminish Ford's presidential aura, Reagan emphasized that he had not been elected by a vote of the people.‡ In response, Ford adopted a more conservative stance, and in the fall of 1975 selected New York City's financial crisis as an issue to solidify his Republican support. Ford not only declared that there would be no federal help for New York but also criticized the city and its past leadership in speeches throughout the country. Such criticisms of New York obviously reflected on the vice president who had served as that state's governor for fifteen years.

On November 3, 1975, in a letter to President Ford, Rockefeller announced that he would withdraw his name from consideration for the 1976 vice presidential position so that Ford's " 'range of options' " might be " 'simplified at the earliest time.' " [167] The letter also stated:

> My acceptancy of the Vice-Presidency, as you know, was based upon my concern to help restore national unity and confidence after the shattering experience of Watergate. Working under your leadership toward this goal has been challenging and rewarding as our basic institutions are surmounting our unprecedented crises and the nation is returning to its regular elective Presidential pattern next year.
>
> Regarding next year and my own situation, I have made it clear to you and to the public that I was not a candidate for the Vice-Presidency, that no one realistically can be such, and that the choice of a Vice-Presidential running mate is, and must be, up to the Presidential candidate to recommend to a national party convention.
>
> . . . . I shall, of course, continue to serve as Vice President, to discharge my constitutional obligations and to assist in every way . . . until the installation once again of a President and Vice President duly elected by the people of this great Republic.

At a news conference several days later Rockefeller explained that his possible presence on the ticket was creating " 'party squabbles' " which were distracting the President from the serious problems facing the country. Yet he dismissed the Republican right, which opposed him, as a

---

‡ Reagan was not alone in calling attention to Ford's "unelected status." Similar comments were uttered by a few Democratic public figures during 1975 in speeches critical of Ford. See Yaeger, Letter to the Editor, *N. Y. Times*, Mar 6, 1975 at 36.

" 'minority of a minority.' " He also expressed lukewarm support for President Ford but did not rule out his own possible candidacy in 1976 if Ford should be defeated in the early primaries and withdraw from the race.[168] It was generally thought that Rockefeller had submitted his withdrawal to protect himself from the humiliation of being dumped by Ford at a later time.

While liberal Republicans decried the sacrifice of Rockefeller to their party's right wing, the Rockefeller decision made no great impact on conservatives. Reagan commented: " 'I'm certainly not appeased.' "[169] Simultaneously with the Vice President's withdrawal came the announcement of a major reorganization of Ford's Cabinet. Any gains which the President had scored by Rockefeller's departure were muted by the removal of Secretary of Defense James R. Schlesinger, who had become an outspoken critic of détente and a supporter of increased defense spending. Ford's replacement of him with Donald Rumsfeld and his appointment of George Bush to succeed William Colby at the Central Intelligence Agency incensed many.

Moreover, the reorganization failed to impress a large segment of the nation as a wise exercise of executive leadership.[170] It appeared ill-timed and politically motivated. The reorganization stressed political not policy attributes, and the Rockefeller withdrawal left Ford free to dangle the vice presidential nomination before other segments of the Republican party. As 1975 ended, public opinion polls indicated that Ford's road to obtaining his party's presidential nomination and election to a full four-year term was laden with major obstacles.[171]

NOTES

1. House Comm. on the Judiciary, Report on Confirmation of Nelson A. Rockefeller as Vice President of the United States, H. R. Rep. No. 93–1609, 93d Cong., 2d Sess. 27 (1974).
2. *N. Y. Times*, Aug. 8, 1974 at 23.
3. *Id.* 1.
4. *Id.* 23.
5. *Id.*, Aug. 10, 1974 at 3.
6. *Id.*, Aug. 11, 1974 at 43.
7. *Id.*, Aug. 9, 1974 at 1, 4.
8. *Id.* 4.
9. *Id.*, Aug. 11, 1974 at 43.
10. *Id.*, Aug. 14, 1974 at 16.
11. *Id.*, Aug. 16, 1974 at 10.
12. *Id.*, Aug. 17, 1974 at 15.
13. *Newsweek*, Aug. 26, 1974 at 18.
14. *Id.* 19.
15. *N. Y. Times*, Aug. 19, 1974 at 24.
16. *Newsweek*, Aug. 26, 1974 at 18.
17. *Id.*, Sept. 2, 1974 at 14.

18. Apple, A Turn in G.O.P. Tide, *N. Y. Times*, Aug. 21, 1974 at 1.
19. *Newsweek*, Sept. 2, 1974 at 15.
20. *N. Y. Times*, Aug. 21, 1974 at 26.
21. *Id.* 1.
22. *Id.*, Aug. 22, 1974 at 1.
23. *Id.* 24.
24. *Id.*, Aug. 24, 1974 at 1.
25. *Id.*, Aug. 29, 1974 at 20.
26. *Id.*, Sept. 9, 1974 at 1.
27. *Id.*, Sept. 12, 1974 at 30.
28. *Id.*, Sept. 11, 1974 at 44.
29. *Id.*, Sept. 12, 1974 at 1, 28.
30. Hearings on the Pardon of Richard M. Nixon, and Related Matters, Before the Subcomm. on Criminal Justice of the House Comm. on the Judiciary, 93d Cong., 2d Sess. 90–111, 148–58 (1975).
31. *N. Y. Times*, Sept. 5, 1974 at 19.
32. *Id.*, Sept. 4, 1974 at 16.
33. Senate Comm. on Rules and Administration, Report on Nomination of Nelson A. Rockefeller of New York to be Vice President of the United States, S. Exec. Rep. No. 93–34, 93d Cong., 2d Sess. 4–5 (1974).
34. *N. Y. Times*, Sept. 12, 1974 at 24.
35. *Id.*, Sept. 20, 1974 at 1.
36. *Id.* 21.
37. *Id.*
38. Hearings on Nomination of Nelson A. Rockefeller of New York to be Vice President of the United States Before the Senate Comm. on Rules and Administration, 93d Cong., 2d Sess. 39–79 (1974).
39. *Id.* 128.
40. *Id.* 143.
41. *Id.* 165.
42. *Id.* 23.
43. *Id.* 224.
44. *Id.* 147.
45. *Id.* 22–23.
46. *Id.* 233–61.
47. *Id.* 267–459.
48. *N. Y. Times*, Sept. 25, 1974 at 1.
49. *Newsweek*, Oct. 7, 1974 at 46.
50. *N. Y. Times*, Sept. 30, 1974 at 27.
51. *Id.*, Oct. 6, 1974 at 1, 58.
52. *Id.*
53. *Id.*, Oct. 8, 1974 at 27.
54. *Id.*, Oct. 9, 1974 at 1, 29.
55. 120 Cong. Rec. S. 19171–72 (daily ed. Oct. 15, 1974).
56. *N. Y. Times*, Oct. 9, 1974 at 1, 29.
57. 120 Cong. Rec. S. 18472 (daily ed. Oct. 8, 1974).
58. 120 Cong. Rec. S. 18627–28 (daily ed. Oct. 9, 1974).
59. *N. Y. Times*, Oct. 10, 1974 at 34.
60. Lynn, The Power of Rockefeller Money, *N. Y. Times*, Oct. 9, 1974 at 30.
61. *N. Y. Times*, Oct. 10, 1974 at 1.
62. *Id.* 38.
63. *Id.* 46.
64. *Id.* 1.

65. *Id.*, Oct. 22, 1974 at 1.
66. *Id.*, Oct. 10, 1974 at 34.
67. *Id.*, Oct. 17, 1974 at 27.
68. *Id.*, Oct. 11, 1974 at 1, 16.
69. *Id.* 16.
70. *Id.* 1, 16.
71. *Id.* 1.
72. *Id.*, Oct. 12, 1974 at 1, 14.
73. *Id.* 14.
74. *Id.* 1, 15.
75. *Id.*, Oct. 13, 1974 at 24.
76. *Id.*, Oct. 14, 1974 at 33.
77. *Id.*
78. *Id.*, Oct. 13, 1974 at 1, 23.
79. *Id.* 23.
80. *Id.*, Oct. 14, 1974 at 1, 38.
81. *Id.*, Oct. 15, 1974 at 1, 28.
82. *Id.*, Oct. 17, 1974 at 1.
83. *Id.*, Oct. 19, 1974 at 1, 13.
84. *Id.*, Oct. 20, 1974 at 1.
85. *Id.*
86. *Id.*, Oct. 23, 1974 at 1.
87. *Id.*, Oct. 21, 1974 at 1.
88. *Newsweek*, Oct. 28, 1974 at 30.
89. *N. Y. Times*, Oct. 25, 1974 at 1, 36.
90. *Id.*, Oct. 29, 1974 at 1, 24.
91. Wicker, Mr. Rockefeller's Ordeal, *id.*, Nov. 1, 1974 at 39.
92. *N. Y. Times*, Nov. 13, 1974 at 29.
93. *Id.*
94. Rockefeller Senate Hearings 477.
95. *Id.* 533.
96. *Id.* 477.
97. *Id.* 530–31.
98. *Id.* 533.
99. *Id.* 541.
100. *Id.* 522.
101. *Id.*
102. *Id.* 472.
103. *Id.* 473.
104. *Id.*
105. *Id.* 474.
106. *Id.* 476.
107. *Id.* 475–76, 479.
108. Wicker, Money in Office, *N. Y. Times*, Nov. 15, 1974 at 37.
109. Rockefeller Senate Hearings 617.
110. *Id.* 670–89.
111. *Id.* 673.
112. *Id.* 698.
113. *Id.* 692.
114. *N. Y. Times*, Nov. 15, 1974 at 1, 21.
115. *Id.*, Nov. 16, 1974 at 14.
116. Rockefeller Senate Hearings 710–13.
117. *Id.* 848.

118. *Id.* 849.
119. *Id.* 886.
120. *Id.*
121. *Id.* 897–98.
122. *Id.* 887–89.
123. *N. Y. Times,* Nov. 17, 1974 at 47.
124. *Id.,* Nov. 19, 1974 at 38.
125. Rockefeller Senate Hearings 930.
126. *Id.*
127. *Id.* 930–31.
128. *Id.* 951, 971–74.
129. *Id.* 986.
130. *Id.* 986–87.
131. *Id.* 1015.
132. *Id.* 1025.
133. *Id.* 1025–26.
134. *N. Y. Times,* Nov. 23, 1974 at 1.
135. Hearings on the Nomination of Nelson A. Rockefeller to be Vice President of the United States Before the House Comm. on the Judiciary, 93d Cong., 2d Sess. 2 (1974).
136. *Id.* 186–87, 197.
137. *Id.* 65.
138. *Id.* 169, 195.
139. *Id.* 66–67, 164, 959–64.
140. *Id.* 660.
141. *Id.* 636.
142. *Id.* 717–22.
143. *Id.* 848–49.
144. *Id.* 873.
145. *Id.* 926.
146. *Id.* 1010.
147. 120 Cong. Rec. S. 20783–85 (daily ed. Dec. 9, 1974).
148. *Id.* S. 20788, S. 20790.
149. *Id.* S. 20801.
150. *Id.* S. 20814.
151. *Id.* S. 20814–20.
152. 120 Cong. Rec. S. 20978 (daily ed. Dec. 10, 1974).
153. *Id.* S. 20978–82.
154. *Id.* S. 20993.
155. H. R. Rep. No. 93–1609 at 11 (1974).
156. *Id.* 24.
157. 120 Cong. Rec. H. 12459–60 (daily ed. Dec. 19, 1974).
158. *Id.* H. 12367.
159. *Id.* H. 12439 (Clausen).
160. *Id.* H. 12372 (Hungate).
161. *Id.* H. 12391–92 (Crane).
162. *Id.* H. 12364 (Holtzman).
163. *Id.* H. 12370–71 (Kastenmeier).
164. *Id.* H. 12383.
165. *Id.* S. 22267–68.
166. Exit Rockefeller: A New Equation for 1976, Congressional Quarterly, Nov. 8, 1975 at 2366.
167. *N. Y. Times,* Nov. 4, 1975 at 27.

168. *Id.*, Nov. 7, 1975, at 1, 16.

169. *Id.*, Nov. 4, 1975 at 1.

170. *Id.* at 24. See also Lydon, Ford's First National Campaign: Incumbent in Role of Underdog, *id.*, Dec. 22, 1975 at 1.

171. *N. Y. Times*, Dec. 13, 1975 at 14, discussing the results of a Gallup Poll showing that 40 per cent of Republicans and 27 per cent of independents surveyed in the period November 21–24, 1975 preferred Reagan as the Republican presidential nominee, and that 32 per cent of the Republicans and 25 per cent of the independents preferred Ford. See Ford's 1975: Economy, Energy, Foreign Policy, Congressional Quarterly, Jan. 10, 1976 at 35.

IV

An Evaluation

12

An Analysis of Sections 1, 2, 3, and 4 of the Amendment

> We had more cooks with more zeal concerned with preparing this "broth" than any piece of proposed legislation I have ever seen in the time I have been in the Senate.
>
> SAM J. ERVIN
> July 6, 1965 [1]

SECTION 1

In case of the removal of the President from office or of his death or resignation, the Vice President shall become President.

This Section specifically confirms the Tyler precedent whereby a Vice President becomes President when there is a vacancy in the presidential office because of the President's death.[2] It also extends the precedent to cover vacancies in the presidency caused by resignation and removal after an impeachment.[3] In any of these cases, the Vice President takes the presidential oath [4] and serves as President for the remainder of the unexpired term.[5] The contingency of "inability" is removed entirely from this Section.[6]

SECTION 2

Whenever there is a vacancy in the office of the Vice President, the President shall nominate a Vice President who shall take office upon confirmation by a majority vote of both Houses of Congress.

The congressional debates and hearings in 1964 and 1965 established a number of underlying principles with respect to the meaning and intent of Section 2.[7]

First, the "vacancy" terminology is intended as an abbreviated way of covering situations involving the death, resignation, or removal of the President or Vice President.[8] When the Vice President succeeds to the presidency, he is empowered to nominate a successor.[9] The legislative history is clear that an "inability" of the President resulting in the Vice

President's having to act as President is not a situation involving a vacancy in the vice presidency.[10] Nor is there a vice presidential vacancy when the Vice President becomes disabled.[11] Even the inability of both the President and the Vice President does not bring Section 2 into play.[12] * Moreover, the legislative history is unclear whether a Speaker acting as President upon a President's inability when there is no Vice President should nominate a new Vice President.[13]

Second, the use of "whenever" and "shall" is intended to make clear that the President is required to nominate a person for Vice President in the event of a vacancy.[14] It is not left to his discretion whether or not to nominate, although mention was made in the 1965 House hearings of the possibility of the President's not having to make a nomination when a vacancy occurs just prior to the end of his term.[15]

Third, the terminology "the President shall nominate a Vice President" contemplates that the President submit one name, not several, to the Congress.[16] A proposal made in 1964 for the submission of several names was not accepted for the reason, among others, that it was felt the President should have a free hand in nominating the person he believed best qualified for the office and with whom he could work most closely.[17] Were the President to submit several names, it is questionable whether he would be discharging his obligation under Section 2 of nominating "a Vice President." It is arguable that the submission of several names would in effect transfer to Congress a portion of the nominating function, which function should be exercised exclusively by the President.

In giving the President the role of initiation in filling a vice presidential vacancy, the Amendment follows the historical practice whereby a presidential candidate has a decisive voice in the selection of his running mate.[18] The Amendment's history is replete with statements to the effect that the President should initiate the nomination to ensure a Vice President of the same party for purposes of continuity,[19] and of compatible temperament and views for an effective working relationship.[20] The history also reflects the intent that, before making a nomination, the President seek the advice and views of congressional leaders.[21]

Fourth, should a President's nomination be rejected, the legislative history is plain that the President would be obliged to nominate another person.[22] No limit is placed on the number of nominations which can be made.

Fifth, frequent references are made in the history concerning the "confirmation" role of Congress bringing into play the "advise and consent" check currently in the Constitution with respect to other appointments.[23]

---

* Under these circumstances the 1947 succession law provides for the Speaker to act as President until either the President or Vice President recovers. See Appendix C. However, that law contains no procedures comparable to Sections 3 and 4 of the Twenty-Fifth Amendment.

It was contemplated that there might be occasions on which a nominee's qualifications are so well known and readily acceptable that little debate would be required, and other occasions on which his qualifications might have to be closely scrutinized, which would involve congressional hearings and extensive debate.[24] The wording of Section 2 gives to the President and Congress the power each currently has in the process of selecting officials such as federal judges, ambassadors, and Cabinet members.[25] † That Congress was to be the "voice of the people" is a concept which appears throughout the legislative history,[26] and was a reason for giving the House of Representatives a confirmatory role.

Sixth, the coupling of "nomination" with "confirmation" instead of the "advise and consent" language of Article II was designed to ensure that a nominee cannot act as Vice President pending congressional confirmation.[27] Consequently, if a vacancy should occur when Congress is out of session, it could not be filled until the next regular session or at a special session called for that purpose by the President. Until a vacancy is filled, whoever might be first in the statutory line of succession would be the heir apparent, since the Amendment leaves intact the power of Congress to establish a line of succession beyond the vice presidency.[28] The statutory successor, however, would have no right to act as Vice President because under Article II, section 1 he is limited to acting as President only.[29] Thus, if at a time a vacancy in the vice presidency exists, the President should die, resign, or be removed, the Speaker, upon his resignation from Congress, would fill out the presidential term by reason of the 1947 succession statute.[30] He also would have the power to nominate a Vice President, since, upon succession, he assumes the discharge of all the powers and duties of President.‡ The Speaker's succession to the

---

† However, all aspects of the "advise and consent" process were not intended to be applicable to the nomination of a new Vice President. The involvement of both Houses of Congress was intended to give Congress a more active role in the selection of a Vice President than the Senate's role in passing on other presidential nominations. Secondly, the use of the term "confirmation" in Section 2 was intended to achieve another distinction between the "advise and consent" process and that of selecting a new Vice President. See text accompanying note 27, infra. Thirdly, the rule that the President is under no duty to appoint an officer approved by the Senate would not be applicable, since the selection of a Vice President under the Twenty-Fifth Amendment involves only two steps of nomination and confirmation. Presidential nominations made under Article II involve the steps of nomination, senatorial advice and consent, appointment by the President, and commissioning by the President. See Marbury v. Madison, 1 Cranch 137, 155–57 (1803); see Can the President appoint and sign commissions of persons who have been nominated and confirmed during the administration of his predecessor, Department of Justice, Nov. 26, 1963 (informal staff memorandum).

‡ See note at p. 196, infra. In her treatise Ruth Silva takes the position that the law of 1947 "is based on two irreconcilable premises. It recognizes a designated officer as becoming President by providing for his resignation from his legislative or Cabinet post. At the same time it denies that he becomes President by failing to give him the tenure [i.e., four years] which the Constitution guarantees to a President. It is submitted that this contradiction is rather blatant." Silva, Presidential Succession 142.

presidency would not be affected by a pending vice presidential nomination at the time of the presidential vacancy, since confirmation is essential to filling a vice presidential vacancy.[31] It is not entirely clear whether the intervening events would operate to render the nomination of no further effect. But since nominations made by a President who has died or resigned are treated as still valid when a Vice President succeeds, the result should be no different in the case of a vice presidential nomination, since Section 2 was referred to throughout its legislative history as being analogous to the present "advise and consent" process.[32] It therefore would seem that upon the Speaker's succession he could, and should, either withdraw the nomination and nominate someone else or continue the nomination.* If he continues the nomination and the nominee is confirmed, that nominee would not replace the Speaker but rather would be the Speaker's Vice President, since in the event of a dual vacancy, the 1947 law provides for the Speaker to act as President for the rest of the established term. One interesting example given in the legislative history involves a situation in which the Speaker is nominated to fill a vice presidential vacancy and the President dies while confirmation hearings are in progress. Under such circumstances, it was noted, the Speaker would take over the powers and duties of President for the rest of the term by virtue of the 1947 law.[33]

Seventh, the history of Section 2 manifests the intention that there be both a President and a Vice President at all times [34] and that whenever a vacancy occurs in the latter office, both the President and Congress act with reasonable dispatch to fill it,[35] putting aside partisan politics [36] and seeking, as Representative Rodino stated in the House debates of 1965, the selection of a person of the "highest character and national stature." [37] Originally, S. J. Res. 139 had required the President to make a nomination within thirty days of a vacancy, but the time limit was eliminated because, among other reasons, unforeseeable circumstances might prevent the President from adhering to the limit, thereby causing him to violate the Constitution.[38] A proposal made during the Senate debates to add the word "immediately" to Section 2 was defeated largely because of the concern that it might prevent Congress from conducting a proper investigation of a nominee's background.[39]

---

* Under Rule 38.6 of the Standing Rules of the Senate, a presidential nomination under art. II continues until it is returned to the President as rejected by the Senate, not acted upon when the Congress adjourns for thirty days or more, or withdrawn by the President. There is no similar House rule since, until the Twenty-Fifth Amendment, it had no role in the nomination process. If a vacancy should occur in the office of the President while a vice presidential nomination is pending, it can reasonably be argued that the nomination should subsist in accordance with the general practice of the Senate with respect to other presidential nominations. For a contrary view, see the testimony of Assistant Attorney General Antonin Scalia. Hearing on the First Implementation of Section Two of the Twenty-Fifth Amendment Before the Subcomm. on Constitutional Amendments of the Senate Comm. on the Judiciary, 94th Cong., 1st Sess. 51–55 (1975); but see the 1975 Report of the subcommittee at 5.

Eighth, the phrase "by a majority vote of both Houses of Congress" is similar to that used elsewhere in the Constitution,[40] and is designed to make clear that each House votes separately on a nomination and that the required vote in each is a majority of those members present and voting, provided there is a quorum.[41] A proposal for a two-thirds vote was rejected because it was thought to give too much control to those who might oppose a President.[42]

Ninth, the legislative history also is clear that a nominee for Vice President must meet the constitutional qualifications of being a natural-born citizen of the United States, at least thirty-five years of age, and a resident within the United States for a minimum of fourteen years.[43] Although under the Twelfth Amendment the presidential electors of a state must cast one of their two votes for an inhabitant of another state, a President is not prevented under the Twenty-Fifth Amendment from nominating an inhabitant of his own state.[44]

Tenth, a Vice President selected under the Twenty-Fifth Amendment occupies the same status as an elected Vice President.[45] Thus, when a Vice President succeeds to the presidency, as he did in 1974, he may use the procedures of Section 2.

SECTION 3

Whenever the President transmits to the President pro tempore of the Senate and the Speaker of the House of Representatives his written declaration that he is unable to discharge the powers and duties of his office, and until he transmits to them a written declaration to the contrary, such powers and duties shall be discharged by the Vice President as Acting President.

This Section is designed to make clear that in a case of presidential inability the Vice President simply discharges the powers and duties of the presidency; he assumes neither the office nor the title of President. Rather, he remains the Vice President, exercising presidential power, under the title of Acting President.[46] Accordingly, this Section solves the problem first raised by Tyler's succession to the presidency.

Although the terms "unable" and "inability" are nowhere defined in either Section 3 or 4 of the Amendment (or in Article II), this was not the result of an oversight. Rather, it reflected a judgment that a rigid constitutional definition was undesirable, since cases of inability could take various forms not neatly fitting into such a definition.[47] The presence of a definition would only give rise to difficult questions of interpretation at a time when the country was confronted with a case of inability. The debates surrounding the Twenty-Fifth Amendment indicate that the terms "unable" and "inability" are intended to cover all cases in which some condition or circumstance prevents the President from discharging his powers and duties and the public business requires that the Vice President discharge them.[48] Situations involving physical and mental illness, temporary or permanent, were the most frequently mentioned cases covered by the expression.[49]

Section 3 deals with a case in which the President recognizes his own inability and wishes to suspend temporarily his exercise of the powers and duties of President.[50] It involves a personal judgment on the part of the President.[51] As Representative White noted in the House debates of April 13, 1965, "[t]here is no requirement that a reason be given other than that the President is 'unable' to act. . . ."[52]

The legislative history of Section 3, however, leaves no dispute about the specific types of cases contemplated. It was intended to cover situations such as the President's entering a hospital for an operation or other medical attention, or going abroad where he might be out of effective communication with the White House.[53] Said former Attorney General Brownell during the House hearings:

> A typical situation that is covered by this section is one in which the President is physically ill and his doctors recommend temporary suspension of his normal governmental activities, to facilitate his recovery. Other situations that have been visualized are those where the President might be going to have an operation, or where he was going abroad and might be out of reliable communication with the White House for a short period.[54]

Under Section 3 a President is permitted to declare himself disabled either for an indefinite or a specified period of time, and to name the hour when the Vice President is to begin as Acting President.[55] The declaration could even be conditional and prospective in nature, stating, for example: " '[I]f in the event I am under anesthesia or similarly unable, I wish you to assume those duties. . . .' "[56] Once the Vice President commences his role as Acting President, the Amendment contemplates that he would continue in such capacity until the President terminates it by a subsequent declaration of recovery.

Whether Section 3 is broad enough to cover the case of a President's deciding to step aside temporarily, as was suggested during Nixon's last year in office,[57] in order to devote his full time to his defense against impeachment and removal is a debatable question. Although such a use of the Amendment was never mentioned by the Congress which proposed it, it probably would not be beyond the scope of Section 3, since the Section was intended to be broadly interpreted. However, Section 3 does not provide a mechanism for a President to step aside temporarily without justification, thereby neglecting his duties.

Section 3 encourages a President to declare his own inability since, if he does, his declaration of restoration to capacity is not subject to the challenge procedures of Section 4.[58] "A President would always hesitate to utilize the voluntary mechanism if he knew that a challenge could be lodged when he sought to recapture his office [i.e., its powers and duties]." [59]

The Vice President becomes Acting President as soon as the President transmits a written declaration of inability to the President pro tempore and to the Speaker, or, as the case may be, at the time or under the circumstances specified in the declaration. He ceases to be Acting President as soon as the President transmits his written declaration of recovery to these two officials.[60] Whenever the Vice President is called upon to act as President, he loses his title as President of the Senate.[61] * Whether the Vice President would be required to take the presidential oath before serving as Acting President is not entirely clear. The limited legislative history on this point suggests that the President's oath need not be taken.[62] It would seem that it should not, since the Vice President does not become President and the duty of acting as President is encompassed by his vice presidential oath to perform his duties faithfully.

The legislative history also is not clear on whether the Vice President would be entitled to a presidential salary during the period he serves as Acting President. But again, since he does not become President, it would seem that he should not be so paid, although there is legislative history to the contrary.[63] The succession statute of 1947 specifically provides for a statutory successor to be paid at the presidential salary rate in all cases (i.e., death, resignation, removal, and inability), and Congress could, of course, legislate a similar provision with respect to a Vice President who acts as President in a case of inability.

Because of its flexibility, Section 3 is likely to be used in most cases of presidential inability.

SECTION 4

Whenever the Vice President and a majority of either the principal officers of the executive departments or of such other body as Congress may by law provide, transmit to the President pro tempore of the Senate and the Speaker of the House of Representatives their written declaration that the President is unable to discharge the powers and duties of his office, the Vice President shall immediately assume the powers and duties of the office as Acting President.

Thereafter, when the President transmits to the President pro tempore of the Senate and the Speaker of the House of Representatives his written declaration that no inability exists, he shall resume the powers and duties

---

* The President pro tempore serves in that capacity in the interim, because of U. S. Const. art. I, § 3, cl. 5, which provides: "The Senate shall chuse their other Officers, and also a President pro tempore, in the Absence of the Vice President, or when he shall exercise the Office of President of the United States."

of his office unless the Vice President and a majority of either the principal officers of the executive department or of such other body as Congress may by law provide, transmit within four days to the President pro tempore of the Senate and the Speaker of the House of Representatives their written declaration that the President is unable to discharge the powers and duties of his office. Thereupon Congress shall decide the issue, assembling within forty-eight hours for that purpose if not in session. If the Congress, within twenty-one days after receipt of the latter written declaration, or, if Congress is not in session, within twenty-one days after Congress is required to assemble, determines by two-thirds vote of both Houses that the President is unable to discharge the powers and duties of his office, the Vice President shall continue to discharge the same as Acting President; otherwise, the President shall resume the powers and duties of his office.

This Section, like Section 3, provides for an Acting President in a case of inability. It should be noted, however, that the inability procedures of these Sections do not apply to the inability of a Vice President, or of a Vice President as Acting President, or to a case of simultaneous inabilities of the President and Vice President when the Speaker is designated to serve as President.[64] *

Section 4 covers the most difficult cases of inability—when the President cannot or does not declare his own inability.[65] Cases involving a mental inability were commonly referred to as falling within this section,[66] as were situations in which the President is kidnapped or captured, under an oxygen tent at a time of an enemy attack, or bereft of speech or sight.[67]

As for the cases falling within this Section, Senator Bayh said in the Senate debates of February 19, 1965:

> [T]he word "inability" and the word "unable" as used in [Section 4] . . . , which refer to an impairment of the President's faculties, mean that he is unable either to make or communicate his decisions as to his own competency to execute the powers and duties of his office. I should like for the RECORD to include that as my definition of the words "inability" and "unable." [68]

In the Senate debates of June 30, 1965, Senators Bayh and Robert F. Kennedy referred to cases involving physical or mental inability to make or communicate a decision regarding incapacity and physical or mental inability to exercise the powers and duties of office. The following important exchange took place between Kennedy and Bayh:

> MR. KENNEDY of New York. Is it not true that the inability to which we are referring in the proposed amendment is total inability to exercise the powers and duties of the office?

* Language to deal with these contingencies was placed in the record by Representative Poff. Hearings on Presidential Inability and Vice Presidential Vacancy Before the House Comm. on the Judiciary, 89th Cong., 1st Sess. 86 (1965).

MR. BAYH. The inability that we deal with here is described several times in the amendment itself as the inability of the President to perform the powers and duties of office.

It is conceivable that a President might be able to walk, for example, and thus, by the definition of some people, might be physically able, but at the same time he might not possess the mental capacity to make a decision and perform the powers and duties of his office. We are talking about inability to perform the constitutional duties of the office of President.

MR. KENNEDY of New York. And that has to be total disability to perform the powers and duties of the office.

MR. BAYH. The Senator is correct. We are not getting into a position, through the pending measure, in which when a President makes an unpopular decision, he would immediately be rendered unable to perform the duties of his office.

MR. KENNEDY of New York. Is it limited to mental inability to make or communicate his decision regarding his capacity and mental inability to perform the powers and duties prescribed by law?

MR. BAYH. I do not believe that we should limit it to mental disability. It is conceivable that the President might fall into the hands of the enemy, for example.

MR. KENNEDY of New York. It involves physical or mental inability to make or communicate his decision regarding his capacity and physical or mental inability to exercise the powers and duties of his office.

MR. BAYH. The Senator is correct. That is very important. I would refer the Senator back to the definition which I read into the RECORD at the time the Senate passed this measure earlier this year.

MR. KENNEDY of New York. It was that definition which I was seeking to reemphasize. May I ask one other question? Is it not true that the inability referred to must be expected to be of long duration or at least one whose duration is uncertain and might persist?

MR. BAYH. Here again I think one of the advantages of this particular amendment is the leeway it gives us. We are not talking about the kind of inability in which the President went to the dentist and was under anesthesia. It is not that type of inability we are talking about, but the Cabinet, as well as the Vice President and Congress, are going to have to judge the severity of the disability and the problems that face our country.

MR. KENNEDY of New York. Is it not true that what we are talking about here as far as inability is concerned, is not a brief or temporary inability?

MR. BAYH. We are talking about one that would seriously impair the President's ability to perform the powers and duties of his office.

MR. KENNEDY of New York. Could a President have such inability for a short period of time?

MR. BAYH. A President who was unconscious for 30 minutes when missiles were flying toward this country might only be disabled temporarily, but it would be of severe consequence when viewed in the light of the problems facing the country.

So at that time, even for that short duration, someone would have to make a decision. But a disability which has persisted for only a short time would ordinarily be excluded. If a President were unable to make an Executive decision which might have severe consequences for the country, I think we would be better off under the conditions of the amendment.[69]

In the House debates of April 13, 1965, Representative Poff said that Section 4 provides for two categories of cases: (1) when the President "by reason of some physical ailment or some sudden accident is unconscious or paralyzed and therefore unable to make or to communicate" a decision; and (2) "when the President, by reason of mental debility is unable or unwilling to make any rational decision, including particularly the decision to stand aside." [70]

At various times in the debates and hearings of 1964 and 1965, it was made clear that unpopularity, incompetence, impeachable conduct, poor judgment, and laziness do not constitute an "inability" within the meaning of the Amendment.[71] As Senator Bayh stated in the Senate debates of February 19, 1965:

The Senator from Indiana agrees with the Senator from Michigan [Hart] that we are not dealing with an unpopular decision that must be made in time of trial and which might render the President unpopular. We are talking about a President who is unable to perform the powers and duties of his office.[72]

Under Section 4 the Vice President and a majority † of the "principal officers of the executive departments" (popularly known as the Cabinet) are empowered to declare the President disabled by transmitting a written declaration of this fact to the President pro tempore and to the Speaker.[73] Few subjects received as much attention as that of the composition of the Cabinet. The debates make clear that the following ten officials were intended, plus the head of any executive department established after July 1965: ‡ Secretaries of State, Treasury, Defense, Interior, Agriculture, Commerce, Labor, and Health, Education and Welfare, the Attorney General, and the Postmaster General.[74] The following were not intended: the United States Representative to the

---

† A "majority" and not unanimous action was decided upon in order to take care of a situation where one member "might be entirely out of sympathy with the national administration." 1965 House Hearings 248.

‡ In September 1965 Congress created a Department of Housing and Urban Development and in October 1966 a Department of Transportation, whose Secretaries also would participate as members of the Cabinet. The expression "executive departments" is used in Section 4 in both the singular and the plural. The use of the singular was inadvertent; the plural was what was intended, as is demonstrated from all the prior versions of that Section. See Appendix A.

United Nations, the Secretaries of Army, Navy, and the Air Force, the Director of the Poverty Program, and the head of the Atomic Energy Commission.[75] Whether an Under Secretary can participate as a member of the Cabinet when there is a Cabinet vacancy was dealt with by the House Judiciary Committee in its report:

> In case of the death, resignation, absence, or sickness of the head of any executive department, the acting head of the department would be authorized to participate in a presidential inability determination.[76] §

A different view was expressed in the Senate debates of February 19, 1965;[77] but the view of the House Judiciary Committee, which I believe to be the correct one, was articulated by Senator Robert Kennedy in the Senate debates of June 30, 1965,[78] and was assumed by a number of senators on both June 30 and July 6, 1965, when the discussion centered on the firing and replacement of Cabinet members.[79] These later debates, as well as the earlier Senate debate, also indicate that a recess appointee to the Cabinet would be able to participate in the determination of inability.[80] With respect to the Senate debate of February 19 and the statement that an Under Secretary would not participate when there is a vacancy, it should be noted that the principal subject of discussion concerned not vacancies but whether the expression "heads of the executive departments" included subdivision and bureau heads. Indeed, a memorandum from the Library of Congress was placed in the record to indicate that the latter were not intended to be included.[81]

Under Section 4 the declaration of inability probably would be a joint one, although the Vice President and Cabinet might choose to send separate declarations.[82] In answer to the question concerning the way in which a written declaration might be prepared under Section 4, Brownell stated:

> Undoubtedly the Justice Department would prepare the papers, and the action would be taken at a joint meeting of the Vice President and the Cabinet members. It might not even be a matter of public knowledge as to who signed first. That particular point would fade into insignificance in getting the group action.[83]

The question of whether an inability had occurred could be initiated for discussion purposes by the Vice President or by any member of the Cabinet.[84]

Upon the transmittal of a declaration of inability to the Speaker and the President pro tempore, the Vice President immediately takes over as Acting President and is entitled to discharge all the powers and duties

---

§ It also should be pointed out that 5 U.S.C. § 4 (1964) specifically provides that, in the case of the death, resignation, absence, or sickness of a department head, the first assistant of the department shall, unless otherwise directed by the President, perform the duties of the head.

of President.[85] It makes no difference that Congress is not in session at the time of such transmittal.[86] During the period in which the Vice President serves as Acting President, the President is prevented from exercising his powers and duties.[87]

Once the President announces his recovery by transmitting an appropriate written declaration to the Speaker and the President pro tempore, he then must wait four days before resuming his powers and duties.[88] In the meantime, the Vice President continues to act as President,[89] and he and the Cabinet have an opportunity to revie\ the situation. Either the Vice President alone or the Cabinet and Vice President can agree to the President's taking over immediately or at any time short of four days.[90] If they disagree with the President's declaration of recovery, they are required to send, within four days, a written declaration of that fact to the President pro tempore and the Speaker, and Congress then is required to decide the issue, with each House meeting separately.[91] If there is a disagreement between the Vice President and Cabinet about the President's recovery, the issue is not appropriate for Congress to decide and the President then resumes his powers and duties. Agreement between the Vice President and Cabinet that the President has not recovered is a condition which must precede congressional consideration.[92] If Congress is not in session at the time an issue of disagreement is raised, it is obliged to assemble within forty-eight hours from the time the Vice President and Cabinet transmit their declaration to the President pro tempore and the Speaker. It is incumbent upon the Vice President as Acting President to fix a certain time within forty-eight hours when Congress must assemble.[93] If he fails to do so, the President pro tempore and the Speaker are obliged to call their respective Houses into session within the forty-eight–hour period.[94] Upon their failure to do so, Congress must come into session within forty-eight hours on its own initiative.[95]

Congress has twenty-one days from the date of receipt of the transmittal, if it is in session, or from the time it is required to assemble, if not in session, in which to decide a disagreement issue.[96] Pending the decision of Congress, the Vice President continues to act as President, so that the powers and duties of President will not be in the hands of a person whose capacity has been seriously challenged.[97] * Furthermore, by allowing the Vice President to continue as Acting President during

* During the hearings Attorney General Katzenbach observed: "Now, I suppose the two problems that one is dealing with are the risk to the country of a period, however short, where a President who really is unable, nonetheless declares ability, and the problem, how quick the congressional action could be gotten in that situation and the risk to the country in that period of time, as against the problem that you raised, Mr. Chairman, of the usurper, which is the traditional fear of Vice Presidents in exercising their power, that they would be so regarded." Hearings on Presidential Inability and Vacancies in the Office of Vice President Before the Subcomm. on Constitutional Amendments of the Senate Comm. on the Judiciary, 89th Cong., 1st Sess. 17 (1965).

this period, there would be fewer transfers of power and more continuity. Otherwise, there would be a ping-pong sort of situation where the Vice President takes over as a result of an inability declaration, the President returns immediately by making a recovery declaration, and the Vice President returns by virtue of Congress' decision in his favor on the disagreement issue.[98]

Congress has three choices under the twenty-one–day limitation: to decide in favor of the President; to decide in favor of the Vice President; or to reach no decision at all.[99] Said Poff:

> Circumstances may be such that the Congress by tacit agreement may want to uphold the President in some manner which will not amount to a public rebuke of the Vice President who is then Acting President. . . . [This] option furnishes the graceful vehicle.[100]

If Congress fails to reach a decision within this time, or if more than one-third of either House sides with the President, the President automatically reassumes his powers and duties.[101] "[I]f one House voted but failed to get the necessary two-thirds majority, the other House would be precluded from using the 21 days and the President would immediately resume the powers and duties of his office." [102] The twenty-one–day limit is an outside limitation, it being the Amendment's intent that Congress act as speedily as possible under the circumstances presented. If Congress fails to act until the twenty-second day, its decision will be of no effect, since the President automatically would have resumed the discharge of his powers and duties at the end of the twenty-first day. Of course, the Vice President and Cabinet would have the power to reactivate the procedures of Section 4, since there is no limit on the number of times those procedures can be used. The two-thirds vote is of those present and voting, provided there is a quorum.[103] In deciding the issue, Congress can proceed as it thinks best. It can prescribe rules governing the process.[104] Thus, it may request that the President undergo medical tests and examinations or submit to questioning at hearings.[105] As Senator Hruska said:

> Obviously, such a decision must rest on the relevant and reliable facts regarding the President's physical or mental faculties. It must be divorced from any thoughts of political advantage, personal prejudice, or other extraneous factors.[106]

If a challenge is resolved in favor of a Vice President by a two-thirds vote of both Houses,† he continues as the Acting President until the President recovers from his inability. Since an inability decision does not result in the President's removal from office, there is nothing to prevent him, after an adverse congressional decision, from issuing another re-

---

† This requirement is even more strict than that in the case of impeachment since only a simple majority vote to impeach is required of the House of Representatives.

covery declaration, thereby activating the process again.[107] The debates indicate that a congressional decision supporting either the President or Vice President is not subject to judicial review.[108]

If future circumstances indicate that the Cabinet is not a workable body, Congress would have the power under Section 4 to entrust to another body the responsibility of deciding, with the Vice President, a question of presidential inability.[109] This power can be exercised even in the midst of a case of presidential inability as, for example, when a Cabinet refuses to declare an obviously sick President unable.[110] But any legislation adopted by Congress is subject to the President's veto power.[111] The debates make clear that Congress' power with respect to the creation of "another body" is vast. It can designate itself,[112] expand or restrict the membership of the Cabinet,[113] combine the Cabinet with other officials,[114] require a unanimous vote of the body established by law,[115] and prescribe the rules and procedures to be followed by that body.[116] As Senator Javits stated:

> Congress has the right to provide for the exclusivity of that body in exercising this authority, as well as the way in which the body shall exercise that authority, and other pertinent details necessary to the creation of such a body, its continuance, its way of meeting, the rules of the procedure, and the way in which it shall exercise its power.[117]

This power, however, cannot be exercised to replace the Vice President.[118] The legislative history of the "other body" provision clearly shows that, when Congress designates such a body, it replaces the Cabinet as the group which must act in conjunction with the Vice President.[119] In this connection, it must be emphasized that the provisions of Sections 3 and 4 cannot operate without a Vice President. He is the key to the effectiveness of the procedures prescribed in the Amendment.[120]

During the hearings and debates criticism was voiced that the President could discharge Cabinet members before they had a chance to declare him disabled, thus nullifying that prescribed method.[121] While the possibility of removal is there, if a President were to act in such a manner, Congress could cope with the situation by exercising its power under Section 4 to establish another body. Another observation was that a Vice President acting as President would have the presidential powers of appointing and removing Cabinet members during his tenure as Acting President.[122] Should he use these powers for the purpose of stacking the Cabinet in his favor, the President, having declared himself disabled under Section 3, could regain his powers and duties immediately by a declaration of recovery. If the President were declared disabled under Section 4, he could issue a recovery declaration and, assuming a challenge by the Vice President and Cabinet within four days, could get Congress to pass on the issue. Congress certainly would not look favorably on a Vice President who had acted in an irresponsible manner.

The record is replete with suggestions that irresponsible behavior also might subject a Vice President to impeachment.[123]

NOTES

1. 111 Cong. Rec. 15594–95 (1965).
2. Hearings on Presidential Inability and Vacancies in the Office of Vice President Before the Subcomm. on Constitutional Amendments of the Senate Comm. on the Judiciary, 89th Cong., 1st Sess. 8, 86 (1965); Hearings on Presidential Inability and Vice Presidential Vacancy Before the House Comm. on the Judiciary, 89th Cong., 1st Sess. 40 (1965); Senate Comm. on the Judiciary, Report on Presidential Inability and Vacancies in the Office of Vice President, S. Rep. No. 66, 89th Cong., 1st Sess. 12 (1965); House Comm. on the Judiciary, Report on Presidential Inability and Vacancies in the Office of Vice President, H. R. Rep. No. 203, 89th Cong., 1st Sess. 12 (1965); 111 Cong. Rec. 7942, 7953, 7955, 15378 (1965).
3. 1965 Senate Hearings 8; Hearings on Presidential Inability and Vacancies in the Office of Vice President Before the Subcomm. on Constitutional Amendments of the Senate Comm. on the Judiciary, 88th Cong., 2d Sess. 68 (1964); Senate Comm. on the Judiciary, Report on Presidential Inability and Vacancies in the Office of Vice President, S. Rep. No. 1382, 88th Cong., 2d Sess. 11 (1964).
4. 1965 Senate Hearings 8.
5. Id. 106; 109 Cong. Rec. 24420 (1963) (Bayh).
6. S. Rep. No. 66 at 12 (1965).
7. This author collected this legislative history in a memorandum dated September 24, 1973 to Senator Bayh, which was reprinted in S. Doc. No. 93–42, Selected Materials on the Twenty-Fifth Amendment, 93d Cong., 1st Sess. 279–300 (1973).
8. 1965 House Hearings 44, 87, 196, 246; H. R. Rep. No. 203 at 18 (1965); 111 Cong. Rec. 3252 (1965) (Bayh); 1964 Senate Hearings 68; 109 Cong. Rec. 24421 (1963) (Bayh).
9. 111 Cong. Rec. 3253–56 (1965).
10. 1965 House Hearings 87, 192–93, 239, 246; 111 Cong. Rec. 3253 (1965) (Bayh, Hruska).
11. 111 Cong. Rec. 3253 (1965) (Bayh, Hruska).
12. 1965 House Hearings 77–78; 111 Cong. Rec. 3265–68 (1965) (Dirksen).
13. 111 Cong. Rec. 3253 (1965) (Bayh, Hruska).
14. S. Rep. No. 1382 at 13 (1964).
15. 1965 House Hearings 65–66.
16. 111 Cong. Rec. 7955 (1965) (Rodino); 110 Cong. Rec. 22988, 22996, 22999 (1964).
17. For relevant proposals, see H. J. Res. 818, 88th Cong., 1st Sess. (1963); H. R. 9305, 88th Cong., 1st Sess. (1963).
18. 1965 Senate Hearings 62; 1964 Senate Hearings 4, 68, 137; 109 Cong. Rec. 24421 (1963) (Bayh).
19. 1965 Senate Hearings 62, 64; 1965 House Hearings 179; 111 Cong. Rec. 3255, 3262 (1965); 1964 Senate Hearings 4, 226; S. Rep. No. 1382 at 13 (1964); 110 Cong. Rec. 22988 (1964) (Ervin); 109 Cong. Rec. 24421 (1963) (Bayh). One of the reasons for the rejection of the proposal that Congress select a new Vice President was that it might not ensure a member of the same party as the President's. 1964 Senate Hearings 28, 89.
20. 1965 Senate Hearings 11, 106; S. Rep. No. 66 at 15 (1965); H. R. Rep.

No. 203 at 15 (1965); 111 Cong. Rec. 3255 (Bayh), 3262 (Fong) (1965); 1964 Senate Hearings 4, 60, 121, 138; S. Rep. No. 1382 at 13 (1964); 110 Cong. Rec. 22988 (Bayh), 22994 (Fong), 23060 (Bayh) (1964).

21. 1965 House Hearings 210; 1964 Senate Hearings 130–31.

22. 1965 House Hearings 50, 54; 1964 Senate Hearings 62, 205.

23. 1965 House Hearings 89, 92; 111 Cong. Rec. 3275 (1965) (Bayh); 1964 Senate Hearings 68.

24. 1965 House Hearings 256; 1964 Senate Hearings 39, 62, 81, 218; 110 Cong. Rec. 22996 (1964) (Monroney).

25. 1965 House Hearings 45, 49, 89.

26. 1965 Senate Hearings 11; 1965 House Hearings 179; 111 Cong. Rec. 3255–56 (1965) (Ervin); 1964 Senate Hearings 60; 110 Cong. Rec. 22994 (Bible), 22996 (Bayh) (1964).

27. 1965 House Hearings 45; 111 Cong. Rec. 7955 (1965) (Rodino).

28. 111 Cong. Rec. 7951 (Mathias), 7960 (Poff) (1965).

29. 1965 House Hearings 49, 78.

30. 1965 Senate Hearings 102; 1965 House Hearings 48; 111 Cong. Rec. 3281 (Ervin), 7960 (Poff) (1965); 110 Cong. Rec. 22995 (1964) (Bayh).

31. 1965 House Hearings 47, 49–50; 111 Cong. Rec. 3281–82 (Bass), 7961 (Rogers) (1965).

32. Note 25, *supra.*

33. 1965 House Hearings 50.

34. 111 Cong. Rec. 3252 (Bayh), 7949 (Cohelan), 7953 (Bennett), 7960 (Celler) (1965).

35. 1965 Senate Hearings 64; 1965 House Hearings 66; 111 Cong. Rec. 7962 (Lindsay) (1965); 1964 Senate Hearings 229.

36. 1965 House Hearings 47; 111 Cong. Rec. 3275 (1965) (Bayh); 1964 Senate Hearings 226; 110 Cong. Rec. 22988 (Bayh), 22996 (Bayh), 22999 (Church) (1964).

37. 111 Cong. Rec. 7955 (1965). An almost identical view had been expressed earlier by Senator Bayh. 110 Cong. Rec. 22987 (1964).

38. 1965 House Hearings 65–66.

39. See pp. 93–94, *supra.*

40. E.g., U. S. Const. art. V. See *Missouri Pac. Ry.* v. *Kansas,* 248 U.S. 276 (1919).

41. 1965 Senate Hearings 10, 52, 64; 1965 House Hearings 45, 60, 95–96, 101, 106; 111 Cong. Rec. 7944–46 (1965).

42. 1965 Senate Hearings 19.

43. 1965 House Hearings 48–49; S. Rep. No. 66 at 14 (1965); H. R. Rep. No. 203 at 14 (1965).

44. 1965 Senate Hearings 18. This question was raised after Agnew's resignation when Ronald Reagan was being mentioned as Nixon's possible vice presidential choice. *N. Y. Times,* Oct. 11, 1973 at 35.

45. 1965 House Hearings 208.

46. 111 Cong. Rec. 7953 (1965) (Gilbert); 1964 Senate Hearings 224–32; Hearings on Presidential Inability Before the Subcomm. on Constitutional Amendments of the Senate Comm. on the Judiciary, 88th Cong., 1st Sess. 33, 38 (1963).

47. 111 Cong. Rec. 7938 (Celler), 7941 (Poff) (1965).

48. 1965 Senate Hearings 20; 1965 House Hearings 40; 1964 Senate Hearings 215; 1963 Senate Hearings 49, 106 & n. 44.

49. E.g., 1964 Senate Hearings 60; 1963 Senate Hearings 106 & n. 44; see Silva, *Presidential Succession* 171.

50. 111 Cong. Rec. 7946–47 (1965) (McClory).

51. 1965 House Hearings 179.

52. 111 Cong. Rec. 7958 (1965).

53. 1965 Senate Hearings 9, 20, 64–65; 1965 House Hearings 40; 111 Cong. Rec. 3265, 7941 (Poff), 7946–47 (McClory), 7955 (Rodino) (1965); 1964 Senate Hearings 136; 1963 Senate Hearings 22.

54. 1965 House Hearings 240.

55. 1965 Senate Hearings 20–21, 64–65; 1965 House Hearings 96–99, 240.

56. 1965 House Hearings 99.

57. Williams, An Alternative: Taking the Twenty-Fifth, National Review 476 (1974). See Feerick, The Way of the 25th, *N. Y. Times*, Dec. 13, 1973 at 47. See also Chapter 10, nn. 25–28, *supra*.

58. 1965 House Hearings 264–65; S. Rep. No. 66 at 3 (1965); H. Rep. No. 203 at 2 (1965); 111 Cong. Rec. 7938 (Celler), 7941 (Poff), 7943 (Horton), 7953 (Gilbert), 7956 (Randall), 15214 (Poff), 15378 (Bayh) (1965). There was confusion early in the legislative history on whether a President who had voluntarily declared his own inability nevertheless was subject to the challenge procedures of Section 4 (then Section 5). Compare 1965 House Hearings 41–42, 99, with 111 Cong. Rec. 3252–53 (Bayh), 3271 (Bayh) (1965). The House amendment to Section 3 (see pp. 98–99, *supra*) eliminated this doubt. 111 Cong. Rec. 15214 (1965).

59. 111 Cong. Rec. 7941 (1965) (Poff).

60. See S. Rep. No. 66 at 2 (1965) for an excellent summary of the congressional intent regarding written declarations. See pp. 89–90, *supra*.

61. 111 Cong. Rec. 3270 (1965) (Saltonstall).

62. 1964 Senate Hearings 215, 232; 1965 House Hearings 87. But see 111 Cong. Rec. 7950 (1965) (Moore).

63. 1965 House Hearings 88.

64. 111 Cong. Rec. 3253 (1965) (Hruska, Bayh); 1965 House Hearings 77–78, 193.

65. 1965 Senate Hearings 9; 111 Cong. Rec. 3254 (Bayh), 3282–83, 7938 (Celler), 15380 (Kennedy) (1965); 1964 Senate Hearings 44; 109 Cong. Rec. 24421 (1963).

66. 111 Cong. Rec. 3256 (Ervin), 7941 (Poff), 7947 (McClory), 15593 (Bayh) (1965).

67. 1965 House Hearings 141; 111 Cong. Rec. 3265 (Carlson), 3271 (Bayh), 7938 (Celler) (1965).

68. 111 Cong. Rec. 3282 (1965).

69. *Id.* 15381.

70. *Id.* 7941.

71. *Id.* 3282–83 (Hart); 1964 Senate Hearings 25.

72. 111 Cong. Rec. 3283 (1965).

73. *Id.* 7938 (Celler).

74. *Id.* (Waggonner), 7941 (Poff), 7944–45 (Whitener), 7952, 7954 (Gilbert).

75. 1965 House Hearings 52, 61.

76. H. Rep. No. 203 at 3 (1965).

77. 111 Cong. Rec. 3284 (1965) (Hart).

78. *Id.* 15380.

79. *Id.* (Kennedy), 15382 (Kennedy), 15385 (Javits).

80. Notes 78 and 79, *supra*, and 111 Cong. Rec. 3284 (1965) (Bayh, Hart).

81. Note 75, *supra*.

82. 1965 House Hearings 79–80; 111 Cong. Rec. 15385 (1965) (Bayh, Javits).

83. 1965 House Hearings 247.

84. 1965 Senate Hearings 65; 1965 House Hearings 79–80, 82.

85. 1965 House Hearings 40, 64–65, 87–88; 111 Cong. Rec. 7956 (1965) (Randall).

86. 111 Cong. Rec. 3270 (Saltonstall, Ervin), 7956 (Randall) (1965).

87. Note 85, *supra*.

88. 111 Cong. Rec. 15214 (Poff), 15378–79 (Bayh) (1965); S. Rep. No. 66 at 14 (1965); H. Rep. No. 203 at 14 (1965).

89. 111 Cong. Rec. 3284 (Bayh), 3285 (Allot), 7939 (Celler) (1965); 1965 House Hearings 41, 58, 250, 253.

90. 1965 House Hearings 99, 107, 243; 111 Cong. Rec. 3285 (Bayh), 15214 (Poff) (1965). As for the declaration's taking effect later than four days, see 1965 House Hearings 242–43.

91. See note 41, *supra*; 1965 Senate Hearings 52, 71; 111 Cong. Rec. 3285 (Hruska), 7944 (Whitener, Celler), 7946 (Hutchinson, Celler) (1965).

92. 111 Cong. Rec. 7941 (Poff), 15379 (Bayh) (1965).

93. 1965 House Hearings 100; 111 Cong. Rec. 7967 (1965) (Poff, Celler).

94. 1965 House Hearings 100; S. Rep. No. 66 at 2 (1965); 111 Cong. Rec. 3270, 7967 (Poff), 7968 (McCormack) (1965).

95. S. Rep. No. 66 at 2 (1965); 111 Cong. Rec. 7968 (1965) (McCormack).

96. Conference Committee, Report on Presidential Inability and Vacancies in the Office of Vice President, H. R. Rep. No. 564, 89th Cong., 1st Sess. 4 (1965).

97. 1965 House Hearings 41, 58, 250, 253; 111 Cong. Rec. 3284–85 (Lausche, Bayh), 7939 (Celler); 1964 Senate Hearings 130.

98. 111 Cong. Rec. 3284 (1965) (Bayh).

99. *Id.* 7941 (Poff).

100. *Id.*

101. 111 Cong. Rec. 3279 (Bayh), 15214 (Poff), 15379 (Bayh) (1965); H. Rep. No. 564 at 4 (1965).

102. 111 Cong. Rec. 15379 (1965) (Bayh).

103. 1965 House Hearings 243.

104. S. Rep. No. 66 at 3 (1965); 111 Cong. Rec. 3285 (Bayh), 15385 (Javits, Bayh) (1965).

105. 1965 Senate Hearings 21–22; S. Rep. No. 66 at 3 (1965); 111 Cong. Rec. 3278–79, 7939, 7954 (1965); 1964 Senate Hearings 119. On the question of the President's asserting a doctor–patient privilege, see 1965 House Hearings 143–44.

106. 1965 Senate Hearings 34.

107. 1965 House Hearings 101–02, 251 (frequent declarations).

108. 111 Cong. Rec. 15588 (Ervin) (1965). The debates, however, indicate that questions involving the constitutionality of legislation passed by Congress under Section 4 would be appropriate for judicial review. 111 Cong. Rec. 15386 (Javits), 15594 (Bayh) (1965).

109. 1965 Senate Hearings 52, 61; 1965 House Hearings 45, 241, 253; S. Rep. No. 66 at 14 (1965); 111 Cong. Rec. 3257 (Bayh), 7941 (Poff), 15380 (Bayh) (1965); 1964 Senate Hearings 44.

110. 111 Cong. Rec. 3284 (Lausche, Bayh), 15382 (Bayh), 15589–92 (1965).

111. *Id.* 3257 (Bayh), 3284 (Bayh); 1964 Senate Hearings 44.

112. 111 Cong. Rec. 7957 (1965) (Tenzer).

113. *Id.* 3258 (Tydings), 7941 (Poff), 15385 (Bayh).

114. *Id.* 3258 (Tydings), 7941 (Poff).

115. 1965 House Hearings 254.

116. S. Rep. No. 66 at 3 (1965); 111 Cong. Rec. 15595 (1965) (Javits).

117. 111 Cong. Rec. 15386 (1965).

118. 111 Cong. Rec. 15379 (Bayh), 15383–86, 15586–96 (1965).

119. 1965 House Hearings 93. See pp. 106–07, *supra*. 111 Cong. Rec. 15383–85 (1965).
120. 1965 Senate Hearings 24; 1965 House Hearings 58, 84–85, 108; 111 Cong. Rec. 7963 (Celler), 15379 (Bayh), 15383 (McCarthy), 15586 (Gore) (1965).
121. See pp. 105–06, *supra*; 1965 Senate Hearings 28. A firing after a decision had been made should have no effect on that decision.
122. 1965 Senate Hearings 28; 111 Cong. Rec. 15590 (Gore, Ervin), 15592 (Bayh) (1965).
123. 1965 House Hearings 62, 81, 88; 111 Cong. Rec. 15383 (1965).

13

An Appraisal

On the brief record of the 25th Amendment, it has served the nation well under extraordinary and unforeseen circumstances.

JAMES RESTON
November 1, 1974 [1]

THE EXTRAORDINARY OCCURRENCE of the resignations of an elected President and Vice President within the same four-year term and their replacement by a President and Vice President selected under Section 2 of the Twenty-Fifth Amendment has drawn considerable attention to the Amendment's procedures for the filling of vice presidential vacancies.

In any appraisal * of the Amendment, one must start with the function it played in shaping the extraordinary events of 1973 and 1974. As Representative Rodino stated at the 1975 review hearings on the Twenty-Fifth Amendment before the Senate Subcommittee on Constitutional Amendments:

> Had there been no amendment, not only would the Nixon and Agnew resignations still have left the nation without a nationally elected executive, but the uncertainty and partisan divisions which would have been inherent in the operation of the succession statutes might have threatened the very constitutional process which ultimately preserved our institutions. Or, barring that, they might have rendered any "new administration" wholly unable to govern.
>
> The 25th amendment permitted the constitutional process to proceed in such a way that the American people could have confidence that no one sought partisan advantage.

* The appraisal contained in this chapter does not deal with the presidential inability provisions of Sections 3 and 4 of the Amendment since, unlike Section 2, they have not yet been implemented. The importance of these Sections has, however, been emphasized throughout this book. The number of assassinations and near assassinations of American leaders since 1963, including two attempts on the life of President Ford in September 1975, serve as a clear reminder of the ever present possibility of a President's being rendered disabled, thereby triggering the procedures of either Section 3 or 4. Nor is it surprising that the health of presidential candidates has become a subject of far greater public discussion than ever before in American history. See, for example, Reston, Are the Old Men Fit?, N. Y. Times, Oct. 26, 1975, § 4 (News of the Week in Review) at 15; id., Jan. 28, 1976 at 54 (report on the health of President Ford); id., Feb. 10, 1976 at 31. Indeed, a proposal for compulsory health examinations of a presidential candidate was considered, though not accepted, by the governing board of the citizens' lobby Common Cause.

He also said:

> I think it is unquestionable that without section 2 of the 25th amendment, this Nation might not have endured nearly so well the ordeal of its recent constitutional crisis.†

When charges of criminal wrongdoing were leveled against Vice President Agnew, the option of resignation was viable partially because there existed procedures under which a new Vice President could be selected from the same party as that of the President. Had the Amendment not been operative, it is quite possible that significant pressure against resignation might have developed because a resignation would have placed a member of the opposition party at the head of the line of succession. With the Amendment in place, however, the President, Vice President, and Attorney General were able to consider whether a resignation was in the national interest without having to worry about a lack of executive continuity should something happen to the President during the remainder of his term.

The existence of the Amendment also assisted the country in passing through one of its greatest tests: impeachment proceedings against a President. Since the Amendment had operated to replace a Republican Vice President with another Republican Vice President, Congress was able to deal with the question of impeachment in the following months with the knowledge that it could not be charged with attempting to install its Speaker as President and thereby turn over control of the executive to a different political party. This is to be contrasted with the situation in 1868 when impeachment proceedings were brought against President Andrew Johnson. Then the President pro tempore of the Senate, Benjamin Wade, stood first in the line of succession, participated in the impeachment proceedings in the Senate, and voted in favor of Johnson's removal from office.‡ Wade's participation in that proceeding was widely criticized at the time and was one of the factors which led Congress in 1886 to remove the President pro tempore and the Speaker from the line of succession.

---

† See Hearing on the First Implementation of Section Two of the Twenty-Fifth Amendment Before the Subcomm. on Constitutional Amendments of the Senate Comm. on the Judiciary, 94th Cong., 1st Sess. 34–35 (1975). In its report the subcommittee noted: "There was general agreement that without the 25th Amendment it would have been much more difficult for President Nixon to resign, thus forcing the country through a prolonged and divisive impeachment trial. In addition the character of the entire investigative process of the House Judiciary Committee investigation might well have been changed, increasing political motivation and decreasing the objective pursuit of what was in the national interest." Report of the Subcomm. on Constitutional Amendments of the Senate Comm. on the Judiciary, 94th Cong., 1st Sess., A Review of the Implementation of Section 2 of the 25th Amendment, 3 (Comm. Print 1975). The subcommittee concluded that no change in the Amendment was warranted.

‡ It is reported that at the time he cast his vote Wade had already selected his Cabinet. D. Young, *American Roulette: The History and Dilemma of the Vice Presidency* 82 (1972); L. Thomas, *The First President Johnson* 595 (1968).

But in 1974, because of the Twenty-Fifth Amendment, President Nixon was able to resign without having to surrender his party's control of the White House. Had the Republicans lost it then, instead of having two of their leaders serve out the existing term, the consequences to the party itself might well have been devastating. Indeed, the resignations of both of its national leaders, without an opportunity for two other members of the party to restore credibility to the federal government, might have operated to prevent the Republicans from being an effective force in national politics for a substantial period of time and, it may be argued, might even have led to a disintegration of the party at all levels of government.

Finally, upon President Nixon's resignation, the Amendment made it possible for the country to enjoy a swift, orderly, and undisputed transfer of executive power. Gerald Ford was immediately recognized as the new President, a fact which served as a unifying and stabilizing force throughout the country. Indeed, the acceptance accorded Ford is a great tribute to the American system.

Against the backdrop of the circumstances under which the Twenty-Fifth Amendment had to operate, the conclusion is inescapable that the process worked exceedingly well in the selection of two Vice Presidents. Ford's selection was the smoother and speedier of the two,§ and seems to have been the result of a grand compromise. The congressional leaders made it clear that Congress did not want the President to nominate a person then considered a potential Republican presidential candidate in 1976, and Nixon undoubtedly wanted to avoid a stiff confirmation battle and to restore credibility to his administration, lest there be further damage to his efforts to avoid impeachment. It is not clear whether he was also motivated by a belief that the installation as Vice President of a person who had never been considered for the presidency would provide an impediment to impeachment. In any event, Gerald Ford came to be viewed by both the President and Congress as the ideal nominee under the circumstances. Although he was a relative stranger to large segments of the country and had never been a serious candidate for high national office, Ford was well known to and respected by the body which had to pass on his nomination, and he possessed the much desired qualities of openness and integrity.

In the case of the Rockefeller selection, since the nominee enjoyed a pre-eminent position in his party and possessed the experience and ability to be an outstanding Vice President, his nomination by Ford measured up to the high standards intended by the Twenty-Fifth Amendment in the selection of a Vice President. As Clifton Daniel of *The New York Times* observed, the Amendment enabled the President to nominate "one of the most experienced public officials in America" without "re-

§ From nomination to confirmation, a period of 57 days elapsed, in contrast to 121 days in the case of Rockefeller.

gard to the usual political considerations that prevail in a national political convention and a Presidential election." [2]

Although it is risky to generalize, the selections of Ford and Rockefeller indicate that a lame duck President may have difficulty filling a vice presidential vacancy with a potential candidate for President, while a President eligible for re-election may have an easier time with the nomination of a national figure. Yet both selections suggest that public opinion and the press can be counted on to guard against any potential for political abuse which exists under the Amendment. These forces contributed significantly to the thorough inquiries to which Ford and Rockefeller were exposed, and influenced Congress not to extract a pledge from Ford with respect to running for President in 1976, not to defer action on Ford's nomination pending completion of the impeachment inquiry, and not to drag out Rockefeller's confirmation for decision by a new Congress.

PROPOSALS FOR REFORM

The occupancy of both the presidency and the vice presidency by officials selected under Section 2 of the Twenty-Fifth Amendment has given rise to a number of proposals to change our present system of presidential succession.[3] These proposals range from outright abolition of both the vice presidency and the Twenty-Fifth Amendment [4] to modification of the Amendment to provide for a special presidential election upon the succession of a Vice President.

Thus, historian Arthur Schlesinger and others favor the abolition of the vice presidency and the adoption of a procedure for a speedy presidential election whenever a vacancy occurs in the presidency, with the Secretary of State acting as President in the interim.[5] They have argued that the use of appointed leaders is not consistent with our democracy and the principle of government by the people. Said Senator Edward Kennedy: "I believe the campaign trail is the surest road to choose a President who will be an effective national leader in foreign and domestic policy." [6]

Senator John Pastore of Rhode Island has proposed a constitutional amendment which would require a special election for President and Vice President whenever an appointed Vice President succeeds to the presidency and more than twelve months remain in the presidential term.[7] At the time he presented his proposal in 1973 Pastore argued that, should the nation be governed by an appointed President and Vice President, it will no longer "be democratically governed" and "a constitutional crisis will occur." [8] Under Pastore's proposal, an appointed Vice President who succeeds to the presidency would be prohibited from invoking the procedures of Section 2 to nominate a new Vice President. Instead, the Speaker of the House would act as Vice President * during the special election period while continuing to discharge his duties as Speaker. He would not, however, have the vice presidential duty of serving as President of the Senate. In the event of a need to cast a tie-breaking vote in the Senate, Pastore's proposal provides for the Secretary of State to discharge that duty. Pastore's proposal also specifies that the President and Vice President who are elected in a special election serve for the remainder of the established term.

It also has been proposed that whenever a vacancy occurs in the vice presidency it should be filled by a special election open to candidates of both parties.[9] Another variation is to limit the election to candidates of the President's party. Still others propose that the presidential succession statute of 1947 be amended to provide for a special presidential election whenever simultaneous vacancies exist in the offices of President and Vice President.[10] Some of these legislative proposals have the Speaker serving as President in the interim, while another approach is for the House Minority Leader to serve in that capacity if his party had occupied the White House as a result of the last presidential election.[11]

Other proposals include removing the presiding officers of Congress entirely from the line of succession in favor of a straight Cabinet line; requiring a President's nomination under Section 2 of the Twenty-Fifth Amendment to be submitted to a popular referendum for approval or disapproval; convening the last electoral college to select a Vice President whenever an elected or appointed Vice President succeeds to the presidency; convening the last electoral college to select a new President and Vice President whenever both offices become vacant or an appointed Vice President succeeds to the presidency; and electing two Vice Presidents in the regular quadrennial election.[12]

Senator Robert Griffin of Michigan,[13] Tom Wicker of *The New York Times*, and others have advanced the interesting idea that only candidates for the presidency should run in our regular quadrennial election and that, after taking office, a new President should nominate a person for Vice President under the procedures of the Twenty-Fifth Amendment. In advancing this idea, Wicker has stated:

> The fact is that Presidents dictate their choices for Vice President with ruthless disregard of any but political qualifications, and political conventions approve them with no "inquisition" at all. The further fact is that no Vice President is really elected by the people or their electors; he is an appendage to their Presidential choice.[14]

* In addition to his constitutional duties of succeeding to the presidency, presiding over the Senate, and participating in a declaration of presidential inability, the Vice President is a statutory member of the National Security Council and, by custom, a member of the Cabinet.

President Ford has suggested that Section 2 of the Twenty-Fifth Amendment be amended to provide specific time limits in which a President must nominate and Congress must confirm or reject a nominee.[15]

The proposals to change our institutions constitute in my view an over-reaction to the Watergate crises, which are attributable more to the weaknesses of human beings than to flaws in our governmental system. As it stands, the present record does not furnish sufficient justification for modifying a carefully designed constitutional amendment which came close to being unanimously endorsed by both Houses of Congress in 1964 and 1965. As Walter Lippmann said of the Amendment in general: "[I]t is . . . a great deal better than an endless search for . . . the absolutely perfect solution which will never be found, and . . . is not necessary." [16] There are so many possible combinations of circumstances that no single solution can be expected to handle each one perfectly. As Lewis Powell observed during the 1965 hearings before the House Judiciary Committee, "it is not necessary . . . that we find a solution free from all reasonable objection. It is unlikely that such a solution will ever be found, as the problems are inherently complex and difficult." [17] So far nothing indicates that the Twenty-Fifth Amendment cannot handle all the possible contingencies reasonably well; and, in any case, it is highly doubtful that it will ever again encounter such difficult tests as those which confronted it in 1973 and 1974. Surely, as James MacGregor Burns noted, the Amendment "has been subjected to extraordinary circumstances" and "deserves an opportunity to operate in normal times before we scrap it." [18]

Abolition of the Vice Presidency

The suggestion to abolish the vice presidency is an old chestnut which, if accepted, would substantially change our system of presidential succession. While the vice presidency has been an object of scorn and satire throughout history, the office has contributed significantly to the stability and continuity of our government in difficult circumstances. Under the system of vice presidential succession to the presidency, we have had only peaceful transfers of presidential authority. Moreover, since World War II the occupants of the vice presidency have provided useful assistance to our Presidents in the discharge of their responsibilities.

Abolishing the vice presidency and providing for a Speaker or Secretary of State to act temporarily as President in the event of a presidential vacancy could seriously undermine the stability and continuity of our government. Possibly neither would possess the constitutional qualifications for President or have been chosen for his ability to serve as President. But even if they should possess the qualifications, it is doubtful whether either would be recognized as a true President since he would occupy the White House only as a caretaker—that is, until a President and Vice President would be selected in a special election. It is also questionable whether a caretaker could deal effectively with Congress or exercise any real leadership domestically. Foreign leaders too might be encouraged to defer dealing with a caretaker while awaiting the election of a President. Furthermore, it could happen that the caretaker might be of a different party from the last President, so that his succession would lack continuity with the administration of the President he replaced. As Senator Frank Moss of Utah observed about John Kennedy's assassination:

> Consider what could have happened had the next man in line of succession been a man of opposite political persuasion. At best he would have had only secondhand information on Kennedy policies, and he could have been hostile to them. There would have been the turmoil of an immediate Cabinet shuffle, and changes in other appointive positions in the Government. We would have been taking the risk of a slowdown in Government business, and perhaps a breakdown which would have taken all of our capabilities to master. I do not believe that world order in the age of the atom, the supersonic flight, and instant communications can tolerate that sort of leadership strain in the most powerful country in the world.
>
> And even had the man next in line for the Presidential succession after the Kennedy assassination been a man of similar political faith in the legislative body, the takeover could not have been as untroubled and smooth. A legislative officer, engrossed as he is in business on Capitol Hill, cannot know as much about the business of the executive branch as does the Vice President who is constantly participating in it.[19]

In contrast, a person chosen as a potential presidential successor under the Twenty-Fifth Amendment will necessarily possess the constitutional qualifications and will have been judged on his or her ability to serve as President. Section 2 of the Twenty-Fifth Amendment also assures continuity of party and administration.

The abolition of the vice presidency also would vitiate the presidential inability provisions of the Twenty-Fifth Amendment which depend on the availability of a Vice President. The Amendment embodies a number of checks and balances designed to protect the President. One such check is that a President's Cabinet, or any body established by Congress, has no power to declare a President disabled without the concurrence of the Vice President. Obviously, substituting in effect the Secretary of State or Speaker for the Vice President would remove this important check and possibly impair the independence of the presidency.

Furthermore, to abolish the office of an elected Vice President in favor of the Speaker or the Secretary of State acting temporarily as President in the event of a vacancy would substantially increase the likelihood of persons not elected nationally serving as President, since we have lost a President on the average of once every twenty years. Although the Speaker reaches his position in Congress by choice of the majority party in the House of Representatives, he is elected to Congress by the voters of but one of the 435 congressional districts in the country, and in no way is he chosen as a presidential prospect. The Secretary of State, on the other hand, may never have been elected to any public office. When Truman succeeded to the presidency, the presence of Secretary of State Edward R. Stettinius, Jr. at the head of the line of succession brought sharp criticism, since he had never been elected to a public office and lacked the type of political experience necessary for the presidency. As a consequence, Stettinius was forced to resign as Secretary of State. A Vice President, however, enjoys a nationwide popular base. Although a vice presidential candidate is closely tied to his party's presidential candidate, the people elect the Vice President, realizing that he may succeed to the presidency during the ensuing term. Furthermore, a Vice President usually has before his election, or acquires while serving as Vice President, the type of governmental and political experience which is necessary for dealing effectively with Congress in the event of his succession to the presidency. A Vice President, by virtue of his relationship with the President and Congress, is best able to prepare himself for possible succession to the presidency and to make any such succession truly effective. The record of vice presidential successions, especially in this century, demonstrates the wisdom of the framers in providing for an office of Vice President.

Special Election for President and Vice President

The proposals to abolish the vice presidency or to provide for a presidential election for a new President and Vice President whenever a Vice President succeeds to the presidency would change important principles which have operated throughout our experience with presidential succession—those of the stability and continuity of the elected President's four-year term.

The leading advocate of abolishing the vice presidency, Arthur Schlesinger, has emphasized the importance of continuity in urging that the Speaker, because he might be of the opposition party, not act as President during the period of a special election. A change in party control, said Schlesinger, "would be a graver infringement of the democratic principle than the provisional service of an appointed officer as acting President." He added: "Fidelity to the results of the last election and to the requirements of continuity in policy creates, it seems to me, an irresistible argument for returning the line of provisional descent to the executive branch." [20] * It may be observed that this was the rationale used to support the procedures of Section 2 of the Twenty-Fifth Amendment.

By assuring, as we now do through vice presidential succession, that the President's party will continue to occupy the office of President for the full four years, the four-year electoral mandate, which is a fundamental part of our existing system, is respected and protected.† Procedures for a special presidential election could lend weight to efforts to force an unpopular President from office. Indeed, it is noteworthy that some of those who advocate this proposal believe the Constitution should provide specifically for a special election whenever Congress finds that the President has lost popular confidence.[21]

Another objection to a special presidential election system is that the triggering events (e.g., death of a President and Vice President) might not be conducive to the holding of a special election. As Max Lerner noted:

> The death, resignation or impeachment of a President is bound to be a scarring event or part of a scarring process. It is a tense, even a tragic, moment. It isn't a good time to hold a presidential convention and election campaign, with all their polarizing impact. It is best at that moment to have someone ready and able to act, who has been chosen for the succession and whom the people have come to accept in that role.[22]

When some "thunderclap of history suddenly carries away a President, either by death or forced resignation," observed James Reston, there is a need for "reflection, calm and unity—three qualities seldom present in Presidential elections." [23] Though it may be argued that after a Watergate type of crisis an election might be desirable for its cleansing effects, it is of dubious wisdom to hold one immediately after the assassination or death of a President.‡ To date, our experiences with presidential succes-

---

* In its 1975 report the Subcommittee on Constitutional Amendments stated: "In effect, the Amendment helps insure that the popular mandate from the previous election will be continued throughout the regular four-year term. More rapid changes in policy would tend to promote instability as well as prevent a fair appraisal and evaluation of the policies of the political party which had won the previous election." *Id.* 2.

† In a statement to the Senate Judiciary Committee in 1964, Senator Eugene J. McCarthy stated: "The succession law should respect the mandate of the people, who vote not only for a man but also, in a broad way, for his party and his program. The elevation of a leader of another party in midterm is undesirable in principle and could have most unfortunate practical effects." Hearings on Presidential Inability and Vacancies in the Office of Vice President Before the Subcomm. on Constitutional Amendments of the Senate Comm. on the Judiciary, 88th Cong., 2d Sess. 208 (1964).

‡ In speaking of the widespread remorse and the great outpouring of intense public feeling caused by President Kennedy's assassination, Professor Fred I. Greenstein observed: "Historical accounts make it clear that at least since the death of Lincoln, every presidential death in office—those of Roosevelt, McKinley, Garfield, and even Harding—have produced similar public responses. Something in presidential incumbency itself

sion do not indicate that an election is necessary to furnish a mandate to govern.

The extant proposals for a special election gloss over numerous practical problems. They ignore, for example, such questions as whether a special election would entail the present six-month system of primaries and conventions, followed by a two-month period of post-convention campaigning, and then followed by a two-month period of counting and certifying the votes and declaring the winners. The suggestion of a special election within a period of two or three months disregards a salient feature of the American presidential election system: namely, the importance of a significant pre-convention testing period for candidates to develop and be scrutinized by the people. Donald R. Matthews of The Brookings Institution noted:

> The process that culminates in the popular choice of a president begins years before election day, and a long sequence of events determines the alternatives from which the voters choose. . . . How, and how well, the preliminary screening process works is thus at least as important as what happens on election day. . . .[24]

Under a quick presidential election procedure there is a serious risk that the type of candidates who are now produced might not emerge and that party bosses would be given inordinate power in the selection process. Former party candidates, incumbents, and persons of wealth would have a distinct advantage, while newer candidates would have practically no opportunity to develop.* But bringing into play the present system of nomination and election of a President in a special presidential election process would mean that during the interim period of almost a year the presidency would be occupied by a caretaker, with the possible consequences noted earlier in this chapter.

Another objection is that, under some of the special election proposals, we could have as many as four elections in as many years.† Such a circumstance would leave little time for governing. This remote possibility becomes less remote under the proposal calling for a special presidential election every time an elected Vice President succeeds to the presidency.

---

evidently has been responsible for these reactions since the deaths of other public figures, including ex-Presidents, were by no means as emotionally moving to such large numbers of citizens." *Choosing the President* 124 (Barber ed., 1974).

* Another area in need of analysis is the financing of a special election. In order to compete effectively in any election, candidates generally need time to raise money to cover their campaign costs. Obviously, a special election telescoped into a short period of time would put poorer and less known candidates at a considerable disadvantage.

† That is, two regular quadrennial elections plus two special elections. For example, if the principle of vice presidential succession for the rest of the term were scrapped, the death, resignation or removal of a President would immediately trigger a special election. Similarly, if one of these events occurred during the tenure of the next President, another special election would take place. At the end of the four-year period which began with the first President, there would be a regular election unless the specially elected President and Vice President were selected for a four-year period.

Although we have not had vice presidential successions in consecutive administrations, the events of the last thirty years indicate that we must be prepared for even the most remote of eventualities. It is highly questionable whether the gains to be derived from a presidential succession system involving a special election would compensate for losing the stability and continuity inherent in our existing system of presidential succession.

The theory, offered in support of the special election proposals, that an appointment of President and Vice President violates the design of the framers is an over-simplification. The framers did not provide for a system of presidential election by the people. Indeed, proposals for a system of direct, popular election were specifically rejected at the Constitutional Convention of 1787. What the framers deliberately designed was an indirect system of choice of President and Vice President. As Alexander Hamilton described the system: "A small number of persons, selected by their fellow-citizens from the general mass, will be most likely to possess the information and discernment requisite to such complicated investigation." [25] In fact, many framers believed it would happen frequently that no candidate would receive the votes of a majority of the electors. Under such circumstances it was, and still is, provided that the House of Representatives choose a President and the Senate a Vice President.* It should likewise be noted that the framers placed no requirement in the Constitution that the people select the presidential electors, but rather left the manner of their appointment to the state legislatures. Thus, in the first few elections presidential electors were chosen in most states by the members of the state legislatures. It was not until 1832 that every state, except one, had vested the people with the choice of selection of the electors.[26] Furthermore, since the congressional caucus was the principal nominating vehicle from 1796 through 1820, early Presidents in effect were chosen by Congress.

Although some of the framers felt that the electoral college system should become operative whenever double vacancies occur in the offices of President and Vice President, Article II nonetheless empowers Congress to designate the official who would act as President in the event of such vacancies. Furthermore, the first succession law in 1792 allowed (at a time when senators were selected by state legislatures †) for the possi-

---

* These contingency provisions, which are found in Article II and in the Twelfth Amendment, were used to select a President in 1801 and 1825 and a Vice President in 1837. Other contingency provisions involving congressional participation in selecting a President and Vice President are found in the Twentieth Amendment, which provides, among other things, for Congress to cover the case wherein neither a President-elect nor a Vice President-elect shall have qualified, and for the case of the death of any of the persons from whom the House and Senate are to select a President and Vice President whenever the choice devolves upon them because of the absence of an electoral majority.

† It was not until 1913 that this indirect method of selection of senators was replaced by direct, popular election.

bility of an appointed President pro tempore of the Senate acting in that capacity for a period of up to seventeen months.

Consequently, in assigning the confirmation of the Vice President to Congress, the Twenty-Fifth Amendment provides a selection process no less democratic than (*a*) the system originally conceived for the election of the President, or (*b*) the currently effective method for selecting the President and Vice President in case of the failure of an electoral majority, or (*c*) the historical succession statutes.

A specific analysis of the major proposals follows:

1. *Pastore's Special Election Proposal*

The proposal advanced by Senator Pastore would institutionalize the caretaker presidency, since a Vice President selected under the Twenty-Fifth Amendment would not become President for the rest of the term but only until a special election is held. Under such circumstances it is questionable whether a succeeding appointed–Vice President would be capable of providing effective leadership. And yet it is precisely at such a time, after the loss of the elected President and Vice President, that strong leadership is necessary.

By requiring a special election if more than one year remains in the term, Pastore's proposal entails such impractical situations as the specially elected President and Vice President running immediately again. In fact, two presidential elections could take place in the same year. To illustrate: if a vacancy were to occur late in the third year of a term, the special election cycle would be triggered shortly before the regular quadrennial process is to begin. Such a situation would be confusing and make little sense. Even if the proposal provided that two years must remain in the term before a special election would take place, the following possibility is left open: if the vacancy should occur late in the second year of a term, the special election would take place in the third year and then be followed shortly by the regular quadrennial election in the fourth year. Only a double vacancy occurring in the first year of a term or early in the second year would not be followed on its heels by another presidential election.

The designation under Pastore's proposal of the Speaker of the House of Representatives to act as Vice President in the period preceding a special election would have the additional disadvantage of blending the legislative and executive branches in an undesirable relationship. The Speaker would be placed in an untenable position if, as Acting Vice President, he should participate in the executive decision-making processes of the Cabinet and National Security Council and then, as a member of Congress, participate in the legislative process with respect to executive decisions. The problem would be exacerbated if the Speaker were a member of a different party. The designation of the Speaker as Acting

Vice President would also violate the design of the presidential inability features of the Twenty-Fifth Amendment, which contemplate a Vice President of the same party as the President. A President who became disabled and wished to declare his own inability under the procedures of Section 3 might hesitate to do so if the Speaker, unlike the Vice President a person not of the President's choosing, were a member of the other party. Further, the mechanism of Section 4 for declaring a President disabled is premised on a Vice President of the President's party, in part to prevent Congress from assigning to itself a decision to declare a President disabled. Yet, if the Speaker were the Acting Vice President, by virtue of its power under Section 4 to replace the Cabinet as the body to function with the Vice President, Congress would be in a position during the interim period to determine a case of inability involving the caretaker.

Finally, since Senator Pastore's proposal would deprive a Vice President of a major part of his existing constitutional function,* it could discourage able persons from accepting a vice presidential nomination under Section 2. There also might be a tendency for less emphasis to be given in the selection process to a nominee's presidential qualifications since his tenure would be of a caretaker nature.

2. *Statutory Special Election Proposals*

The suggestion to amend the 1947 succession law to provide for a special election in the event of double vacancies in the offices of President and Vice President is impractical and dangerous. The matter of a special election is so clouded with uncertainty and controversy that serious questions would be raised after simultaneous vacancies regarding the legitimacy of such a transfer of presidential power, a matter about which there should be absolute certainty. One of the hallmarks of our presidential succession system has been the swift, smooth, unquestioned, and undisputed manner by which presidential power has been transferred whenever a vacancy has occurred in the presidency.

With respect to this proposal, one must start with the question whether Congress has the power to pass such a law. Though there is evidence that the framers of the Constitution left open the possibility of a special election in Article II, the existence of congressional power to establish such a system has been disputed by a number of constitutional scholars as well as by members of Congress during past discussions of our succession laws.[27] Indeed, in 1867, the House Judiciary Committee felt there was no such power, although the same committee reached a different conclusion in 1945.[28] One of the principal architects of the 1947 succession law, Senator Burton Wheeler, expressed strong reservations about the constitutionality of a special election law. Others felt that such an election

* That is, upon succession, serving as President for the rest of the term.

would not be practical. As a consequence, the proposal was rejected in the deliberations leading to the 1947 law, and the principle was established that when the Speaker or the President pro tempore acts as President, he does so for the remainder of the President's term (except in a case of inability or failure to qualify).

But even if there were such legislative power, there is the question of the elected President's tenure. Since the Constitution provides only for a four-year term for an elected President and Vice President commencing on January 20, it is unclear whether Congress has the power to provide that a specially elected President and Vice President serve only for the duration of the existing term, which was the basis of the special election proposal advanced during the deliberations on the 1947 law. In view of the provision of Article II that an elected President "shall hold his Office during the term of four years," it is hard to see how Congress could by statute prescribe a shorter term. If Congress were to recognize a four-year term for a specially elected President and Vice President, the present cycle of concurrent presidential and congressional elections would be changed.*

A further question exists concerning the election of a Vice President in a special presidential election. By virtue of the Twelfth Amendment, a President and Vice President are always elected together. Yet the Twenty-Fifth Amendment prescribes a procedure for filling a vice presidential vacancy. Therefore, it may be argued that whenever a statutory successor acts as President, he is under an obligation to exercise the constitutional power to nominate a Vice President under Section 2 of the Twenty-Fifth Amendment, who, when confirmed, would serve out his predecessor's term. Therefore, the argument goes, the availability of the Twenty-Fifth Amendment procedure would preclude the election of a Vice President in a special presidential election.

3. Special Election for Vice President

The suggestion for filling a vice presidential vacancy by means of a special vice presidential election ignores certain practical considerations. If, as has been suggested, the election were open to candidates of both parties, it would be possible for a Vice President to be selected from the opposite party or from a wing of the President's party which is openly antagonistic to him. This possibility would be extremely harmful to the office of President because it would set up a potentially divisive force within the executive branch. Our two national officers might find them-

---

* Of course, a special presidential election could be held at the mid-term congressional elections. For proponents of this approach, see Feerick, The Vice-Presidency and the Problems of Presidential Succession and Inability, 32 Fordham L. Rev. 484 & n. 164 (1964).

selves at odds on many issues and competing for public attention, thereby contributing to ineffective executive leadership. Indeed, a Vice President of another party or one incompatible with the President might have nothing to do but stir up trouble.

Furthermore, a special election for Vice President would involve changes in Article II, in the Twelfth and Twentieth Amendments, and in state constitutions and election laws. It would present complicated problems on the nature of the election process—such as whether candidates for Vice President would run in state primaries, be nominated by a national convention, and then campaign for a period of time prior to election day. But were there such a cycle, the new Vice President might well enter office with a mandate quite different from that of the President, who would have been chosen at an earlier time. As long as we continue our present system of presidential and vice presidential candidates running as a team, there seems little justification for a special election for Vice President.

4. Use of the Last Electoral College

The use of the last electoral college also would introduce problems. There would be little, if any, opportunity for the electors to scrutinize candidates for Vice President, with all the risks the absence of scrutiny entails. Even if they had investigatory powers, the electors would be largely unknown and unaccountable to the public. Since their meeting would not be preceded by an election, they would be without any popular mandate in choosing a Vice President. This would vest in a body generally viewed as being without discretionary authority a considerable amount of discretion. Such circumstances could produce a situation in which a majority of the electors would be unable to agree on one candidate. Indeed, the special election and electoral college proposals for filling a vice presidential vacancy would increase the risk of having to resort to the present procedure of the Twelfth Amendment involving the Senate only, since such an election likely would encourage a number of candidates to get into the field, with the resultant possibility of no one's winning a majority of the electoral votes. It would be ironic if, after providing for a special vice presidential election, the selection had to be made by Congress anyway, and by only one-half of the Congress at that.

Changes in Section 2 of the Twenty-Fifth Amendment

Implementing President Ford's suggestion of time limits for the filling of vice presidential vacancies is undesirable. Neither the President nor the Congress should be straitjacketed in discharging their responsibilities. The period of time required for the rendering of a congressional judgment obviously will vary from nominee to nominee. Some nominees will be better known than others and require less time for Congress to render its judgment. Others may require a great deal of time because of the need to study charges raised during the confirmation process. The time period also will be influenced by the press of other congressional business. Furthermore, the existence of time limits could present legal difficulties if they were exceeded.

If, in view of the long delay in confirming Nelson Rockefeller, a time limit on confirmation is deemed necessary, the better course of action would be to provide for it in the rules of both Houses rather than in a new constitutional amendment. Congress, I believe, has the power so to provide in its rules in discharging its responsibilities under the Twenty-Fifth Amendment; still, it should be noted that the framers of the Amendment rejected the use of time limits. One advantage of dealing with them by congressional rules is that Congress would have the flexibility to change any limit which in the light of experience it found to be too short or too long. To freeze limits in the Constitution would require another constitutional amendment to change them—unless, of course, the amendment gave Congress the power to change the specified limits.

But none of this is intended to suggest that Congress should not render its judgment on a vice presidential nomination with reasonable dispatch. The time involved in passing judgment on Rockefeller's nomination could have been shortened had Congress accepted a recommendation, made in July 1974 by a Special Committee of the American Bar Association, that a single joint hearing be utilized in passing on vice presidential nominations. The ABA noted that a "joint inquiry not only would eliminate duplication of effort but would tend to increase the effectiveness of the inquiry, since the resources of both Houses would be combined, coordinated and utilized to best advantage." [29] Although the Twenty-Fifth Amendment requires each House to vote separately, Congress has the power, by making appropriate changes in its rules, to use a joint hearing to probe a candidate's qualifications. In fact, there was considerable support for such an idea following Agnew's resignation,* but it appears that political considerations killed the proposal. A review of the record of the Ford and Rockefeller confirmation hearings reveals considerable duplication of effort. Both committees drew on the same investigatory arms of government, heard many of the same witnesses, and covered many of the same matters. Although each committee served as a check

---

* Indeed, during the hearings before the Senate Committee on Rules and Administration, Chairman Cannon expressed his personal preference for a joint hearing. Hearings on Nomination of Gerald R. Ford of Michigan to be Vice President of the United States Before the Senate Committee on Rules and Administration, 93rd Cong., 1st Sess. 149–50 (1973). Chairman Rodino expressed a contrary view during the 1975 review hearings on the Twenty-Fifth Amendment before the Subcommittee on Constitutional Amendments.

on the other, and although matters were dealt with by one which were not covered by the other, the record does not indicate that these advantages of dual hearings outweigh the advantages of a single hearing. After all, nominees for the United States Supreme Court, the Cabinet, and other key posts are subject to a single hearing. Of course, if there were to be a single joint hearing in the selection of a Vice President, the committee should be large enough to have representation from both parties geographically and ideologically.

Although some consider the idea of any hearings on the qualifications of vice presidential nominees to be unseemly and demeaning,[30] recent experiences underscore the desirability of thorough scrutiny of candidates for high office. The exhaustive inquiries into the nominations of Ford and Rockefeller came at a time when the integrity of all public officials was being questioned. Hence, one useful by-product of the hearings was to emphasize the high standards of conduct expected of persons who aspire to the presidency and vice presidency. It is interesting that, because of these hearings, the suggestion has been made that all Vice Presidents be chosen under the procedures of Section 2.[31] If past statistics are any indication, this proposal would involve a Vice President selected under the Twenty-Fifth Amendment serving as President on the average of one term out of five. If there is a need, as seems evident, for greater scrutiny in the pre-nomination period for vice presidential nominees, the political parties should improve their own selection procedures. To assign this function to Congress after inauguration day would divert the attention of a new President at a time when it is essential that his team be intact and that he be developing the policies and programs of his administration, and would create an unavoidable period during which there would be no Vice President.

As for the suggestion that a President under the threat of impeachment not be permitted to nominate a successor, such a limitation in Section 2 would seem unnecessary. In the first place, the Constitution reflects the policy that until he is impeached and removed, the President has the obligation to discharge his duties. Indeed, the framers specifically rejected a proposal under which the President would be suspended from exercising his powers and duties upon his impeachment by the House of Representatives. Secondly, Congress shares with the President the power of selecting a new Vice President. If a particular nomination is improper, Congress can and ought to reject it. Thirdly, the acceptance of Gerald Ford as President, despite his nomination by a President whose removal was a distinct possibility at the time the nomination was made, shows that the process can work properly in the face of a threatened impeachment. Finally, to include such a limitation in Section 2 might invite impeachment resolutions against a President at a time of a vice presidential vacancy.

The further criticism of the Amendment on the ground that it sets no standards for the selection of a Vice President is unfair. It cannot be expected to prescribe more than the procedures for handling a vacancy. Nowhere does the Constitution set any standards by which to judge a person's ability to perform in office. The absence of standards obviously means that it is left to the President and to Congress to make their own judgments, utilizing whatever tests and historical perspectives they feel are appropriate.* Congress and the President share an independent responsibility to ensure that only persons qualified to be President are chosen for Vice President. In my opinion, the executive and legislative branches discharged their responsibilities well in the first implementations of the Twenty-Fifth Amendment.

NOTES

1. *N. Y. Times,* Nov. 1, 1974 at 39.

2. Daniel, Ford and 25th Amendment: Rockefeller Choice Held Free of Party Pressure, *id.,* Dec. 23, 1974 at 17.

3. See generally, The Twenty-Fifth Amendment, Congressional Quarterly, Jan. 4, 1975 at 35–36; Charlton, 25th Amendment: Its Critics Say Amend or Abandon It, *N. Y. Times,* News of the Week in Review, Nov. 17, 1974 at 4; Large, The 25th Amendment—An Appraisal, *Wall Street Journal,* Jan. 6, 1975 at 12.

4. H. J. Res. 124, 94th Cong., 1st Sess. (1975) (Gonzalez).

5. Schlesinger, Is the Vice Presidency Necessary?, 233 Atlantic Monthly 37 (May 1974); On the Presidential Succession, 89 Pol. Sci. Q. 475 (1974); and What to Do About a Nonjob, *N. Y. Times,* Nov. 29, 1974 at 39.

6. Kennedy, The Constitution and the Campaign Trail, *N. Y. Times,* Oct. 21, 1974 at 33.

7. S. J. Res. 26, 94th Cong., 1st Sess. (1975); S. J. Res. 172, 93d Cong., 1st Sess. (1973); for Senator Pastore's comments, see 120 Cong. Rec. S. 1370–73 (daily ed. Feb. 3, 1975); 119 Cong. Rec. 37217–19 (1973); Pastore, Special Election Best Way to Fill the Vacancies, *L. A. Times,* Nov. 17, 1974, § 8 at 5.

8. 119 Cong. Rec. 37217 (1973).

9. Peabody, On the Threshold of the White House, 234 Atlantic Monthly 63 (July 1974).

10. H. R. 11230 (Abzug), H. R. 11243 (Moakley), H. R. 11439 (Moakley), S. 2678 (Hathaway), 93d Cong., 1st Sess. (1973); H. R. 1714 (Mink), 94th Cong., 1st Sess. (1975). See White, For a Special Presidential Election, *N. Y. Times,* Oct. 30, 1973 at 43; Schlesinger, Back to the Founding Fathers?, *Wall Street Journal,* Oct. 31, 1973 at 16.

11. See S. 2678, 93d Cong., 1st Sess. (1973).

* It should be pointed out, however, that the debates surrounding the adoption of the Twenty-Fifth Amendment repeatedly speak of the President's being permitted to nominate a person of his own political party and ideology who might carry on the mandate of the prior presidential election. It may be argued that a Congress dissatisfied with the ideology of the President should not require a different philosophy from a vice presidential nominee, since that would change the last election mandate and to some extent add to the American system the British vote of "no confidence."

12. See The Twenty-Fifth Amendment, Congressional Quarterly, Jan. 4, 1975 at 35–36; H. J. Res. 120, 94th Cong., 1st Sess. (1975) (popular referendum—Brinkley).

13. S. J. Res. 166, 93d Cong., 1st Sess. (1973).

14. *N. Y. Times*, Dec. 20, 1974 at 37.

15. *Id.*, Oct. 30, 1974 at 34.

16. *N. Y. Herald–Tribune*, June 9, 1964 at 20.

17. Hearings on Presidential Inability and Vice Presidential Vacancy Before the House Comm. on the Judiciary, 89th Cong., 1st Sess. 227 (1965).

18. The Twenty-Fifth Amendment, Congressional Quarterly, Jan. 4, 1975 at 36.

19. Hearings on Presidential Inability and Vacancies in the Office of Vice President Before the Subcomm. on Constitutional Amendments of the Senate Comm. on the Judiciary, 88th Cong., 2d Sess. 60 (1964).

20. Schlesinger, On the Presidential Succession 89.

21. E.g., Schlesinger, *The Imperial Presidency* 411–19 (1973).

22. *N. Y. Post*, Dec. 23, 1974 at 35.

23. *N. Y. Times*, Nov. 1, 1974 at 39.

24. *Perspectives on Presidential Selection* 1 (Matthews ed., 1973).

25. *The Federalist* No. 68 at 452 (Ford ed., 1898).

26. Peirce, *People's President* 58–80.

27. See Silva, *Presidential Succession* 142–49.

28. Compare Cong. Globe, 39th Cong., 2d Sess. 691 (1867) with H. Rep. No. 829, 79th Cong., 1st Sess. (1945).

29. Report of the Special Committee on Election Reform of the American Bar Association (1974).

30. Schlesinger, What to do About a Nonjob 39.

31. Note 13, *supra.*

14

Recommendations

> In the end, in dealing with so fundamental a structure as
> succession to the Presidency, the best guide is the maxim if
> there is no need to change, there is need not to change.
>
> PAUL A. FREUND
> March 11, 1975 [1]

ALTHOUGH I DO NOT BELIEVE that a case for structural reform of the
Twenty-Fifth Amendment has been established, some changes in the
implementation procedures are warranted. As already noted, one such
change which should and can easily be made involves the adoption of a
single, joint hearing. This change requires no alteration in the Amendment, merely the establishment by Congress of appropriate rules.*

But if there is to be any change in the Amendment itself, it should be
made only in a period of calm and after we have had the benefit of our
first experiences. Moreover, such change should not be of a piecemeal
nature but part of an integrated approach to electoral reform. As
Senator John F. Kennedy observed during a debate on electoral reform
in 1956, "[I]t is not only . . . the Presidency we are talking about, but
a whole solar system of governmental power. If it is proposed to change
. . . one of the elements of the solar system, it is necessary to consider
all the others." [2]

Such an overall approach must take account of the following: †

THE PRESIDENTIAL ELECTION SYSTEM

The case for reform of our indirect and dangerous electoral college system of electing a President is clear. Every four years we run the risks
that the popular vote winner will lose, that electors will disregard the
will of the people, and that an election for President will have to be

---

* Related to the question of separate or joint hearings is the problem of unauthorized
congressional leaks of confidential information, which was underscored during the
Rockefeller confirmation hearings. See pp. 167–75, *supra*. There is a need for Congress
to adopt new measures to prevent such leaks and avoid the harm and unfairness to a
vice presidential nominee which are inherent in the untimely dissemination of information.

† Among the areas which should be considered are those referred to in the text
accompanying note 64 in Chapter 12, *supra*.

decided by the House of Representatives under an archaic one-state, one-vote rule.[3] To provide by a new constitutional amendment for a special presidential election under the electoral college system would reaffirm a mechanism under which the popular will can be frustrated. There is an obvious inconsistency in providing, out of a concern that the President at all times be a popularly elected official, for a special election of President whenever a vacancy occurs, and leaving intact the electoral college system of indirect election through which a special election would be handled.

The process by which candidates are selected is another area in need of revision. The current state presidential primary system is uncoordinated; the procedure by which vice presidential candidates are chosen, accident-prone. The recently adopted plan of the Democratic Party for the selection of vice presidential candidates, it is hoped, will lead to further improvement in the selection procedure. The plan requires that at least forty-eight hours elapse between the selection of the party's presidential and vice presidential candidates, and offers the presidential candidate the option of deferring his choice of a running mate for up to three weeks. Under that option, the presidential candidate would submit the name of his nominee or nominees to the party's national committee which would select the vice presidential candidate.‡

Finally, there is a need for legislation to deal with the death of a candidate before election day, in the forty-one–day period between election day and the meeting of the electors in December, and in the period after the electors vote in December and before their votes are counted on January 6.§

THE PRESIDENTIAL SUCCESSION SYSTEM

With or without any change in the Twenty-Fifth Amendment, the wisdom of using the present succession law, which puts the Speaker and the President pro tempore at the head of the line, is questionable. Both are elected to Congress from limited constituencies, and both are usually appointed to their positions of congressional leadership late in life without regard for their qualifications for the presidency and without the scrutiny to which a potential President is subject, either on the campaign

‡ This option reflects the situation in 1972 when Senator Thomas Eagleton of Missouri withdrew from the Democratic ticket as a result of disclosures that in the past he had suffered from mental fatigue and depression. Thereupon, on the recommendation of the presidential candidate, Senator George McGovern of South Dakota, the Democratic National Committee selected Sargent Shriver as Eagleton's replacement.

§ Each of our major political parties, however, has procedures authorizing its national committee to fill a vacancy. The Republican National Committee is also empowered to call a new convention. *From Failing Hands* 271–72 & appendices F & G.

trail or through congressional hearings under the Twenty-Fifth Amendment. Their presence in the line of succession allows for the possibility of a disruptive and perhaps disputed succession, especially in situations where Congress is controlled by a party other than that of the President, and it offers obvious difficulties whenever Congress is faced with a case of presidential impeachment.

There is a question, too, of the efficacy of the current succession law in the event of a case of presidential inability. In such a case, the Speaker would have to resign from Congress to act as President even for a period as short as a few hours, and if, as at present, the Speaker is a member of another party, it is questionable whether a disabled President would turn over executive power to him even temporarily.*

But as serious as these objections are, even more substantial controversy exists concerning the constitutionality of the law itself.

The basic question is whether the Speaker and the President pro tempore are officers of the United States,† and the answer is of primary importance since the section of the Constitution (Article II, section 1) which empowers Congress to establish a line of succession states that:

> Congress may by Law provide for the case of Removal, Death, Resignation or Inability, both of the President and Vice President, declaring what *Officer* shall then act as President, and such *Officer* shall act accordingly, until the Disability be removed, or a President shall be elected [emphasis added].

Ruth C. Silva, one authority who has studied this question in detail, has stated that "the Constitution does not contemplate the presiding legislative officers as officers of the United States" and that this view is "supported by all the commentators." [4] ‡ It seems unlikely, from a practical standpoint, that the Supreme Court would compel a Speaker who had succeeded to vacate the presidential office; yet the legitimacy of his occupancy of the White House would be open to question at the very time when no doubt should exist about his status.

The requirement that the Speaker and the President pro tempore resign their positions and seats in Congress in order to act as President presents another area of legal difficulty. It has been argued that under Article II Congress can attach the powers and duties of the presidency only to an existing office which the occupant continues to occupy while acting as President. In rebuttal, it has been contended that the Consti-

---

* This assumes that the President has the power to do so, which I believe to be the case under Article II. See opinion of Attorney General Robert F. Kennedy, Aug. 2, 1961 (see p. 56, *supra*). The presidential inability provisions of the Twenty-Fifth Amendment apply, of course, only when there are a President and Vice President. See p. 206, *supra*.

† It is noteworthy that the Twentieth Amendment, unlike art. II, § 1, cl. 6, used the term "person" instead of "officer" in empowering Congress to provide for the cases of death and failure to qualify of the President-elect and Vice President–elect.

‡ For the views of James Madison, see p. 39, *supra*.

tution merely requires the successor to be an officer of the United States at the time he begins to act as President, and that if the officer resigns at the time he takes the presidential oath, this requirement is satisfied. Yet the Constitution specifically states that the officer shall act as President "until the Disability be removed, or a President shall be elected," implying that he or she is to remain an officer. But if the Speaker and the President pro tempore retain their legislative positions and seats, there clearly would be a violation of the principle of separation of powers.

The so-called bumping provision—that is, that whenever a Cabinet officer, in the absence of a Speaker or President pro tempore, acts as President, he may be superseded by a subsequently elected Speaker or President pro tempore—prompts yet another objection to the succession law. Since the Constitution provides that the officer appointed by Congress shall act "until the Disability be removed, or a President shall be elected," it would seem that the officer should not be replaced except by the President or Vice President whose inability had ended or by a newly elected President.

Of course, if there were a Cabinet line of succession, the major legal problems raised by the current succession law would be eliminated. There is no doubt that Cabinet officers are officers of the United States, and if they retain their offices while acting as President, there would be no violation of the principle of separation of powers.

The argument that the present line of succession is more in keeping with the American tradition, because it provides for an elected official in the line of succession, is of doubtful validity. For more than 155 years of our existence the immediate successor after the Vice President was not a popularly elected official or a person chosen for his position with a view to his succeeding to the presidency. From 1792 to 1886, the President pro tempore, who was first in line, was chosen by the Senate which was elected not by the people but by the state legislatures. From 1886 to 1947, the Secretary of State, an appointed official, was the immediate successor. Even the present law puts the Cabinet in the line of succession after the President pro tempore.

The policy question should not, of course, be resolved on the basis of how many Speakers or Secretaries of State were subsequently elected President. But if this were the criterion, the Cabinet line of succession would seem preferable since six Secretaries of State (Jefferson, Madison, Monroe, J. Q. Adams, Van Buren, and Buchanan) and only one Speaker (Polk) were subsequently elected to the presidency.§

§ One can hardly deny the general executive competency of the men who have been Secretaries of State—e.g., John Marshall, Daniel Webster, John C. Calhoun, William H. Seward, John Hay, Elihu Root, William Jennings Bryan, Robert Lansing, Charles E. Hughes, Henry L. Stimson, Cordell Hull, James F. Byrnes, George C. Marshall, and John Foster Dulles. Yet some excellent Speakers have been Vice Presidents (John N.

Of far greater importance is whether the succession of legislative leaders satisfies the principles of continuity and stability, and it clearly does not. History shows that the possibility of a President and Vice President of one party and a Congress dominated by another is by no means remote. For more than eight of the thirty-seven–plus years during which the vice presidency has been vacant, the person next in line was of the opposite party. This was the case for a substantial part of the time when Tyler, Fillmore, and Truman were serving out the terms to which others had been elected. Although there was neither a President pro tempore nor a Speaker when Arthur succeeded to the presidency in 1881 and when Vice President Hendricks died in office in 1885, the President's party was not in control of the Senate in either case. During Eisenhower's entire second term, when his health was uncertain, Congress was controlled by the Democrats. Former Presidents Taft, Wilson, and Hoover were confronted with Congresses controlled in one or both Houses by the opposite party. And, of course, since 1968 the Democratic Party has controlled Congress while a Republican has occupied the presidency.

On balance, therefore, it appears that there are substantial reasons for changing the current succession law in order to make it more compatible with the principle of separation of powers and to ensure a stable succession whenever the line of succession extends beyond the vice presidency.*

CONCLUSION

The swift manner by which presidential power has been transferred upon the deaths in office of eight Presidents and the resignation of another President has demonstrated the stability and continuity of our government. In every case the succession has been peaceful, and no question has been raised as to the legitimacy of the successor's occupancy of the White House.

Since the presidency is such a vital part of the structure of our government, there must never be any doubt about the adequacy of the country's laws on election and succession to that office. In the history of our country the absence of procedures for dealing with cases of presidential inability had proved to be a great deficiency in the system, and the devising of an effective system of succession beyond the vice presidency, a

---

Garner and Schuyler Colfax), Secretaries of State (James G. Blaine and Henry Clay), Secretaries of Treasury (Howell Cobb and John J. Carlisle), Secretary of War (John Bell), and nominated for the presidency (Blaine, Clay and Bell) and vice presidency (Polk).

* For a persuasive statement of the case for placing the legislative leaders of the President's party first in line behind the Vice President, see Joel K. Goldstein's Presidential Succession and Inability: America's Inadequate Provisions (unpubl. thesis, Woodrow Wilson School of Public and International Affairs, Princeton University, 1975).

recurrent problem. The adoption and re-adoption of succession statutes, often based on the personalities of the people occupying the particular offices at the time, and the growth in the importance of the vice presidency had underscored the need for a better approach to situations involving the loss of a President or Vice President and the accompanying vacancy in the vice presidency.

After long and great study, the Twenty-Fifth Amendment was adopted to remedy these demonstrated needs and deficiencies. Nothing in the record to date indicates that there is a superior remedy for dealing with the complex problems involved. The Amendment deals with these problems practically, in a manner consistent with the principle of separation of powers, and in a way which protects the office of President and assures stability and continuity in the event of succession.† It gives the decisive role only to those in whom the American people most likely would have confidence. It involves only persons who have been elected by the people or approved by their chosen representatives, and it embodies checks on all concerned—the President, Vice President, Cabinet, and Congress. Thus, under the inability procedures of the Amendment, neither the Vice President nor Cabinet can declare a President disabled without the concurrence of the other, and if a President disagrees with their declaration, he is in a position to have the dispute resolved by Congress in accordance with procedures weighted heavily in his favor. Similarly, under the vice presidential vacancy procedures of the Amendment, a President's nomination requires approval by both Houses of Congress, so that each House has a check on the other.

Therefore, in the consideration of any change in the Twenty-Fifth Amendment, attention must be given to the interrelationship of its provisions, and to the fact that history provides examples of new rules' producing unexpected and undesirable results. As Sidney Hyman, a noted authority on the presidency, once observed: "Every constitutional system must pay some price in weakness for the element of strength it has. Not everything is [solvable]. Not everything can be controlled by law." [5]

---

† Senator John McClellan appropriately noted during the 1965 Senate debates: "To cope with the problems of Presidential inability and vacancies in the Office of the Vice President, we must provide means for orderly transition of Executive power in a manner that respects the separation of powers concept and maintains the safeguards of our traditional checks and balances system. Finally, any such provision must have the confidence and support of our people if it is to accomplish the desired results." 111 Cong. Rec. 3275 (1965).

NOTES

1. Hearing on the First Implementation of Section Two of the Twenty-Fifth Amendment Before the Subcomm. on Constitutional Amendments of the Senate Comm. on the Judiciary, 94th Cong., 1st Sess. 138 (1975).

2. 102 Cong. Rec. 5150 (1956).

3. Neal Peirce's outstanding treatise, *The People's President*, vividly describes the dangers and pitfalls of the existing electoral college system. See also Electing the President, a Report of the Commission on Electoral College Reform of the American Bar Association (1967); and Feerick, The Electoral College—Why It Ought to be Abolished, 37 Fordham L. Rev. 1 (1968).

4. Silva, The Presidential Succession Act of 1947, 47 Michigan L. Rev. 451 (1949).

5. Hearings Before the Special Comm. to Study Presidential Inability of the House Comm. on the Judiciary, 84th Cong., 2d Sess. 47 (1956).

Appendices

Appendix A

Section-by-Section Development of the Twenty-Fifth Amendment

SECTION 1

As introduced in Senate in 1963 and 1964

SECTION 1. In case of the removal of the President from office, or of his death or resignation, the Vice President shall become President for the unexpired portion of the then current term. Within a period of thirty days thereafter, the new President shall nominate a Vice President who shall take office upon confirmation by both Houses of Congress by a majority of those present and voting.

As passed Senate in 1964

SECTION 1. In case of the removal of the President from office or of his death or resignation, the Vice President shall become President.

As passed Senate in February 1965

SECTION 1. In case of the removal of the President from office or of his death or resignation, the Vice President shall become President.

As passed House in April 1965

SECTION 1. In case of the removal of the President from office or of his death or resignation, the Vice President shall become President.

Final form

SECTION 1. In case of the removal of the President from office or of his death or resignation, the Vice President shall become President.

SECTION 2

As introduced in Senate in 1963 and 1964

SEC. 2. In case of the removal of the Vice President from office, or of his death or resignation, the President, within a period of thirty days thereafter, shall nominate a Vice President who shall take office upon confirmation by both Houses of Congress by a majority vote of those present and voting.

As passed Senate in 1964

SEC. 2. Whenever there is a vacancy in the office of the Vice President, the President shall nominate a Vice President who shall take office upon confirmation by a majority vote of both Houses of Congress.

As passed Senate in February 1965

SEC. 2. Whenever there is a vacancy in the office of the Vice President, the President shall nominate a Vice President who shall take office upon confirmation by a majority vote of both Houses of Congress.

As passed House in April 1965

SEC. 2. Whenever there is a vacancy in the office of the Vice President, the President shall nominate a Vice President who shall take office upon confirmation by a majority vote of both Houses of Congress.

Final form

SEC. 2. Whenever there is a vacancy in the office of the Vice President, the President shall nominate a Vice President who shall take office upon confirmation by a majority vote of both Houses of Congress.

SECTION 3

As introduced in Senate in 1963 and 1964

SEC. 3. If the President shall declare in writing that he is unable to discharge the powers and duties of his office, such powers and duties shall be discharged by the Vice President as Acting President.

As passed Senate in 1964

SEC. 3. If the President declares in writing that he is unable to discharge the powers and duties of his office, such powers and duties shall be discharged by the Vice President as Acting President.

As passed Senate in February 1965

SEC. 3. Whenever the President transmits to the President of the Senate and the Speaker of the House of Representatives his written declaration that he is unable to discharge the powers and duties of his office, such powers and duties shall be discharged by the Vice President as Acting President.

As passed House in April 1965

SEC. 3. Whenever the President transmits to the President pro tempore of the Senate and the Speaker of the House of Representatives his written declaration that he is unable to discharge the powers and duties of his office, and until he transmits a written declaration to the contrary, such powers and duties shall be discharged by the Vice President as Acting President.

Final form

SEC. 3. Whenever the President transmits to the President pro tempore of the Senate and the Speaker of the House of Representatives his written declaration that he is unable to discharge the powers and duties of his office, and until he transmits to them a written declaration to the contrary, such powers and duties shall be discharged by the Vice President as Acting President.

SECTION 4

As introduced in Senate in 1963 and 1964

SEC. 4. If the President does not so declare, the Vice President, if satisfied that such inability exists, shall, upon the written approval of a majority of the heads of the executive departments in office, assume the discharge of the powers and duties as Acting President.

As passed Senate in 1964

SEC. 4. If the President does not so declare, and the Vice President with the written concurrence of a majority of the heads of the executive departments or such other body as Congress may by law provide, transmits to the Congress his written declaration that the President is unable to discharge the powers and duties of his office, the Vice President shall immediately assume the powers and duties of the office as Acting President.

As passed Senate in February 1965

SEC. 4. Whenever the Vice President, and a majority of the principal officers of the executive departments or such other body as Congress may by law provide, transmit to the President of the Senate and the Speaker of the House of Representatives their written declaration that the President is unable to discharge the powers and duties of his office, the Vice President shall immediately assume the powers and duties of the office as Acting President.

As passed House in April 1965

SEC. 4. Whenever the Vice President and a majority of the principal officers of the executive departments, or such other body as Congress may by law provide, transmit to the President pro tempore of the Senate and the Speaker of the House of Representatives their written declaration that the President is unable to discharge the powers and duties of his office, the Vice President shall immediately assume the powers and duties of the office as Acting President.

Thereafter, when the President transmits to the President pro tempore of the Senate and the Speaker of the House of Representatives his written declaration that no inability exists, he shall resume the powers and duties of his office unless the Vice President and a majority of the principal officers of the executive departments, or such other body as Congress may by law provide, transmit within two days to the President pro tempore of the Senate and

the Speaker of the House of Representatives their written declaration that the President is unable to discharge the powers and duties of his office. Thereupon Congress shall decide the issue, assembling within forty-eight hours for that purpose if not in session. If the Congress, within ten days after the receipt of the written declaration of the Vice President and a majority of the principal officers of the executive departments, or such other body as Congress may by law provide, determines by two-thirds vote of both Houses that the President is unable to discharge the powers and duties of the office, the Vice President shall continue to discharge the same as Acting President; otherwise, the President shall resume the powers and duties of his office.

Final form

SEC. 4. Whenever the Vice President and a majority of either the principal officers of the executive departments or of such other body as Congress may by law provide, transmit to the President pro tempore of the Senate and the Speaker of the House of Representatives their written declaration that the President is unable to discharge the powers and duties of his office, the Vice President shall immediately assume the powers and duties of the office as Acting President.

Thereafter, when the President transmits to the President pro tempore of the Senate and the Speaker of the House of Representatives his written declaration that no inability exists, he shall resume the powers and duties of his office unless the Vice President and a majority of either the principal officers of the executive department or of such other body as Congress may by law provide, transmit within four days to the President pro tempore of the Senate and the Speaker of the House of Representatives their written declaration that the President is unable to discharge the powers and duties of his office. Thereupon Congress shall decide the issue, assembling within forty-eight hours for that purpose if not in session. If the Congress, within twenty-one days after receipt of the latter written declaration, or, if Congress is not in session, within twenty-one days after Congress is required to assemble, determines by two-thirds vote of both Houses that the President is unable to discharge the powers and duties of his office, the Vice President shall continue to discharge the same as Acting President; otherwise, the President shall resume the powers and duties of his office.

SECTION 5

As introduced in Senate in 1963 and 1964

SEC. 5. Whenever the President makes public announcement in writing that his inability has terminated, he shall resume the discharge of the powers and duties of his office on the seventh day after making such announcement, or at such earlier time after such announcement as he and the Vice President may determine. But if the Vice President, with the written approval of a majority of the heads of executive departments in office at the time of such announcement, transmits to the Congress his written declaration that in his opinion the President's inability has not terminated, the Congress shall thereupon consider the issue. If the Congress is not then in session, it shall assemble in special session on the call of the Vice President. If the Congress determines by concurrent resolution, adopted with the approval of two-thirds of the Members present in each House, that the inability of the President has not terminated, thereupon, notwithstanding any further announcement by the President, the Vice President shall discharge such powers and duties as Acting President until the occurrence of the earliest of the following events: (1) the Acting President proclaims that the President's inability has ended, (2) the Congress determines by concurrent resolution, adopted with the approval of a majority of the Members present in each House, that the President's inability has ended, or (3) the President's term ends.

As passed Senate in 1964

SEC. 5. Whenever the President transmits to the Congress his written declaration that no inability exists, he shall resume the powers and duties of his office unless the Vice President, with the written concurrence of a majority of the heads of the executive departments or such other body as Congress may by law provide, transmits within two days to the Congress his written declaration that the President is unable to discharge the powers and duties of his office. Thereupon Congress shall immediately decide the issue. If the Congress determines by two-thirds vote of both Houses that the President is unable to discharge the powers and duties of the office, the Vice President shall continue to discharge the same as Acting President; otherwise the President shall resume the powers and duties of his office.

As passed Senate in February 1965

SEC. 5. Whenever the President transmits to the President of the Senate and the Speaker of the House of Representatives his written declaration that no inability exists, he shall resume the powers and duties of his office unless the Vice President, with the written concurrence of a majority of the principal officers of the executive departments or such other body as Congress may by law provide, transmits within seven days to the President of the Senate and the Speaker of the House of Representatives their written declaration that the President is unable to discharge the powers and duties of his office. Thereupon Congress shall immediately proceed to decide the issue. If the Congress determines by two-thirds vote of both Houses that the President is unable to discharge the powers and duties of the office, the Vice President shall continue to discharge the same as Acting President; otherwise the President shall resume the powers and duties of his office.

SECTION 6

As introduced in Senate in 1963 and 1964

SEC. 6. (a)(1) If, by reason of death, resignation, removal from office, inability, or failure to qualify, there is neither a President nor Vice President to discharge the powers and duties of the office of President, then the officer of the United States who is highest on the following list, and who is not under disability to discharge the powers and duties of the office of President, shall act as President: Secretary of State, Secretary of Treasury, Secretary of Defense, Attorney General, Postmaster General, Secretary of Interior, Secretary of Agriculture, Secretary of Commerce, Secretary of Labor, Secretary of Health, Education, and Welfare, and such other heads of executive departments as may be established hereafter and in order of their establishment.

(2) The same rule shall apply in the case of the death, resignation, removal from office, or inability of an individual acting as President under this section.

(3) To qualify under this section, an individual must have been appointed, by and with the advice and consent of the Senate, prior to the time of the death, resignation, removal from office, or inability of the President and Vice President, and must not be under impeachment by the House of Representatives at the time the powers and duties of the office of President devolve upon him.

(b) In case of the death, resignation, or removal of both the President and Vice President, his successor shall be President until the expiration of the then current presidential term. In case of the inability of the President and Vice President to discharge the powers and duties of the office of President, his successor, as designated in this section, shall be subject to the provisions of sections 3, 4, and 5 of this article as if he were a Vice President acting in case of disability of the President.

(c) The taking of the oath of office by an individual specified in the list of paragraph (1) of subsection (a) shall be held to constitute his resignation from the office by virtue of the holding of which he qualifies to act as President.

(d) During the period that any individual acts as President under this section, his compensation shall be at the rate then provided by law in the case of the President.

SECTION 7

As introduced in Senate in 1963 and 1964

SEC. 7. This article shall be inoperative unless it shall have been ratified as an amendment to the Constitution by the legislatures of three-fourths of the several States within seven years from the date of its submission.

Constitutional Provisions on Succession

Twenty-Fifth Amendment

SECTION 1. In case of the removal of the President from office or of his death or resignation, the Vice President shall become President.

SEC. 2. Whenever there is a vacancy in the office of the Vice President, the President shall nominate a Vice President who shall take office upon confirmation by a majority vote of both Houses of Congress.

SEC. 3. Whenever the President transmits to the President pro tempore of the Senate and the Speaker of the House of Representatives his written declaration that he is unable to discharge the powers and duties of his office, and until he transmits to them a written declaration to the contrary, such powers and duties shall be discharged by the Vice President as Acting President.

SEC. 4. Whenever the Vice President and a majority of either the principal officers of the executive departments or of such other body as Congress may by law provide, transmit to the President pro tempore of the Senate and the Speaker of the House of Representatives their written declaration that the President is unable to discharge the powers and duties of his office, the Vice President shall immediately assume the powers and duties of the office as Acting President.

Thereafter, when the President transmits to the President pro tempore of the Senate and the Speaker of the House of Representatives his written declaration that no inability exists, he shall resume the powers and duties of his office unless the Vice President and a majority of either the principal officers of the executive department or of such other body as Congress may by law provide, transmit within four days to the President pro tempore of the Senate and the Speaker of the House of Representatives their written declaration that the President is unable to discharge the powers and duties of his office. Thereupon Congress shall decide the issue, assembling within forty-eight hours for that purpose if not in session. If the Congress, within twenty-one days after receipt of the latter written declaration, or, if Congress is not in session, within twenty-one days after Congress is required to assemble, determines by two-thirds vote of both Houses that the President is unable to discharge the powers and duties of his office, the Vice President shall continue to discharge the same as Acting President; otherwise, the President shall resume the powers and duties of his office.

Twentieth Amendment

SECTION 1. The terms of the President and Vice President shall end at noon on the 20th day of January, and the terms of Senators and Representatives at noon on the 3d day of January, of the years in which such terms would have ended if this article had not been ratified; and the terms of their successors shall then begin.

SEC. 2. The Congress shall assemble at least once in every year, and such meeting shall begin at noon on the 3d day of January, unless they shall by law appoint a different day.

SEC. 3. If, at the time fixed for the beginning of the term of the President, the President elect shall have died, the Vice President elect shall become President. If a President shall not have been chosen before the time fixed for the beginning of his term, or if the President elect shall have failed to qualify, then the Vice President elect shall act as President until a President shall have qualified; and the Congress may by law provide for the case wherein neither a President elect nor a Vice President elect shall have qualified, declaring who shall then act as President, or the manner in which one who is to act shall be selected, and such person shall act accordingly until a President or Vice President shall have qualified.

SEC. 4. The Congress may by law provide for the case of the death of any of the persons from whom the House of Representatives may choose a President whenever the right of choice shall have devolved upon them, and for the case of the death of any of the persons from whom the Senate may choose a Vice President whenever the right of choice shall have devolved upon them.

SEC. 5. Sections 1 and 2 shall take effect on the 15th day of October following the ratification of this article.

SEC. 6. This article shall be inoperative unless it shall have been ratified as an amendment to the Constitution by the legislatures of three-fourths of the several States within seven years from the date of its submission.

Twelfth Amendment

The Electors shall meet in their respective states, and vote by ballot for President and Vice-President, one of whom, at least, shall not be an inhabitant of the same state with themselves; they shall name in their ballots the person voted for as President, and in distinct ballots the person voted for as Vice-President, and they shall make distinct lists of all persons voted for as President, and of all persons voted for as Vice-President, and of the number of votes for each, which lists they shall sign and certify, and transmit sealed to the seat of the government of the

United States, directed to the President of the Senate;—The President of the Senate shall, in the presence of the Senate and House of Representatives, open all the certificates and the votes shall then be counted;—The person having the greatest number of votes for President, shall be the President, if such number be a majority of the whole number of Electors appointed; and if no person have such majority, then from the persons having the highest numbers not exceeding three on the list of those voted for as President, the House of Representatives shall choose immediately, by ballot, the President. But in choosing the President, the votes shall be taken by states, the representation from each state having one vote; a quorum for this purpose shall consist of a member or members from two-thirds of the states, and a majority of all the states shall be necessary to a choice. And if the House of Representatives shall not choose a President whenever the right of choice shall devolve upon them, before the fourth day of March next following, then the Vice-President shall act as President, as in the case of the death or other constitutional disability of the President—The person having the greatest number of votes as Vice-President, shall be the Vice-President, if such number be a majority of the whole number of Electors appointed, and if no person have a majority, then from the two highest numbers on the list, the Senate shall choose the Vice-President; a quorum for the purpose shall consist of two-thirds of the whole number of Senators, and a majority of the whole number shall be necessary to a choice. But no person constitutionally ineligible to the office of President shall be eligible to that of Vice-President of the United States.

Article II, Section 1, Clause 6

In Case of the Removal of the President from Office, or of his Death, Resignation, or Inability to discharge the Powers and Duties of the said Office, the Same shall devolve on the Vice President, and the Congress may by Law provide for the Case of Removal, Death, Resignation or Inability, both of the President and Vice President, declaring what Officer shall then act as President, and such Officer shall act accordingly, until the Disability be removed, or a President shall be elected.

Appendix C

Statutory Succession Laws

Act of July 18, 1947

(a) (1) If, by reason of death, resignation, removal from office, inability, or failure to qualify, there is neither a President nor Vice-President to discharge the powers and duties of the office of President, then the Speaker of the House of Representatives shall, upon his resignation as Speaker and as Representative in Congress, act as President.

(2) The same rule shall apply in the case of the death, resignation, removal from office, or inability of an individual acting as President under this subsection.

(b) If, at the time when under subsection (a) of this section a Speaker is to begin the discharge of the powers and duties of the office of President, there is no Speaker, or the Speaker fails to qualify as Acting President, then the President pro tempore of the Senate shall, upon his resignation as President pro tempore and as Senator, act as President.

(c) An individual acting as president under subsection (a) or subsection (b) of this section shall continue to act until the expiration of the then current presidential term, except that—

(1) If his discharge of the powers and duties of the office is founded in whole or in part on the failure of both the President-elect and the Vice-President-elect to qualify, then he shall act only until a President or Vice-President qualifies; and

(2) If his discharge of the powers and duties of the office is founded in whole or in part on the inability of the President or Vice-President, then he shall act only until the removal of the disability of one of such individuals.

(d) (1) If, by reason of death, resignation, removal from office, inability, or failure to qualify, there is no President pro tempore to act as President under subsection (b) of this section, then the officer of the United States who is highest on the following list, and who is not under disability to discharge the powers and duties of the office of President shall act as President: Secretary of State, Secretary of the Treasury, Secretary of Defense, Attorney General, Postmaster General, Secretary of the Interior, Secretary of Agriculture, Secretary of Commerce, Secretary of Labor.*

(2) An individual acting as President under this subsection shall continue so to do until the expiration of the then current presidential term, but not after a qualified and prior-entitled individual is able to act, except that the removal of the disability of an individual higher on the list contained in para-

* The position of Postmaster General was abolished in 1970, and the Secretaries of Health, Education and Welfare, of Housing and Urban Development, and of Transportation have been added to the line of succession.

graph (1) of this subsection or the ability to qualify on the part of an individual higher on such list shall not terminate his service.

(3) The taking of the oath of office by an individual specified in the list in paragraph (1) of this subsection shall be held to constitute his resignation from the office by virtue of the holding of which he qualifies to act as President.

(e) Subsections (a), (b), and (d) of this section shall apply only to such officers as are eligible to the office of President under the Constitution. Subsection (d) of this section shall apply only to officers appointed, by and with the advice and consent of the Senate, prior to the time of the death, resignation, removal from office, inability, or failure to qualify, of the President pro tempore, and only to officers not under impeachment by the House of Representatives at the time the powers and duties of the office of President devolve upon them.

(f) During the period that any individual acts as President under this section, his compensation shall be at the rate then provided by law in the case of the President.

Act of January 19, 1886

Be it enacted by the Senate and House of Representatives of the United States of America in Congress assembled, That in case of removal, death, resignation, or inability of both the President and Vice-President of the United States, the Secretary of State, or if there be none, or in case of his removal, death, resignation, or inability, then the Secretary of the Treasury, or if there be none, or in case of his removal, death, resignation, or inability, then the Secretary of War, or if there be none, or in case of his removal, death, resignation, or inability, then the Attorney-General, or if there be none, or in case of his removal, death, resignation, or inability, then the Postmaster-General, or if there be none, or in case of his removal, death, resignation, or inability, then the Secretary of the Navy, or if there be none, or in case of his removal, death, resignation, or inability, then the Secretary of the Interior, shall act as President until the disability of the President or Vice-President is removed or a President shall be elected: *Provided,* That whenever the powers and duties of the office of President of the United States shall devolve upon any of the persons named herein, if Congress be not then in session, or if it would not meet in accordance with law within twenty days thereafter, it shall be the duty of the person upon whom said powers and duties shall devolve to issue a proclamation convening Congress in extraordinary session, giving twenty days' notice of the time of meeting.

Sec. 2. That the preceding section shall only be held to describe and apply to such officers as shall have been appointed by the advice and consent of the Senate to the offices therein named, and such as are eligible to the office of President under the Constitution, and not under impeachment by the House of Representatives of the United States at the time the powers and duties of the office shall devolve upon them respectively.

Sec. 3. That sections one hundred and forty-six, one hundred and forty-seven, one hundred and forty-eight, one hundred and forty-nine, and one hundred and fifty of the Revised Statutes are hereby repealed.

Act of March 1, 1792

Sec. 9. *And be it further enacted*, That in case of removal, death, resignation or inability both of the President and Vice President of the United States, the President of the Senate pro tempore, and in case there shall be no President of the Senate [pro tempore], then the Speaker of the House of Representatives, for the time being shall act as President of the United States until the disability be removed or a President shall be elected.

Sec. 10. *And be it further enacted*, That whenever the offices of President and Vice President shall both become vacant, the Secretary of State shall forthwith cause a notification thereof to be made to the executive of every state, and shall also cause the same to be published in at least one of the newspapers printed in each state, specifying that electors of the President of the United States shall be appointed or chosen in the several states within thirty-four days preceding the first Wednesday in December then next ensuing: *Provided*, There shall be the space of two months between the date of such notification and the said first Wednesday in December, but if there shall not be the space of two months between the date of such notification and the first Wednesday in December; and if the term for which the President and Vice President last in office were elected shall not expire on the third day of March next ensuing, then the Secretary of State shall specify in the notification that the electors shall be appointed or chosen within thirty-four days preceding the first Wednesday in December in the year next ensuing, within which time the electors shall accordingly be appointed or chosen, and the electors shall meet and give their votes on the first Wednesday in December, and the proceedings and duties of the said electors and others shall be pursuant to the directions prescribed in this act.

Appendix D

I · Presidential Vacancies

PRESIDENT	TERM FOR WHICH ELECTED	DATE OF VACANCY	VICE PRESIDENT WHO SUCCEEDED	DATE OATH TAKEN	LENGTH OF UNEXPIRED TERM †		
					YEARS	MONTHS	DAYS
1. William H. Harrison	March 4, 1841–1845	April 4, 1841	John Tyler	April 6, 1841	3	11	0
2. Zachary Taylor	March 4, 1849–1853	July 9, 1850	Millard Fillmore	July 10, 1850	2	7	23
3. Abraham Lincoln *	March 4, 1865–1869	April 15, 1865	Andrew Johnson	April 15, 1865	3	10	17
4. James A. Garfield *	March 4, 1881–1885	September 19, 1881	Chester A. Arthur	September 20, 1881 and September 22, 1881	3	5	13
5. William McKinley *	March 4, 1901–1905	September 14, 1901	Theodore Roosevelt	September 14, 1901	3	5	18
6. Warren G. Harding	March 4, 1921–1925	August 2, 1923	Calvin Coolidge	August 3, 1923 and August 21, 1923	1	7	2
7. Franklin D. Roosevelt	January 20, 1945–1949	April 12, 1945	Harry S Truman	April 12, 1945	3	9	8
8. John F. Kennedy *	January 20, 1961–1965	November 22, 1963	Lyndon B. Johnson	November 22, 1963	1	1	29
9. Richard M. Nixon	January 20, 1973–1977	August 9, 1974	Gerald R. Ford	August 9, 1974	2	5	11
				TOTAL:	26	3	28

* Presidents who were assassinated; the other Presidents died in office, except Richard Nixon, who resigned.
† The computation is based on the dates of the President's death or resignation.

II · Vice Presidential Vacancies

VICE-PRESIDENT	PERIOD FOR WHICH CHOSEN	TERMINATION OF SERVICE *	REASON FOR TERMINATION	LENGTH OF VACANCY		
				YEARS	MONTHS	DAYS
1. George Clinton	March 4, 1809–1813	April 20, 1812	Death		10	12
2. Elbridge Gerry	March 4, 1813–1817	November 23, 1814	Death	2	3	9
3. John C. Calhoun	March 4, 1829–1833	December 28, 1832	Resignation		2	4
4. John Tyler	March 4, 1841–1845	April 4, 1841	Succession	3	11	0
5. Millard Fillmore	March 4, 1849–1853	July 9, 1850	Succession	2	7	23
6. William R. King	March 4, 1853–1857	April 18, 1853	Death	3	10	14
7. Andrew Johnson	March 4, 1865–1869	April 15, 1865	Succession	3	10	17
8. Henry Wilson	March 4, 1873–1877	November 22, 1875	Death	1	3	10
9. Chester A. Arthur	March 4, 1881–1885	September 19, 1881	Succession	3	5	13
10. Thomas A. Hendricks	March 4, 1885–1889	November 25, 1885	Death	3	3	7
11. Garrett A. Hobart	March 4, 1897–1901	November 21, 1899	Death	1	3	11
12. Theodore Roosevelt	March 4, 1901–1905	September 14, 1901	Succession	3	5	18
13. James S. Sherman	March 4, 1909–1913	October 30, 1912	Death		4	5
14. Calvin Coolidge	March 4, 1921–1925	August 2, 1923	Succession	1	7	2
15. Harry S Truman	January 20, 1945–1949	April 12, 1945	Succession	3	9	8
16. Lyndon B. Johnson	January 20, 1961–1965	November 22, 1963	Succession	1	1	29
17. Spiro T. Agnew	January 20, 1973–1977	October 10, 1973	Resignation		1	26
18. Gerald R. Ford	December 6, 1973–1977	August 9, 1974	Succession		4	10
			TOTAL:	37	9	1

* In the case of a Vice President who succeeded to the presidency, the date of the President's death or resignation is treated as the date of termination.

Appendix E

Times During Which the Speaker, the President pro tempore, or Both Were from a Party Different from the President's

CONGRESS	PRESIDENT AND PARTY *	SPEAKER AND PARTY *	PRESIDENT PRO TEMPORE AND PARTY *
20th, 1827–1829	John Quincy Adams—C (DR)	Andrew Stevenson—J	Samuel Smith—J
28th, 1843–1845	John Tyler—W	John W. Jones—D	Willie P. Mangum—W
30th, 1847–1849	James K. Polk—D	Robert C. Winthrop—W	David R. Atchison—W
31st, 1849–1851	Zachary Taylor ⎫ W	Howell Cobb—D	David R. Atchison—W
	Millard Fillmore ⎭		William R. King—D
32nd, 1851–1853	Millard Fillmore—W	Linn Boyd—D	William R. King—D
			David R. Atchison—W
34th, 1853–1857	Franklin Pierce—D	Nathaniel P. Banks—R	Jesse D. Bright—D
			Charles E. Stuart—D
			James M. Mason—D
36th, 1859–1861	James Buchanan—D	William Pennington—R	Benjamin Fitzpatrick—D
			Jesse D. Bright—D
			Solomon Foot—R
44th, 1875–1877	Ulysses S. Grant—R	Michael C. Kerr—D	Thomas W. Ferry—R
		Samuel J. Randall—D	
45th, 1877–1879	Rutherford B. Hayes—R	Samuel J. Randall—D	Thomas W. Ferry—R
46th, 1879–1881	Rutherford B. Hayes—R	Samuel J. Randall—D	Allen G. Thurman—D
48th, 1883–1885	Chester A. Arthur—R	John G. Carlisle—D	George F. Edmunds—R
49th, 1885–1887	Grover Cleveland—D	John G. Carlisle—D	John Sherman—R
50th, 1887–1889	Grover Cleveland—D	John G. Carlisle—D	John J. Ingalls—R
52nd, 1891–1893	Benjamin Harrison—R	Charles F. Crisp—D	Charles F. Monderson—R

PRESIDENT PRO
TEMPORE AND PARTY *

CONGRESS	PRESIDENT AND PARTY *	SPEAKER AND PARTY *	PRESIDENT PRO TEMPORE AND PARTY *
54th, 1895–1897	Grover Cleveland—D	Thomas B. Reed—R	William P. Frye—R
62nd, 1911–1913	William H. Taft—R	Champ Clark—D	William P. Frye—R
			Charles Curtis—R
			Augustus O. Bacon—R
			Jacob H. Gallinger—R
			Henry Cabot Lodge—R
			Frank B. Brandegee—R
66th, 1919–1921	Woodrow Wilson—D	Frederick H. Gillett—R	Albert B. Cummins—R
72nd, 1931–1933	Herbert C. Hoover—R	John Nance Garner—D	George H. Moses—R
80th, 1947–1949	Harry S Truman—D	Joseph Martin, Jr.—R	Arthur H. Vandenberg—R
84th, 1955–1957	Dwight D. Eisenhower—R	Sam Rayburn—D	Walter F. George—D
85th, 1957–1959	Dwight D. Eisenhower—R	Sam Rayburn—D	Carl Hayden—D
86th, 1959–1961	Dwight D. Eisenhower—R	Sam Rayburn—D	Carl Hayden—D
91st, 1969–1971	Richard M. Nixon—R	John W. McCormack—D	Richard B. Russell—D
92nd, 1971–1973	Richard M. Nixon—R	Carl B. Albert—D	Allen J. Ellender—D
			James O. Eastland—D
93rd, 1973–1975	Richard M. Nixon—R	Carl B. Albert—D	James O. Eastland—D
94th, 1975–1977	Gerald R. Ford—R	Carl B. Albert—D	James O. Eastland—D

* The party abbreviations are as follows: C—Coalition; D—Democratic; DR—Democratic-Republican; J—Jacksonian; R—Republican; W—Whig.

Bibliography

Books

Bayh, Birch. *One Heartbeat Away*. Indianapolis: Bobbs–Merrill, 1968.
Bernstein, Carl, and Woodward, Bob. *All the President's Men*. New York: Simon & Schuster, 1974.
——. *The Final Days*. New York: Simon & Schuster, 1976.
Bishop, Jim. *FDR's Last Year*. New York: Morrow, 1974.
Cohen, Richard M., and Witcover, Jules. *A Heartbeat Away: The Investigation and Resignation of Vice President Spiro T. Agnew*. New York: Viking, 1974.
DiSalle, Michael V. *Second Choice*. New York: Hawthorne, 1966.
Dorman, M. *The Second Man*. New York: Delacorte, 1968.
Feerick, John D. *From Failing Hands: The Story of Presidential Succession*. New York: Fordham University Press, 1965.
Hansen, Richard H. *The Year We Had No President*. Lincoln: University of Nebraska Press, 1962.
Harwood, M. *In the Shadow of Presidents: The American Vice-Presidency and Succession System*. Philadelphia: Lippincott, 1966.
New York Times Staff. *The End of a Presidency*. New York: Bantam Books, 1974.
The Records of the Federal Convention of 1787. Ed. Max Farrand. 4 vols. New Haven: Yale University Press, 1911, 1937.
Reeves, Thomas C. *Gentleman Boss: The Life of Chester Alan Arthur*. New York: Random House, 1975.
Schlesinger, Arthur M., Jr. *The Imperial Presidency*. Boston: Houghton Mifflin, 1973.
Silva, Ruth C. *Presidential Succession*. Ann Arbor: The University of Michigan Press, 1951.
terHorst, Jerald F. *Gerald Ford and the Future of the Presidency*. New York: Third Press-Viking, 1974.
White, Theodore. *Breach of Faith: The Fall of Richard Nixon*. New York: Atheneum, 1975.

Congressional Materials

Analysis of the Philosophy and Public Record of Nelson A. Rockefeller, Nominee for Vice President of the United States. House Comm. on the Judiciary, 93d Cong., 2d Sess. (1974).
Axel-Lute. Checklist of Federal Documents on Watergate, Impeachment and Presidential Transition, 1973–1974. Rutgers Law Library (1975).
Celada. Obligation on President and Congress to Fill Vice Presidential Va-

---

This Bibliography is essentially an update of the one which appeared in *From Failing Hands* 349–61.

cancy, in Legislative History on Application of the Twenty-Fifth Amendment to Vacancies in the Office of the Vice President. House Comm. on the Judiciary, 93d Cong., 1st Sess. 445 (1973).

Conference Committee. Report on Presidential Inability and Vacancies in the Office of Vice President. H. R. Rep. No. 564, 89th Cong., 1st Sess. (1965).

Debate on the Nomination of Nelson A. Rockefeller to be Vice President of the United States. House Comm. on the Judiciary, 93d Cong., 2d Sess. (1974).

Feerick. Legislative History of Section 2 of the Twenty-Fifth Amendment, in Selected Materials on the Twenty-Fifth Amendment. S. Doc. No. 93–42, 93d Cong., 1st Sess. (1973).

Hearings Before the Special Subcomm. on Study of Presidential Inability of the House Comm. on the Judiciary, 84th Cong., 2d Sess. (1956).

Hearings Before the Special Subcomm. on Study of Presidential Inability of the House Comm. on the Judiciary, 85th Cong., 1st Sess. (1957).

Hearings on Presidential Inability Before the Subcomm. on Constitutional Amendments of the Senate Comm. on the Judiciary, 85th Cong., 2d Sess. (1958).

Hearings on Presidential Inability Before the Subcomm. on Constitutional Amendments of the Senate Comm. on the Judiciary, 88th Cong., 1st Sess. (1963).

Hearings on Presidential Inability and Vacancies in the Office of Vice President Before the Subcomm. on Constitutional Amendments of the Senate Comm. on the Judiciary, 88th Cong., 2d Sess. (1964).

Hearings on Presidential Inability and Vice Presidential Vacancy Before the House Comm. on the Judiciary, 89th Cong., 1st Sess. (1965).

Hearings on Presidential Inability and Vacancies in the Office of Vice President Before the Subcomm. on Constitutional Amendments of the Senate Comm. on the Judiciary, 89th Cong., 1st Sess. (1965).

Hearings on Nomination of Gerald R. Ford to be Vice President of the United States Before the House Comm. on the Judiciary, 93d Cong., 1st Sess. (1973).

Hearings on Nomination of Gerald R. Ford of Michigan to be Vice President of the United States Before the Senate Comm. on Rules and Administration, 93d Cong., 1st Sess. (1973).

Hearings on Nomination of Nelson A. Rockefeller to be Vice President of the United States Before the House Comm. on the Judiciary, 93d Cong., 2d Sess. (1974).

Hearings on Nomination of Nelson A. Rockefeller of New York to be Vice President of the United States Before the Senate Comm. on Rules and Administration, 93d Cong., 2d Sess. (1974).

Hearing on the First Implementation of Section Two of the Twenty-Fifth Amendment Before the Subcomm. on Constitutional Amendments of the Senate Comm. on the Judiciary, 94th Cong., 1st Sess. (1975).

Hearings on the Pardon of Richard M. Nixon, and Related Matters, Before the Subcomm. on Criminal Justice of the House Comm. on the Judiciary, 93d Cong., 2d Sess. (1975).

House Comm. on the Judiciary. Report on Presidential Inability and Vacancies in the Office of Vice President. H. R. Rep. No. 203, 89th Cong., 1st Sess. (1965).

―――. Report on Confirmation of Gerald R. Ford as Vice President of the United States. H. R. Rep. No. 93–695, 93d Cong., 1st Sess. (1973).

―――. Report on Confirmation of Nelson A. Rockefeller as Vice President of the United States. H. R. Rep. No. 93–1609, 93d Cong., 2d Sess. (1974).

How Can the Federal Political System Be Improved: A Collection of Excerpts and Bibliography Relating to the High School Debate Topic, 1974–75. S. Doc. No. 93–79, 93d Cong., 2d Sess. (1974).

Legislative History on Application of the Twenty-Fifth Amendment to Vacancies in the Office of the Vice President. House Comm. on the Judiciary, 93d Cong., 1st Sess. (1973).

Presidential Continuity and Vice Presidential Vacancy Amendment, in Legislative History on Application of the Twenty-Fifth Amendment to Vacancies in the Office of the Vice President. House Comm. on the Judiciary, 93d Cong., 1st Sess. 451 (1973).

Presidential Inability. Staff of House Comm. on the Judiciary, 84th Cong., 2d Sess. (Comm. Print 1956).

Presidential Inability: An Analysis of Replies to a Questionnaire and Testimony at a Hearing on Presidential Inability. House Comm. on the Judiciary, 85th Cong., 1st Sess. (Comm. Print 1957).

Report of the Subcomm. on Constitutional Amendments of Senate Comm. on the Judiciary. A Review of the Implementation of Section 2 of the 25th Amendment. 94th Cong., 1st Sess. (Comm. Print 1975).

Selected Issues and the Positions of Nelson A. Rockefeller, Nominee for Vice President of the United States. House Comm. on the Judiciary, 93d Cong., 2d Sess. (1974).

Selected Materials on the Twenty-Fifth Amendment. S. Doc. No. 93–42. 93d Cong., 1st Sess. (1973).

Senate Comm. on the Judiciary. Report on Presidential Inability and Vacancies in the Office of Vice President. S. Rep. No. 1382, 88th Cong., 2d Sess. (1964); S. Rep. No. 1017, 88th Cong., 1st Sess. (1964).

―――. Report on Presidential Inability and Vacancies in the Office of Vice President. S. Rep. No. 66, 89th Cong., 1st Sess. (1965).

Senate Comm. on Rules and Administration. Report on Nomination of Gerald R. Ford of Michigan to be the Vice President of the United States. S. Exec. Rep. No. 93–26, 93d Cong., 1st Sess. (1973).

―――. Report on Nomination of Nelson A. Rockefeller of New York to be Vice President of the United States. S. Exec. Rep. No. 93–34, 93d Cong., 2d Sess. (1974).

Articles

Albert. The Most Dramatic Events of My Life. Oklahoma State University Outreach 4 (March 1974).

Bayh. Our Greatest National Danger. Look, April 7, 1964 at 74.

Blackman. Presidential Disability and the Bayh Amendment. 20 Western Political Quarterly 440 (1967).

Blattner. Presidential Inability and Vice Presidential Vacancy. 36 Cleveland Bar Association Journal 261 (November 1964).

Boroson. Beyond the 25th Amendment. 3 Fact 21 (1966).

Brownell. Presidential Disability: The Need for a Constitutional Amendment. 68 Yale Law Journal 189 (1958).

CBS Reports. The Crisis of Presidential Succession. Jan. 8, 1964.

Charlton. 25th Amendment: Its Critics Say Amend or Abandon It. N. Y. Times, News of the Week in Review, Nov. 17, 1974 at 4.

Christopher. A Special Election to Fill a Presidential Vacancy. 30 Record of the Association of the Bar of the City of New York 47 (1975).

Clayton. Presidential Succession: One of the Biggest Problems. N. Y. Journal–American, Feb. 4, 1964 at 30.

Clifford. A Government of National Unity. N. Y. Times, June 4, 1973 at 35.

Countryman. Letter to the Editor, N. Y. Times, April 9, 1975 at 42.

Craig. Presidential Inability and Vice Presidential Vacancy. 1 Arizona Bar Journal 5 (1965).

Daniel. Ford and 25th Amendment: Rockefeller Choice Held Free of Party Pressure. N. Y. Times, Dec. 23, 1974 at 17.

Drummond. Congress Must Face Up Now: A Gap at Top if President Should Fall Seriously Ill. N. Y. Herald–Tribune, Dec. 6, 1963 at 19.

―――――. The Succession Debate: President's Party Is Seen Best Suited to Fill Vacancy. N. Y. Herald–Tribune, Dec. 13, 1963 at 21.

Editorial, N. Y. Times, March 4, 1975 at 32.

Feerick. Filling a Vacancy in the Vice Presidency. New York Law Journal, Oct. 11, 1973.

―――――. Is the Law on Presidential Succession Adequate?. New York Law Journal, Nov. 25, 1974 at 1.

―――――. The Issue of Presidential Inability. New York Law Journal, May 15, 1974 at 1.

―――――. Presidential Inability: The Problem and a Solution. 50 American Bar Association Journal 321 (1964).

―――――. The Problem of Presidential Inability—It Must be Solved Now. 36 New York State Bar Journal 181 (1964).

―――――. Problem of Presidential Inability—Will Congress Ever Solve It?. 32 Fordham Law Review 73 (1963).

―――――. Proposed Amendment on Presidential Inability and Vice Presidential Vacancy. 51 American Bar Association Journal 915 (1965).

―――――. Proposed Twenty-Fifth Amendment to the Constitution. 34 Fordham Law Review 173 (1965).

―――――. The Transition Was Smooth: Why Change?. L. A. Times, Nov. 17, 1974, § 8 at 5.

―――――. Vice Presidential Succession: In Support of the Bayh–Celler Plan. 18 South Carolina Law Review 226 (1966).

―――――. The Vice Presidency and the Problems of Presidential Succession and Inability. 32 Fordham Law Review 457 (1964).

―――――. The Way of the 25th. N. Y. Times, Dec. 13, 1973 at 47.

Finkelstein & Seitel. Vice-President Can Oust the President. New York Law Journal, May 14, 1974 at 1.

Goldstein. Presidential Succession and Inability: America's Inadequate Provisions. Unpubl. thesis, Woodrow Wilson School of Public and International Affairs, Princeton University, 1975.

Haimbaugh. Vice Presidential Succession: A Brief Rebuttal. 18 South Carolina Law Review 237 (1966).

————. Vice Presidential Succession: A Criticism of the Bayh–Celler Plan. 17 South Carolina Law Review 315 (1965).

Hamlin. The Presidential Succession Act of 1886. 18 Harvard Law Review 182 (1905).

Kennedy. The Constitution and the Campaign Trail. N. Y. Times, Oct. 21, 1974 at 33.

Kirby. A Breakthrough on Presidential Inability: The ABA Conference Consensus. 17 Vanderbilt Law Review 463 (1964).

Krock. Basic Principles Emerging from the Fog. N. Y. Times, Jan. 24, 1964 at 26.

————. The Cart Is Getting Ahead of the Horse. N. Y. Times, Dec. 12, 1963 at 38.

————. The Continuum: Kennedy's Death Points Up Orderly Progression in U. S. Government. N. Y. Times, News of the Week in Review, Nov. 24, 1963 at 9E.

————. An Object Lesson for the Critics of Congress. N. Y. Times, March 6, 1964 at 30.

————. Solvents of an Ancient Congressional Dilemma. N. Y. Times, Jan. 17, 1964 at 42.

————. Succession Problem: The Death of Kennedy Again Points Up the Need to Devise Solution. N. Y. Times, News of the Week in Review, Dec. 8, 1963 at 9E.

Kury. The Crisis in the Law of Presidential Succession. 36 Pennsylvania Bar Association Quarterly 301 (1965).

Large. The 25th Amendment—An Appraisal. Wall Street Journal, Jan. 6, 1975 at 12.

Lawrence. The Big Succession Muddle. Wash. Evening Star, Feb. 28, 1964 at A13.

————. Need Is Seen for a New Vice-President Right Away. N. Y. Herald–Tribune, Dec. 13, 1963 at 21.

————. People's Right to Elect and the Succession Law. N. Y. Herald–Tribune, Dec. 9, 1963 at 24.

Lerner. Taking the 25th. N. Y. Post, Dec. 23, 1974 at 35.

Letter from Paul A. Freund, Abram Chayes, & Raoul Berger to Mayor of Boston, Kevin H. White, Nov. 1, 1973. Repr. 119 Cong. Rec. 26493 (1973).

Lewis. Presidential Disability Problem Stirs Concern. N. Y. Times, News of the Week in Review, Dec. 22, 1963 at 4E.

————. The 25th Amendment and its Unanswered Questions. N. Y. Times, News of the Week in Review, Sept. 30, 1973 at 2.

Linde. Replacing a President: Rx for a 21st Century Watergate. 43 George Washington Law Review 384 (1975).

Lippmann. The Presidential Succession. *Wash. Post,* Dec. 12, 1963 at A24.
————. Presidential Succession and Disability. *N. Y. Herald–Tribune,* June 9, 1964 at 20.
————. The Problem of a Disabled President. *N. Y. Herald–Tribune,* Dec. 17, 1963 at 24.
Longaker. Presidential Continuity: The Twenty-Fifth Amendment. 13 University of California Law Review 532 (1966).
The New President. 60 American Bar Association Journal 1258 (1974).
Paper & Calamaro. Not by Honesty Alone. *N. Y. Times,* Nov. 13, 1974 at 43.
Pastore. Special Election Best Way to Fill the Vacancies. *L. A. Times,* Nov. 17, 1974, § 8 at 5.
Peabody. On the Threshold of the White House. 234 Atlantic Monthly 63 (1974).
Reston. Fiddling with the 25th. *N. Y. Times,* Nov. 1, 1974 at 39.
————. The Problem of Succession to the Presidency. *N. Y. Times,* Dec. 6, 1963 at 34.
Roche. 25th Amendment Tradition of 1787. *Daily Mail,* Dec. 26, 1974.
Royster. The 25th Amendment. *Wall Street Journal,* Oct. 31, 1973 at 16.
Schlesinger. Back to the Founding Fathers?. *Wall Street Journal,* Oct. 31, 1973 at 16.
————. Is the Vice Presidency Necessary?. 233 Atlantic Monthly 37 (May 1974).
————. On the Presidential Succession. 89 Political Science Quarterly 475 (1974).
————. Taking the 25th. *N. Y. Times,* Oct. 3, 1973 at 45.
————. What to Do About a Nonjob. *N. Y. Times,* Nov. 29, 1974 at 39.
Seitel. Why the Delay on Rockefeller. New York Law Journal, Oct. 9, 1974 at 1.
Silva. The Presidential Succession Act of 1947. 47 Michigan Law Review 451 (1949).
Sperling. Succession: Doubts Posed. *Christian Science Monitor,* March 11, 1964 at 1.
Thomas & Morton. The Drastic Remedies. *N. Y. Times,* May 30, 1973 at 39.
The Twenty-Fifth Amendment. Congressional Quarterly, Jan. 4, 1975 at 35.
Twenty-Fifth Amendment Proposals Aired in Senate Hearings: Association Position Favors No Changes. 61 American Bar Association Journal 599 (1975).
The Vice Presidency: How Would a Vacancy be Filled?. Congressional Quarterly, Sept. 22, 1973 at 2499.
Viorst. If a President is Disabled. *N. Y. Post,* March 22, 1964 (magazine).
Wicker. Two for the 25th. *N. Y. Times,* Dec. 20, 1974 at 37.
————. Why Rush to Change the 25th?. *N. Y. Times,* Nov. 19, 1974 at 43.
White. For a Special Presidential Election. *N. Y. Times,* Oct. 30, 1973 at 43.
Williams. An Alternative: Taking the Twenty-Fifth. 26 National Review 476 (1974).
————. The American Vice Presidency. 68 Current History 254 (1974).

Index

Abourezk, James, 183
Abzug, Bella S., 139, 148, 149, 182
Acheson, Dean, 16
Adams, John, 27, 31
Adams, John Quincy, 236; view on Tyler succession, 6
Adams, Sherman, 18–22
Agnew, Spiro T., 47, 117–26, 129, 130, 132, 140, 153, 213, 214, 228
Albert, Carl, 47, 122, 123, 130–31, 133, 153, 157, 167, 176
Allen, James B., 181
Allen, William, 7
American Bar Association: 1964 conference on presidential inability and succession, 59–61; 1974 recommendation on joint hearings, 228
Anderson, Jack, 164
Anderson, Robert B., 175
Apple, R. W., Jr., 165
Arends, Leslie C., 122, 130
Arthur, Chester A., 11; illness, 10, 11; question on succession mechanisms, 9, 11; succession to presidency, 8, 32, 40, 237
Assassinations, see Deaths

Bahmer, Robert, 112n
Baker, Howard H., 129, 163
Baldwin, Abraham, 38
Banzhaf, John F. III, 139–40
Bass, Ross, 93, 94
Bauman, Robert E., 147
Bayh, Birch, 59, 62, 65–66, 69, 71, 72, 77–79, 83, 85, 86, 89–97, 104n, 106, 107, 131, 133, 138, 141, 183, 200–02
Beall, George, 119, 121
Beck, James B., 40
Bell, John, 237n
Benson, Ezra Taft, 19
Best, Judah, 119, 121
Bible, Alan, 79
Biddle, Francis, 64
Biden, Joseph R., Jr., 135
Bingham, Jonathan, 148
Blaine, James G., 9, 11, 237n
Blount, William, 40n
Boland, Edward P., 142, 148
Boyer, Louise, 179
Broder, David, 121

Brooke, Edward, 134
Brown, Clarence J., 101
Brownell, Herbert, 61, 62, 84; as Attorney General, 18, 21; as member of ABA committee on presidential inability, 60, 62, 63; on vice presidential vacancy, 60; on presidential inability, 22, 53, 88, 95, 96, 203; on temporary delegation of presidential power, 18, 198
Bruenn, Howard, 15, 16
Bryan, William Jennings, 236n
Buchanan, James, 236
Buchen, Philip, 159
Burger, Warren, 130, 150, 184
Burns, James MacGregor, 61, 64, 218
Burr, Aaron, 30
Bush, George, 130, 163, 164, 186
Butterfield, Alexander, 118
Butler, M. Caldwell, 149
Buzhardt, J. Fred, 119, 121, 122, 136n
Byrd, Robert, 168, 169, 176–81
Byrne, Brendan, 171
Byrne, W. Matthew, Jr., 118
Byrnes, James F., 16, 43, 236n
Byrnes, John W., 159

Calhoun, John C., 4, 7, 123, 236n
Callaway, Howard H., 184
Cannon, Howard, 136, 137, 141, 168, 170, 171, 174, 176n, 183, 228n
Carlisle, John J., 237n
Carroll, John, 112
Celler, Emanuel, 52, 54, 73n, 83, 99, 100, 103, 104n
Chiles, Lawton, 133–35
Church, Frank, 68, 79, 141
Churchill, Winston, 16, 17
Clay, Henry, 5, 237n
Cleveland, Grover, 11–12
Clifford, Clark, 118
Clinton, George, 4, 29, 33
Cobb, Howell, 237n
Cohen, William S., 143, 169
Colby, William, 186
Colfax, Schuyler, 32, 237n
Colmer, William, 99
Colson, Charles W., 119, 155n
Congressional Acts, see Succession Laws
Connally, John B., 129–32